PAUL'S USE OF ETHOS, PATHOS,
AND LOGOS IN 2 CORINTHIANS 10-13

Mario M. DiCicco

Mellen Biblical Press Series
Volume 31

MELLEN BIBLICAL PRESS
Lewiston/Queenston/Lampeter

Library of Congress Cataloging-in-Publication Data

DiCicco, Mario M.
  Paul's use of ethos, pathos, and logos in 2 Corinthians 10-13 /
Mario M. DiCicco.
    p.   cm.
  Includes bibliographical references and index.
  ISBN 0-7734-2369-9
  1. Bible. N.T. Corrinthians, 2nd, X-XIII--Criticism,
interpretation, etc. 2. Ēthos (The Greek word) 3. Pathos (The
Greek word) 4. Logos. I. Title.
BS2675.2.D53 1995
227'.3066--dc20   94-31547
                                                                CIP

This is volume 31 in the continuing series
Mellen Biblical Press Series
Volume 31 ISBN 0-7734-2369-9
MBP Series ISBN 0-7734-2430-X

A CIP catalog record for this book is available from the British Library.

The Edwin Mellen Press   The Edwin Mellen Press
Box 450   Box 67
Lewiston, New York   Queenston, Ontario
USA 14092-0450   CANADA L0S 1L0

The Edwin Mellen Press, Ltd.
Lampeter, Dyfed, Wales
UNITED KINGDOM SA48 7DY

Printed in the United States of America

To

Pasqualina

Mater, Magistra, Matrona

TABLE OF CONTENTS

PREFACE

What would your response be, if your character was being slandered and your accomplishments belittled by a group of outsiders bent on a hostile takeover and determined to oust you as the head of your organization which you founded and nurtured to its present pre-eminence? How would you react to this abuse? Would you just stand there and swallow the mudslinging, thus by your silence giving some credence to the lies, or would you out of a sense of justice and social responsibility to your employees defend your honor and reputation? Likewise what would be your strategy if, because of these slanderous innuendos, you now had to deal with an emotionally charged atmosphere in your organization, in which your workers had second thoughts about your credentials and entertained questions about your leadership abilities? How would you handle their feelings of doubt and disappointment in you and at the same time fire them up with your own sense of indignation and anger at these outside agitators? To continue the scenario, what press release would you put out to your group which would systematically and rationally answer the charges levelled by this partisan opposition that you lacked competence, trustworthiness, and good faith?

In an a supercharged atmosphere like this, you could not just let things ride, hoping your record would speak for itself and trusting in the levelheadness of your employees. Slander and libelous defamation have a life of their own, becoming like cancers rapaciously and randomly dispossessing in its path the best of goodwill and excellence. You would be obligated to use every aggressive means to bring your critics into disrepute and undo their accusations by a calculated and forceful response. In short, you would need either to make an effective and vigorous speech or to write an expressive statement to your people, in which you would defend your good name and character, change their feelings toward you and against your opponents, and demonstrate the validity of your leadership and rebut the damaging arguments of your critics?

If you can appreciate the difficulty of such a situation, which could tragically split apart your carefully developed company, and the methodical strategy needed to refute the false allegations, then you can value the response of Paul to his church community in 2 Corinthians 10-13. Outside agitators, whose motives were rather suspect but who seemed to proclaim a theology of an exalted Christ, entered the church Paul founded and claimed Paul was deficient in those qualities which displayed the power of the risen Christ, namely visions, miracles, inspired rhetoric, and physically imposing stature. Moreover, they accused him of preaching a rather attenuated Christology, one that emphasized Christ's suffering. Because of these perceived deficiencies, Paul could not be an authentic apostle. Through their unsubstantiated assertions, these "pseudo-apostles" or "super-apostles," as Paul sardonically calls them, attempted to call into question Paul's legitimacy as an emissary of Christ and thus to dislodge him as the leader of the Corinthian community.

Paul needed to respond, if not for his own sake, at least in justice toward the Corinthians whose spiritual welfare was at stake by reason of the alternative Christ and gospel these itinerant missionaries were proclaiming to them. The rebuttal had to be convincing. Using the methods of persuasion current in the Greco-Roman world of rhetoric, Paul composed his response in 2 Corinthians 10-13 to defend his good name, to assert his apostolic legitimacy and leadership, and to vindicate his gospel. The following pages show how he used the three classical proofs of *ethos, pathos*, and *logos* to argue his case against those who vilified him and denigrated the gospel he proclaimed. Paul's method of argumentation was part of a rhetorical strategy which he generally avoided, because such techniques obscured the simplicity of the proof of the gospel inherent in the crucified Christ. However, on this occasion he was compelled to use these rhetorical proofs in the interests of his apostolic mission to the Corinthians. How successful were the results of his persuasion is unknown. How convincing these pages are to show Paul's rhetorical skill is up to the reader to decide.

The rhetorical methodology I have attempted on 2 Corinthians 10-13 is relatively new. I knew some years ago that I wanted to apply rhetorical criticism to biblical exegesis. However, I had no idea of a different approach. I wanted to steer clear of yet another analysis of style, as well as the kind of rhetorical methodology practiced by H. D. Betz which emphasized the structural parts of argumentation, particularly a speech's invention and arrangement, to ascertain genre and function. At the same time I wanted to avoid the more contemporary rhetorical-critical approaches which ran the gamut from reconstruction to deconstruction to the detriment of historical relevancy. I did not want the paradigm to preempt the meaning of the text.

As I pondered 2 Corinthians 10-13, I realized that Paul was trying to convince a group of people toward a particular judgment and a definite action. He was attempting to persuade the Corinthians to think and act correctly. At the same time, as I was reading Aristotle's treatise on the *Art of Rhetoric*, it became clear to me that what Aristotle was saying about *ethos*, *pathos*, and *logos* as integral to persuasion was exactly what Paul was doing in 2 Corinthians 10-13. In fact, Paul was doing what any ancient or even modern speaker does in a speech of persuasion: the speaker projects to an audience an image of competency, good judgment, and moral integrity, pushes the right emotional buttons, and demonstrates with logical appeals. The ingredients to an effective persuasive speech have not changed much in all these centuries.

An approach such at this, using Aristotle's three important methods of proof, answered better some of the puzzling questions concerning the function of the various elements in 2 Corinthians 10-13 and illuminated the meaning of this difficult text. I immediately saw that it was not enough to invoke the theoretical aspects of these three proofs and apply them facilely to 2 Corinthians 10-13 without showing some line of continuity to Paul's practice in contemporary literary rhetorical models and historical precedents. I needed to demonstrate sources and models that reflected Paul's argumentative approach. For this I had to go to speeches prior to and contemporary with Paul to show the various rhetorical possibilities open to Paul which he might have studied and been influenced by. I hope that this methodology will prove a convincing one.

ACKNOWLEDGEMENT

With every gift, one has the obligation to thank one's benefactors. As Cicero once wrote in defense of his friend and benefactor, Gnaeus Plancius: "Gratitude is not only the greatest of virtues but it is the mother of them all. There is no quality I would sooner have, and be thought to have, than gratitude" (*Planc.* 33.80-81). As it is so often said and as Paul argues in 2 Corinthians 10-13, gratitude is both memory and expression. In my case, gratitude is the remembrance of all those who have helped me in the writing of this book and the acknowledgment of thanks to them for their many gifts to me.

In offering thanks, I find that Cicero, in the same oration on behalf of his friend, has anticipated my own categories of beneficiaries. He writes in reference to the Supreme Benefactor: "Who is the person who has true piety and religion if not the one who offers due reverence and remembers to pay thanks to God?" I hope I can be counted among those who have this degree of religion. My other benefactors are my family and friends. "What is filial

x

affection," Cicero continues, "if not willing and eager gratitude toward one's parents?" I wish to thank my mother, 94 years of age at this writing and still alert and active, who has always supported me with her love and gifts. To her I dedicate this book. Thanks also must go to the loving services through the years of my sister, Angie, and brother, Frank, who as the older siblings tried to keep me humble but were always fighting a losing battle.

I am grateful, moreover, to my many friends all over this country and the world for their continuing goodness and countless benefits to me. "Who has there ever been so rich in material wealth", Cicero further comments, "as to be independent of the good offices of so many friends? Take friendship away, and what joy can life continue to hold? Moreover, how can friendship exist at all between those who are devoid of gratitude?" My friends all know their singular place in my heart. I am especially grateful to my confreres in the Franciscan Order who gave me time and support to complete this book.

Last but not least are those whom Cicero acknowledges in his question: "Who among us who have been liberally educated does not constantly ponder with grateful remembrance his tutors and teachers?" I shall be forever indebted to my professors at the Lutheran School of Theology at Chicago, who shared with me their immense knowledge and love of the Scriptures. I am grateful in particular to my major advisor when I was completing my doctorate in New Testament studies, my Doctor-Father, Professor Edgar Krentz, for his nurturing support. With all due respect to Luke 6:40, even though I have finished my studies, I can never hope to be on a par with this singularly gifted teacher and scholar. I am also grateful to my other Lutheran professors who acted as challenging guides to this Roman Catholic clergyman: Professors Wesley Fuerst, David Rhoads, Frederick Danker, Walter Michel, Ralph Klein, and Wilhelm Linss. I also offer special thanks as well to my professors at Catholic Theological Union of Chicago where I first began my biblical studies: Robert Karris, Dianne Bergant, Donald Senior, and the recently deceased Carroll Stuhlmueller. To one and all I say with Paul: "I thank God always whenever I think of you" (Phil 1:3).

INTRODUCTION

In their search for new methodologies to understand the sacred text of the Bible, scripture scholars have used the results of literary critical theories in the process of interpretation. One significant and relatively new offshoot of the use of literary insights for exegesis is a methodology known as rhetorical criticism which applies the principles of argumentation drawn from ancient sources and refined by modern theorists to biblical texts. Rhetorical criticism analyzes the methods of persuasion in a particular discourse to secure an audience's belief and commitment to action.[1]

This new interpretive methodology, however, abounds in conflicting applications because there is no common definition or accepted understanding of what is meant by rhetoric. The word has become a catch-all term to describe every conceivable spoken or written act of human communication. Yet in its long history, it has had a determinative and circumscribed meaning based mainly

---

[1]In his presidential address to the Society of Biblical Literature ("Form Criticism and Beyond," *JBL* 88 [1969] 1-18), the late American Old Testament scholar, James Muilenberg, sounded the call for a new approach to Pentateuchal criticism that would go beyond the predominant method of form-critical analysis and the study of literary types and would give attention to the rhetorical and stylistic features of the received text. Muilenberg's challenge has influenced New Testament criticism. However, his call sounds more like literary-critical analysis rather than strict rhetorical criticism which emphasizes the persuasive power of the text to change or confirm minds to a decided judgment. Since his address, the methodology of rhetorical analysis has become more refined and broadened in scope, making for a thoroughly confusing situation. The person doing rhetorical criticism today must define precisely what that term means before proceeding to use this methodology on a given text.

on the rhetorical theories of such ancient authors as Aristotle, Cicero, and

Quintilian,[2] on other τέχναι in ancient rhetorical handbooks,[3] and on actual

rhetorical practice in such illustrious orators as Demosthenes, Isocrates,

Aeschines, and Cicero. In recent times, however, scholars, under the influence

of the "New Rhetoric," have broadened the application of the term as a result

of penetrating existential and epistemological critiques.[4] This New Rhetoric

retains much from its classical antecedents but expands the meaning of rhetoric

considerably by a generalizing tendency to consider all rhetoric, even epideictic,

as argumentation.[5]

Although there is some growing unanimity that the apostle Paul used

rhetorical techniques in his writing, there is little scholarly consensus today

about how to apply rhetorical analysis in the interpretation of his writings.

There are numerous rhetorical analyses of Pauline letters, but each one proceeds

---

[2]The recognized works are: Arist. *Rh.*; Arist. *[Rh. Al.]*; Cic. *Inv. Rhet.;* Cic. *De Or.*; Cic. *Orat.*; Cic. *Top.*; Cic. *Part. Or.*; Quint. *Inst.*; and *Rhet. Her.*

[3]Many of these handbooks are found in Leonard Spengel, ed., *Rhetores Graeci* (3 vols.; BT; Leipzig: Teubner, 1853-56) and in Ch. Walz, ed., *Rhetores Graeci* (9 vols.; Stuttgart/Tübingen: Cotta, 1832-36).

[4]See especially Ch. Perelman and L. Olbrechts-Tyteca, *The New Rhetoric: A Treatise on Argumentation* (Notre Dame/London: University of Notre Dame Press, 1969).

[5]See the critique of this confusion on the meaning of "rhetorical criticism" and its manifold application in modern exegesis in Margaret Mitchell, *Paul and the Rhetoric of Reconciliation: An Exegetical Investigation of the Language and Composition of 1 Corinthians* (HUT; Tübingen: J. C. Mohr [Paul Siebeck], 1991) 6-11, especially nn.19, 22-26. Mitchell laments the modern eclectic methodology that goes by the rubric of "rhetorical criticism" but is far removed from an historical understanding of the classical rhetoric operative in the first century cultural and intellectual setting of New Testament texts.

from a different set of methodological principles. Basically, most of these rhetorical analyses subsume one of three approaches: the diachronic, the synchronic, and a combination of both.

The diachronic approach seeks to get behind the Pauline text to investigate its historical antecedents and the use of comparative cultural and literary models to account for its genetic development. This approach becomes part of an historical-critical understanding of the text in the light of contemporary Greco-Roman rhetorical tradition, theory, and examples, showing the influence of this rhetoric upon Paul's composition and argumentative strategy. The synchronic approach, on the other hand, looks at the text *qua* text independent of, or at least bracketed from, its historical moorings to see its rhetorical effect in the networking of its component parts, finding the meaning in front of the text. In this approach, the text has a life of its own.

The diachronic critic, consequently, is more linear, emphasizing literary continuity, influence, and cultural evolution from pre-existent models or forms which consciously or subconsciously operated on the creation of a literary text. Here the horizon of historical influences is necessarily limited. The synchronic critic, by contrast, is more helical, seeing almost infinite dimension in the text's architectonic configuration as the text speaks to the cultural and metaphysical presuppositions of the critic's contemporary world. The synchronic critic is constantly recreating the text, more often than not filtering it through one's own philosophical predilections. Here the horizon of meaning is essentially infinite.

In combining both approaches, some rhetorical critics ground their analyses in classical models but use modern linguistic and rhetorical principles that emphasize the subsistent singularity of the text and the reality of the reader.[6]

All three approaches are valid when the critic uses the proper methodological controls and announces one's critical intentions. Without these controls, the diachronic approach may beg the question and assume what needs to be proven, namely, that ancient rhetorical theory and practice actually influenced Paul. The synchronic, on the contrary, may assume the answer at the expense of historical arguments and thus go awry of authorial intention. The combination of both may sacrifice rhetorical precision in either direction and thus confuse the critical reader as to literary appropriateness.

Antoinette Wire's fourfold classification of the more recent uses of rhetorical analysis in Pauline studies illuminates the above three approaches.[7] She groups these rhetorical studies as follows: 1) stylistic analysis; 2) social analysis to arrive at the rhetorical situation; 3) historical analysis of classical parallels; 4) the New Rhetoric and beyond. It would be helpful at this point to say something about her categories to illustrate the variety of meanings attached to rhetorical criticism and further to situate and justify the relatively untried methodology I have taken in this study.

---

[6]These descriptions are somewhat overdrawn to emphasize the direction of the critical approach. The majority of scholars are somewhere at various times on this critical spectrum.

[7]Antoinette Wire, *The Corinthian Women Prophets: A Reconstruction through Paul's Rhetoric* (Minneapolis: Fortress, 1990) 197-201.

Stylistic analysis investigates the aesthetic use of language and the function of various rhetorical devices to show how form is matched to content for persuasive and pleasing effect.[8] Stylistic analysis is intent on identifying and classifying rhetorical figures and showing how the overall integrated function of these devices within a persuasive discourse helps in a fuller understanding of the text. More often than not, the critic interested in stylistics emphasizes more the linguistic mold in which the writer casts a thought or in the arrangement of words to express character or convey emotions rather than in those elements which give persuasion its essential quality.[9]

---

[8]Style in antiquity was very important and the ancient rhetorical theorists devoted large sections of their works to style and to the classification of various figures of speech and thought. Even though these figures of speech and thought and aspects of grammar and composition were, for the most part, considered *ornamenta*, embellishments to make the content stand out more forcefully, yet their arrangement and disposition in a speech or literary work were the very means whereby the persuasive and literary aspects of a work were conveyed. Of course, there had to be propriety and judiciousness in their use, so that there was not ornamentation for ornamentation's sake. Together with propriety and apt use of ornamentation, style had to have other virtues, namely, clarity and correctness. While mere analysis of these figures in a well-written work does not necessarily get to the meaning of a text, yet their identification and function within the work can be a first step toward gaining insight. Those critics who point out such uses and explain and classify them in a work can give invaluable help to the reader. Quintilian did this with Cicero's works. Eventually, however, after the analysis, the work has to be seen as a whole to see how style in all of its aspects functions to make the work literary or persuasive.

[9]Examples of this approach would be Norbert Schneider's work on antithesis, *Die rhetorische Eigenart der paulinischen Antithese* (Tübingen: J. C. B. Mohr [Paul Siebeck], 1970); Karl Plank's treatment of irony, *Paul and the Irony of Affliction* (Atlanta: Scholars Press, 1987); John T. Fitzgerald's work on the catalogue of hardships, *Cracks in an Earthen Vessel: An Examination of the Catalogue of Hardships in the Corinthian Correspondence* (SBLD 99; Atlanta: Scholars Press, 1988); Paul William Hollenbach's study of Paul's use of analogies in "Paul's Self-Understanding as Ascertained through an Analysis of Certain Dramatic Figures of Speech" (Ph.D. diss., Drew University, 1965); Herbert M. Gale's similar study of analogy in *The Use of Analogy in the Letters of Paul* (Philadelphia: Westminster, 1964); Benjamin Fiore's

6

Social world analysis focuses on the cultural milieu of Paul's era as a context of meaning to see how the characteristic aspects of his world penetrated his theology and writing. This analysis looks not only at the cultural heritage of Paul's world reflected in the literary and intellectual writings of his day but also at the material conditions, the psychological ambience, the socio-economic situation, and the socio-political relationships to see how Paul utilized and was influenced by these normative symbols and ideas in his writings.[10]

---

analysis of the function of personal example in the Pastoral Epistles, *The Function of Personal Example in the Socratic and Pastoral Epistles* (AnBib 105; Rome: Biblical Institute Press, 1986); Stanley Stowers' discussion of the diatribe, *The Diatribe and Paul's Letter to the Romans* (Chico, CA: Scholars Press, 1981); and likewise Thomas Schmeller, *Paulus und die "Diatribe": eine vergleichende Stilinterpretation* (Münster: Aschendorff, 1987), as well as Rudolf Bultmann's study, *Der Stil der paulinsichen Predigt und die kynisch-storische Diatribe* (Göttingen: Huth, 1910), to which Stowers' and Schmeller's works are responses; James D. Hester's application of rhetoric to Galatians in "The Use and Influence of Rhetoric in Galatians 2:1-14," *TZ* 42 (1986) 386-408 and "Placing the Blame: The Presence of Epideictic in Galatians 1 and 2," in *Persuasive Artistry: Studies in New Testament Rhetoric in Honor of George Kennedy* (ed. Duane F. Watson; JSOT 50; Sheffield: JSOT, 1991) 281-307; Michael Cosby's "Paul's Persuasive Language in Romans 5," in *Persuasive Artistry*, 209-226; Clarice J. Martin, "The Rhetorical Function of Commercial Language in Paul's Letter to Philemon (Verse 18)," in *Persuasive Artistry*, 321-337; Frank Witt Hughes, "The Rhetoric of Reconciliation: 2 Corinthians 1.1-2.13 and 7.5-8.24," in *Persuasive Artistry*, 246-61; Duane Watson's approach to Paul's use of rhetorical questions in "1 Corinthians 10:23-11:1 in the Light of Graeco-Roman Rhetoric: The Role of Rhetorical Questions," *JBL* 108 (1989) 301-318; Josef Zmijewski's verse-by-verse compositional analysis of Paul's "fool speech" in *Der Stil der paulinischen "Narrenrede." Analyse der Sprachgestaltung II Kor 11, 1-12, 10 als Beitrag zur Methodik von Stiluntersuchungen neutestamentlicher Texte* (BBB 52; Köln-Bonn: Peter Hanstein, 1978); and Aida Besançon Spencer's comparative analysis of various stylistic operations in three Pauline passages with an overlay of a modern linguistic paradigm in *Paul's Literary Style: A Stylistic and Historical Comparison of II Corinthians 11:16-12:13, Romans 8:9-39, and Philippians 3:2-4:13* (Jackson, MS: Evangelical Theological Society, 1984).

[10]Examples of this types of social world analysis are: Peter Marshall, *Enmity in Corinth: Social Conventions In Paul's Relations with the Corinthians* (Tübingen: J. C. B. Mohr [Paul Siebeck], 1987); Norman Petersen, *Rediscovering Paul: Philemon and the Sociology of Paul's Narrative World* (Philadelphia: Fortress, 1985); Frederick

The historical understanding of rhetorical criticism, examined above as strictly diachronic in its approach, uses the documents of Greco-Roman rhetoric to illustrate Paul's rhetorical practices. This type of analysis does not proceed to say anything about Paul's rhetoric and its function in the text as well as in the structural arrangement of his letters without recourse to relevant parallel Greco-Roman texts that operate at the same level, acknowledging Paul's ability to adapt these forms to his own particular needs. An approach such as this presupposes an extensive acquaintance with most of classical literature. Hans Dieter Betz, the outstanding pioneer and practitioner of this historical-critical model, is insistent on this type of methodological rigor: "Scientific facts can only be recognized and demonstrated through comparison with existing parallels."[11] Consequently, he admits of no other method when examining the

---

Danker, "Paul's Debt to the *De Corona* of Demosthenes: A Study of Rhetorical Techniques in Second Corinthians," in *Persuasive Artistry 262-80*, and his *II Corinthians* (Augsburg Commentary; Minneapolis: Augsburg Publishing House, 1989); Makoto Harada, "Paul's Weakness: A Study in Pauline Polemics (2 Cor 10-13)" (Ph.D. diss., Boston University, 1968); Christopher Forbes, "Comparison, Self-Praise, and Irony: Paul's Boasting and the Conventions of Hellenistic Rhetoric," *NTS* 32 (1986) 1-30; Edwin Judge, "Paul's Boasting in Relation to Contemporary Professional Practice," *AusBR* 16 (1968) 37-50; Stanley Olson, *Confidence Expressions in Paul: Epistolary Conventions and the Purpose of 2 Corinthians* (Ph.D. diss., Yale University, 1976) and his "Epistolary Uses of Expression of Self-Confidence," *JBL* 103 (1984) 585-597; Mark Harding, "The Classical Rhetoric of Praise and the New Testament," *Reformed Theological Review* 3 (1986) 73-82.

[11]Betz, *2 Corinthians 8 and 9*, 131. He chides those, on the one hand, who opt for "scientific minimalism" and do nothing along rhetorical-historical lines and those, on the other hand, who "evade methodological control" and "renounce altogether the task of research regarding Pauline rhetoric in general." The latter group might conceivably include those who opt for the "New Rhetoric" and theories beyond it.

text from a rhetorical-critical perspective.[12]

The last category bases its rhetorical approach on the so-called "New Rhetoric," whose theoretical foundations rests principally on Perelman and Olbrechts-Tyteca's imposing work already cited, the focus of which is on argumentation. While it retains many classical concepts, it goes, by its own admission, "far beyond the bounds of ancient rhetoric."[13] However, important though it is as a philosophical work, it aims, as Margaret Mitchell points out, "at *expanding* the realm of argumentation rather than classifying texts according to genre and arrangement," a classification historical critics would consider important.[14] Analyses of Pauline writings using this work are more synchronic in their interpretation since they base their insights on modern philosophical theories of communication rather than on the more diachronic approach of using ancient texts that might have historically influenced Paul.[15]

---

[12]In addition to the works of Betz and Mitchell already cited, the following works illustrate this method: H.D. Betz, *Der Apostel Paulus und die sokratische Tradition: Eine exegetische Untersuchung zu seiner 'Apologie' 2 Kor 10-13* (BHT 45; Tübingen: Mohr/Siebeck, 1972) and "The Problem of Rhetoric and Theology according to the apostle Paul," in *L'Apôtre Paul: Personnalité, Style et Conception du Ministère* (ed. A. Vanhoye; BETL 73; Leuven: Leuven University Press, 1986) 16-48; Michael Bünker, *Briefformular und rhetorische Disposition im 1. Korintherbrief* (Göttingen: Vandenhoeck & Ruprecht, 1983); Frank Witt Hughes, *Early Christian Rhetoric and 2 Thessalonians* (JSOT 30; Sheffield: JSOT Press, 1989); Raymond Humphries, "Paul's Rhetoric in I Corinthians 1-4" (Ph.D. diss., Graduate Theological Union, 1979). Some may not fit neatly into this category but may overlap into the next one.

[13]Perelman and Olbrechts-Tyteca, *The New Rhetoric*, 6.

[14]Mitchell, *Rhetoric of Reconciliation*, 7.

[15]Showing dependence on Perelman and Olbrecht-Tyteca's work are the following: Wilhelm Wuellner, "Paul's Rhetoric of Argumentation in Romans," *CBQ* 38 (1976) 330-51; "Paul as Pastor: The Function of Rhetorical Questions in First Corinthians,"

The above four approaches show the great variety of possibilities in doing rhetorical criticism in Pauline studies in general. The methodologies are equally as disparate in studies specifically devoted to 2 Corinthians 10-13. A major study that comes to mind is Betz's work already cited, *Der Apostle Paulus und die sokratische Tradition*, in which he argues that the form-critical type of 2 Corinthians 10-13 is an "apology" on Paul's part in response to accusations leveled against him that he is a γόης, an imposter. The object was to deny Paul's legitimacy as an apostle. Chapters 10-13 are Paul's attempt to justify himself. In pursuit of this thesis, Betz discusses the σχῆμα and the λόγος of an apostle, since these two points were the major accusations leveled against Paul, namely, that he did not have the appearance or actions of an apostle nor did he have the eloquence of one. Paul's defense is the use of certain Hellenistic conventions that both answer and parody the accusations: self-praise, the image of the fool, the catalogue of hardships and other defense strategies. Betz concludes that Paul's apology shows an extensive familiarity and masterful handling of the literary forms and argumentative devices of the Hellenistic culture. While Betz's analysis is excellent, leading to some helpful insights, it

---

in *L'Apôtre Paul: Personnalité, Style et Conception du Ministère*, 49-77; "Greek Rhetoric and Pauline Argumentation," in *Early Christian Literature and the Classical Tradition* (eds. William R. Schoedel and Robert L. Wilken; Théologie Historique 53; Paris: Éditions Beauchesne, 1979) 177-188; Folker Siegert, *Argumentation bei Paulus, gezeigt an Römer 9-11* (Tübingen: J. C. B. Mohr [Paul Siebeck], 1985); Robert Jewett, *The Thessalonian Correspondence: Pauline Rhetoric and Millenarian Piety* (Philadelphia: Fortress, 1987); Elizabeth Schüssler-Fiorenza, "Rhetorical Situation and Historical Reconstruction in I Corinthians," *NTS* 33 (1987) 386-403; George Kennedy, *New Testament Interpretation through Rhetorical Criticism* (Chapel Hill, NC: University of North Carolina Press, 1984).

does not really get at the essence of Paul's calculated rhetorical tactics. My study will demonstrate that Paul was not merely parodying certain Hellenistic conventions of self-commendation or employing persuasive techniques in an uneven apologetic way but that he was quite designedly using these rhetorical strategies as parts of his own method of proof to convince the Corinthians that he was an authentic apostle with an authoritative gospel. Paul based his probative method on refined classical models expressly intended to persuade.[16]

In contrast to Betz's historical approach, other interpreters of 2 Corinthians 10-13 attempt to puzzle out Paul's plan of rebuttal by recourse to a mixture of

---

[16]Other scholars use different methodologies to unravel Paul's stratagem, the character of his opponents, or the rhetorical situation in 2 Corinthians 10-13. C. K. Barrett ("Christianity at Corinth," *BJRL* 46 [1964] 269-97; "Paul's Opponents in II Corinthians," *NTS* 17 [1971] 233-54) and Dieter Georgi (*The Opponents of Paul in Second Corinthians* (Philadelphia: Fortress, 1986) approach 2 Corinthians 10-13 from the aspect of identifying Paul's opponents to see what their self-understanding was from Paul's response, a kind of rhetorical extrapolation. Johannes Munck (*Paul and the Salvation of Mankind* [Richmond, VA: John Knox Press, 1959] 168-95) analyzes this same passage from the perspective of the contrast between Paul and his opponents in terms of the true and false apostle, what the ethical code and self-description of each should be. Other approaches to a rhetorical analysis of 2 Corinthians 10-13 are J. Paul Sampley ("Paul and His Opponents in 2 Corinthians 10-13 and the Rhetorical Handbooks," in *The Social World of Formative Christianity and Judaism* [eds. Jacob Neusner, Peder Borgen, Ernest Frerichs, and Richard Horsley; Philadelphia: Fortress, 1988] 162-77), who discusses the devices mentioned in the ancient handbooks on achieving an audience's goodwill, using Cicero's theories as a touchstone; Richard Ward ("Paul and the Politics of Performance: A Study of 2 Corinthians 10-13" [Ph.D. diss., Northwestern University, 1987]); D. A. Carson (*From Triumphalism to Maturity: An Exposition of 2 Corinthians 10-13* [Grand Rapids, MI: Baker Book House, 1984]), who does an exposition of this passage from the aspect of bringing the Corinthians from a misguided triumphalism to spiritual maturity; and Aida B. Spencer ("The Wise Fool [and the Foolish Wise]: A Study of Irony in Paul," *NT* 23, 4 [1981] 349-60), who treats of the irony of the wise and the foolish in 2 Cor 11:16-12:13.

methodologies, derived from both ancient sources and modern insights.[17]
More adventuresome modern rhetorical paradigms explain Paul's unusual
response to his critics through the hermeneutics of the new rhetoric.[18] Since
rhetorical criticism takes on many shapes in the hands of various exegetes, it is
important for these interpreters to tell their audience exactly what they mean by
rhetoric and rhetorical criticism. It is equally important for the wary reader to
sift out the value of the methodologies to determine what Paul actually meant
and how he meant it from the how and what of various critics' minds.

In contrast to all the above approaches, my study investigates Paul's use of
the ancient rhetorical theory and practice of ἦθος, πάθος, and λόγος as proofs
in a persuasive discourse to analyze 2 Corinthians 10-13, which H. D. Betz
called "one of the most puzzling passages in the Pauline correspondence."[19]

---

[17]Jewett, for example, does not hesitate to use classical rhetoric, the New Rhetoric, and linguistic analysis together in doing a critical interpretation. Other authors, such as Wuellner and Schüssler-Fiorenza, take rhetorical criticism into the realm of reader-response criticism and other areas, where the received text takes second place to the relocation of meaning in the reader's self or to some other self or situation. See Mitchell's critique of Wuellner's eclectic methodology, *The Rhetoric of Reconciliation*, 7-8, nn. 23-24.

[18]One modern study that relies solely on a contemporary rhetorical model is Jeffrey Crafton, *The Agency of the Apostle: A Dramatistic Analysis of Paul's Response to Conflict in 2 Corinthians* [JSOT 51; Sheffield: JSOT, 1991, in which he follows a modern rhetorical-critical method known as "dramatism," the foundations of which rest on the theory and practice of Kenneth Burke. Burke's theory is basically an analysis of the rhetorical use of language to explicate modes of action in the human speaker or writer rather than the disposition of words by the speaker or writer to form intentional proofs to persuade.

[19]H. D. Betz, *Paul's Apology II Corinthians 10-13 and the Socratic Tradition* (Center for Hermeneutical Studies in Hellenistic and Modern Culture, Colloquy 2, December, 1970; ed. Wilhelm Wuellner; Berkeley: Center for Hermeneutical Studies, 1975) 3.

My investigation focuses specifically on the use Paul makes of Aristotle's three important methods of proof in argumentation to defend his reputation, his authority, and his apostleship. These three methods of proof necessary for a persuasive rhetorical response pay careful and deliberate attention, first, to demonstrating the good character of the speaker or writer ($\mathring{\eta}\theta o\varsigma$); second, to arousing emotions in the audience ($\pi\acute{\alpha}\theta o\varsigma$); and last, to the rational and logical disposition of the argument ($\lambda\acute{o}\gamma o\varsigma$). The following chapters will demonstrate that Paul uses these three proofs in a calculated and effective way to challenge the disturbing perceptions of the Corinthians, to answer his opponents, to validate his apostolic credentials, and to re-establish his leadership.

This paradigm of looking at Paul's communicative strategy through the lens of Aristotle's three constituent proofs of persuasive argumentation is critical to a fuller understanding of the function and meaning of 2 Corinthians 10-13. At the same time, this approach is an heuristic device for demonstrating the nature and use of classical rhetoric in Paul's preaching and for contextualizing the social and cultural influences, ideas, and practices which motivated Paul, the Corinthians, and Paul's opponents in their mutually critical and argumentative stances. In effect, this model arrives at an exegetical understanding of the text on the basis of historical precedents which Paul drew upon from the Greco-Roman rhetorical tradition on the three methods of proof.

The methodology used in thus study imitates the historical approach pioneered by H. D. Betz and used recently by his student, Margaret Mitchell.[20] The task of using rhetorical analysis as part of an historical-critical understanding necessarily assumes, as Margaret Mitchell has clearly shown in her study of factionalism in 1 Corinthians, an important methodological mandate which undergirds the following chapters: the use of ancient handbooks of rhetoric, along with actual speeches and letters from antiquity, in their original texts in the rhetorical analysis of 2 Corinthians 10-13 to demonstrate sources and models that reflect influence on Paul.[21] While this study uses the historical-critical method of Betz and Mitchell, it differs radically from their emphasis on the structural analysis of invention and arrangement and puts significant stress on the three important methods of proof which Aristotle and other classical rhetoricians asserted were absolute requisites in achieving persuasion and which Paul used in 2 Corinthians 10-13 to such masterful advantage.

The rhetorical handbooks present the prescriptive theory of persuasive rhetorical discourse while the actual speeches and letters demonstrate the variety of rhetorical possibilities available to Paul. Consequently, in the following pages I will consult these handbooks and literary works to see what they have to say abut the nature and uses of ἦθος, πάθος, and λόγος and investigate Paul's use of these proofs to act on the minds of the Corinthians to achieve his

---

[20]H. D. Betz, *2 Corinthians 8 and 9: A Commentary on Two Administrative Letters of the Apostle Paul* (Hermeneia; Philadelphia: Fortress, 1985) and *Galatians* (Hermeneia; Philadelphia: Fortress, 1979); Margaret Mitchell, *Paul and the Rhetoric of Reconciliation*.

[21]Mitchell, *Paul and the Rhetoric of Reconciliation*, 6-11.

stated goals: to demolish the sophistries of his opponents (2 Cor 10:5), to correct the Corinthians' superficial view of the reality of their life in Christ (10:7), to answer the accusations against him (10:10), and to assert his apostolic authority (10:8).

So far as I can tell from reviewing the literature on Pauline rhetoric in general and 2 Corinthians 10-13 in particular, no one seems to have used this methodology as a way of entering the world of the text to see how it functions as a very structured and serious response to the crisis at hand. Other have emphasized, as we have seen above, various rhetorical conventions and Hellenistic professional oratorical and literary practices to illuminate portions of the text but so far there seems to be no general paradigm that investigates this appropriate and adroit kind of response on Paul's part.[22] By focusing on Paul's careful use and interaction of these three methods of proof, that is, by an appeal to the goodness, competence, and trustworthiness of his character and life, by summoning up various emotions in his audience, and by the quasi-logical arguments of the enthymeme and example, I intend to show how Paul carries on his rhetorical response in 2 Corinthians 10-13 as a serious enterprise

---

[22]There is one study that treats the first two methods of proof in Galatians. This is Steven John Kraftchick, *Ethos and Pathos Appeals in Galatians Five and Six: A Rhetorical Analysis* (Ph.D. diss., Emory University, 1985). My critique of this study is that it devotes an excessive amount of space to other aspects of rhetorical theory in the first part of the work that are not integrated later into his analysis of Galatians 5 and 6. My main criticism of his approach, however, is that he gives hardly any samples from parallel Greco-Roman texts to show the theory of these two proofs in practice. At the same time he leaves out a discussion of λόγος which Aristotle considered quite important in an oration, in spite of the latter's comments about ἦθος.

of persuasion to reclaim his esteem, the acknowledgement of his authority, and his legitimacy as an apostle among the Corinthians. These three methods of proof constitute the matrix in which Paul's argument is cast.

In summary, the methodology I use in the following pages draws from the literary and rhetorical theories existing at the time of Paul as well as from contemporary literary rhetorical models (the speeches used in a student's training as paradigmatic of good argumentation) to show how Paul used the relevant rhetorical possibilities of his age to respond to the crisis in the Corinthian community. This investigation demonstrates that Paul assimilated much from his culture in his ability to argue for the adherence to his values and his authority. Far from being an ἰδιώτης τῷ λόγῳ (11:6), he was a rhetor of great persuasive power.[23]

---

[23]There is a definite crux in Paul's use of λόγος in 2 Cor 11:6. Does he mean to state that he is not good at written argumentation and literary rhetorical response or does he mean to agree with his critics (if that is all they are objecting to) that he is not good at public speaking and rhetorical delivery? A good example of the separation of these two skills is the *Antidosis* of Isocrates which is an eloquent piece of rhetoric on paper but was never delivered to a live audience. Victor Furnish (*II Corinthians* [AB; Garden City, New York: Doubleday, 1984], 490) translates ἰδιώτης τῷ λόγῳ as "amateur in public speaking," thus suggesting Paul's claim to lack oratorical skill but not necessarily Paul's deficiency in convincing epistolary rhetoric. There is no way to produce evidence of Paul's public speaking ability. But there is a way to make a plausible case, as my investigation shows, that Paul had skill in the use of the three classical proofs involved in a rhetorical response. Some would object even to this and argue that Paul's words in 2 Cor 11:6 must be taken at face value to disclaim any ability to persuade. However, his words can be taken as an example of *praeteritio*, where he ironically acknowledges the critique of the pseudo-apostles but proceeds to demolish their character and influence by the skilled use of rhetorical techniques. If nothing else, the response itself, on careful analysis, shows the influence of rhetorical training. Some may further object that Paul did not necessarily have to have formal school lessons in rhetoric but could have assimilated the skill through careful imitation of speeches he heard. This minimalist objection denies Paul the kind of liberal education he naturally would have received in a culturally diverse city like Tarsus.

CHAPTER ONE

SOME PRELIMINARY BACKGROUND ISSUES

A. Ancient Rhetorical Theory

A brief discussion of ancient rhetorical theory at this point will help to situate for the reader the three methods of proof which Aristotle considered absolutely integral to a speech of persuasion. What is rhetoric? What are its nature, its principles, its uses? Aristotle defined rhetoric as "the faculty (or power) of discovering the possible means of persuasion in reference to any subject whatever."[24] Quintilian explained it as "bene dicendi scientia" or "ars bene dicendi."[25] To oversimplify, in Aristotle's definition the emphasis is on proof in argumentation by means of the speech itself; this is to say that the proof is intrinsic, imbedded in the oration itself through the use of the three proofs. With Quintilian, the emphasis is on the goodness of the orator who is trained in style; hence, the proof is more extrinsic, aligned with the character of the speaker. Basically, all rhetoric or the art of persuasion, as taught in the schools, trained students in five major areas:

---

[24]Arist. *Rh.* 1.2.1.

[25]Quint. *Inst.* 2.14.5 and 2.17 37.

16

> . . . *invention*, which deals with the planning of a discourse and the arguments to be used in it; *arrangement*, the composition of the various parts into an effective whole; *style*, which involves both choice of words and the composition of words into sentences, including the use of figures; *memory*, or preparation for delivery; and *delivery*, the rules for control of the voice and the use of gestures.[26]

Aristotle next goes into the three kinds of rhetoric which are determined by three classes of listeners to speeches who define the speech's end and object. He writes:

> The kinds of Rhetoric are three in number, corresponding to the three kinds of hearers. For every speech is composed of three parts: the speaker, the subject of which he treats, and the person to whom it is addressed, I mean the hearer, to whom the end or object of the speech refers. Now the hearer must necessarily be either a mere spectator or a judge, and a judge either of things past or things to come.[27].

If the hearer is a judge of things to come, the speech is known as deliberative; if the hearer is a judge of things past, the speech is forensic; if the hearer is a mere spectator of the ability of the speaker, the speech is epideictic. Note the emphasis Aristotle gives to the audience whom the speaker must observe carefully to find out its needs.

The deliberative speech is created either to exhort or to dissuade concerning some future action; its special end is the expedient or the harmful. The forensic or judicial speech is composed to either accuse or defend and refers to the past,

---

[26]George Kennedy, *New Testament Interpretation*, 13-14. The preceding thought, with a slight addition, is Kennedy's as well.

[27]Arist. *Rh.* 1.3.1-3. Most of what follows is from this section.

to things done that one party accuses and the other defends; its special end is the just or unjust. The epideictic or display speech is meant for praise or blame and refers to the present condition of things; its end is the honorable and the disgraceful.

Aristotle talks about the two categories of proofs which are the means of persuasion. The first category supplies proofs which the speaker does not have to invent since they are ready at hand, such as witnesses, tortures, contracts, and the like. The speaker makes use of what is already there. These proofs are called ἄτεχνοι, those which are non-fabricated and are independent of the speaker's efforts. The other category contains the ἔντεχνοι, those which the speaker has to construct through one's own literary and logical instrumentality. The ἔντεχνοι-proofs are the subject of this study.

The ἔντεχνοι-proofs are three: proof from the moral character of the speaker (ἦθος); proof from putting the hearers into a certain frame of mind by arousing their emotions (πάθος); and proof from the speech itself, in so far as it proves or seems to prove, by the use of the logical arguments of enthymeme and example (λόγος). Aristotle emphasizes that these three speaker-created methods of proof have an important element in common: *the speech itself must furnish the three proofs*. In other words, the speaker in order to be persuasive must articulate through one's own literary artistry these methods of proof in a clear, correct, and eloquent style that reaches the heart of the listener and must embody through logical skill an effective arrangement of thought that appeals to the listener's mind. It is through the means of the spoken or written word that persuasion occurs, not through any other means, not even the preconceived notions an audience might have of the speaker. This, as will be shown, is different from the conception of Quintilian, who places important emphasis upon the goodness of the speaker as a cogent element in persuasion.

The foregoing discussion basically describes the area of *invention*, the planning of the discourse and the source of the arguments used. The second major area, that of *arrangement*, refers to the necessary parts or division (τάξις) of any effective speech. The quantitative parts are four in number according to Aristotle, although their nomenclature was Latinized by Cicero and Quintilian: the exordium (προοίμιον, *proem* or *proemium*, compared to the πρόλογος in tragedy), statement of the case (πρόθεσις, *propositio*, together with the *expositio* or *narratio* of the case, διήγησις), proofs (πίστεις), and epilogue (ἐπίλογος, *peroratio*).[28]

The *exordium* seeks to gain the attention, goodwill, and sympathy of the audience and makes clear what is the end or purpose of the speech. This is a favorite spot to use ethical appeals, showing one's good character, although the use of ἦθος should not be neglected throughout the speech. The *narration* of the facts and the statement of the proposition which the speaker wishes to prove or disprove are next. In this section, the speaker should narrate anything that tends to show one's virtue or the wickedness of one's opponent, excite emotion,

---

[28]Arist. *Rh*. 3.13.4-3.19.6 for the entire discussion.

and make clear one's moral purpose. *Proofs* are demonstrative or refutative, both of which use enthymemes and examples. The arguments are constructed from what are known as τόποι (*loci*), standard types of argumentation to which the speaker might go to find formal strategies for the construction of the enthymeme. The *epilogue* (or peroration in Roman rhetorical theory) has four functions: to attract the audience's goodwill once again toward the speaker and dispose it unfavorably towards one's adversary; to excite the emotions of the audience one last time to take action or make a judgment; to amplify oneself and deprecate one's adversary; and to recapitulate or summarize the argument.

In very summary fashion, the above are some of the main points of Aristotle's rhetorical system, which numerous theorists modified and expanded in succeeding centuries until the time of Quintilian who in about 80 C.E. codified the prevailing theories in his famous twelve-book masterpiece, *Institutio Oratoria*. Other aspects of the rhetorical system, namely *style*, *memory*, and *delivery* are also important. The last two items are not germane to our present discussion. However, Aristotle noted that the delivery of the oration was extremely important in any success the speech might have at persuading an audience.[29]

Aristotle emphasizes the crucial importance of style (λέξις) with the

---

[29]Aristotle (*Rh.* 3.1.3) says delivery "is of the greatest importance." It is essentially an area that is unrecoverable, since we cannot recapture the one-time experience of speaker, audience, and speech in an actual rhetorical situation with all of its attendant emotional content. Later I shall say more on this issue as far as the public delivery of Paul's letter to the Corinthian community was concerned.

words: "For it is not sufficient to know what one ought to say, but one must also know how to say it."[30] Aristotle devotes the first thirteen chapters of the third book of his *Ars Rhetorica* to a discussion of style. He says it should have basically three qualities: clarity (σαφήνεια *Rh.* 3.2.1, or τὸ ἐλληνίζειν, *Rh.* 3.5.1-6), brevity (συντομία, *Rh.* 3.6.1-6), and appropriateness (πρέπον, *Rh.* 3.7.1-5). At the same time he discusses figures of thought (σχήματα διανοίας) and diction (σχήματα λέξεως) in a detailed way. Later writers such as Cicero, the unknown author of the *Rhetorica ad Herennium*, Dionysius of Halicarnassus, Quintilian, and many others discuss the grand, middle, and the simple styles, as well as elegance in expression and eloquence in diction and the use of various rhetorical techniques, to influence opinion and win a case. The rhetorical handbooks catalog a vast array of rhetorical devices, too numerous to cite here. The following chapters allude to various aspects of style, since style is inseparably linked to the way Paul and other speakers embody their thoughts.[31]

This brief synopsis gives the reader an idea of Aristotle's rhetorical system and where the three methods of proof fit in so far as the art of persuasion is concerned. They are absolutely basic to Aristotle's vision of rhetoric as the art of persuasion. It must be said that this rhetorical theory did not come out of his head full blown. His genius was in extracting and synthesizing the principles

---

[30]Arist. *Rh.* 3.1.2.

[31]Heinrich Lausberg (*Handbuch der literarischen Rhetorik: eine Grundlegung der Literaturwissenschaft* [München: Max Hueber Verlag, 1960]) has collected the most complete definitions and examples of figures of speech and thought in his massive and useful work.

of good oratory he saw being practiced by the famous orators of his time,

Antiphon, Andocides, Isocrates (with whom Aristotle was in competiion), Isaeus

(pupil of Isocrates and teacher of Demosthenes), Lysias, Demosthenes,

Aeschines, and many others.[32] He noted that these orators were effective

because they organized and articulated their thoughts with their listeners and

their auditors' needs constantly in mind. He recognized how these orators were

intent on presenting themselves to their audience as persons of good repute and

trustworthy competence. He recognized in their words, physical actions, and

even stage props (at least this was the case later with Cicero) the intention of

arousing an entire spectrum of emotions in their listeners, coloring their

adversaries in the most lurid of tones and their own cause in feelings of pity,

fear, and indignation. He marked them reasoning with their audience through

syllogisms and examples to appeal to their desire for precedent and logic. He

evaluated how the three proof-approaches were couched in the best Attic Greek.

---

[32]Aristotle and Isocrates were competitors in more ways than one. They competed first of all for students in their respective schools of rhetoric. Isocrates was the more successful and amassed a considerable fortune from charging a high tuition over forty years of teaching rhetoric. His students achieved fame in many fields, a fact which inspired Cicero (*De Or.* 2.22.94) to write: "Then behold! there arose Isocrates, the Master of all rhetoricians, from whose school, as from the Horse of Troy, none but leaders emerged." Aristotle and Isocrates diverged in their philosophies of rhetoric. Aristotle was more the philosopher of rhetoric applying his penetrating scientific mind to the nature of rhetoric. The effect created by the speech itself was all-important as was the attention given to the audience as a controlling factor in writing the discourse. Aristotle was undeniably the greatest theoretician and a very good teacher of the art but never a practitioner of it. Isocrates, on the other hand, mastered the art he taught and insisted that the orator must have a high reputation for honor and goodness which is outside the appearances created by the speech. For Isocrates, being a person of good repute among one's fellow-citizens was intrinsic to the art of rhetoric.

These observations enabled Aristotle to determine the principles underlying effective oratory.

With this in mind, it is surprising that hardly any New Testament scholar has ventured to analyze Paul's writings by applying these three proof-methods. It seems a better mode of fruitful exegesis than the sometimes tedious application of the rhetorical analysis of his letters through structural components.[33] Paul was bent on persuading others to give their adherence to his gospel and to the person of Jesus Christ. He would have searched out methods of proof to bring an audience to his frame of mind. These three methods were ready at hand in his own times and education, as the next section notes, to bring to the purposes of the Gospel. That he used them the following chapters will show.

B. Was Paul Rhetorically Trained?

It is not far off the mark to claim that Paul was acquainted with the rhetorical theory and practice of his day through exposure to formal rhetorical training in his education and to the speeches of his contemporaries and that he consequently later used rhetorical techniques in his writings. This hypothesis

---

[33]I am referring here to the method popularized by Betz and practiced by many others who associate rhetorical analysis with the application of Aristotle's fivefold component of the arrangement of a speech (i.e., *exordium, narratio, propositio, probatio, peroratio*) to Paul's letters. This may help to determine the genre (apologetic, deliberative, polemical, hortatory, etc.) but the question of relevance and understanding of the text still remains.

is based partially on the *external* evidence of the hellenization of thought and practice in Paul's day, even in the pluralistic Jewish circles of Palestine and her neighbors, and partially on the *internal* evidence of the several references Paul makes in his letters to classical literature and in the use of rhetorical techniques in his letters. His remark in 2 Cor 11:6 that he is an ἰδιώτης τῷ λόγῳ should not be taken at face value, but understood as an ironic understatement that demurs before it dazzles, a concession of modesty that disavows on one level while it behaves differently on another. When Paul denies that he has rhetorical skills as he does in 2 Corinthians 10-13 or says that rhetoric in general obscures the simple message of the cross as he does in 1 Corinthians 1-4, he is probably not thinking of the rhetorical art of the great Attic orators mentioned in the preceding section, but of the overtly ornamental and artificial style known as "Asianism," where external flamboyance substituted for the substance of a message and sometimes co-opted its meaning.

The external evidence points to a general cultural phenomenon to which Paul was undoubtedly exposed to in the bustling university city and rhetorical center that was Tarsus.[34] That phenomenon is the influence of Hellenism on

---

[34]W. Rhys Roberts (*Demetrius "On Style"* [LCL; Cambridge, MA: Harvard University Press, 1927; rev. and rep. 1932] 278) writes in the Introduction to his translation: "The long tradition of Greek literary study at Tarsus is suggested by the names of the Stoic Archidemus of Tarsus (130 B.C.); and the rhetorician Hermogenes of Tarsus (A.D. 170); and the vigour with which such studies could be adapted to new and high purposes is best seen in Paul of Tarsus, who was proud to be a citizen not only of Tarsus but of Rome. St. Paul's writings and his life are standing proof that the Tarsus of Plutarch's Demetrius [Roberts tentatively identifies the Demetrius of the work *On Style* with Demetrius of Tarsus] was serving as a linguistic and literary centre and was becoming a great link between East and West."

all facets of society, particularly in the area of rhetorical skill and the inculcation of these techniques through the use of the *progymnasmata* in the secondary level of schooling, which were handbooks containing rhetorical speeches and letters for imitation.[35] This training was necessary for the ephebe if he was to succeed in the public forum and political arena. According to the research of David Daube, even Hebrew exegesis was not exempt from this influence. He writes:

> The thesis here to be submitted is that the Rabbinic methods of interpretation derive from Hellenistic rhetoric. Hellenistic rhetoric is at the bottom of both of the fundamental ideas, propositions, from which the Rabbis proceeded and of the major details of application. . . . In its beginning, the Rabbinic system of hermeneutics is a product of the Hellenistic civilization then dominating the entire Mediterranean world.[36]

---

[35]The literature is becoming more and more voluminous, particularly from Jewish scholars, regarding this issue of how much the Greek language and Greek intellectual concepts and materials of rhetorical art permeated education in the highly Hellenized cities in Palestine, not to mention in the Diaspora. This exposure would hold true as well for the training of the so-called strict rabbinical schools. See the following: Saul Lieberman, *Hellenism in Jewish Palestine: Studies in the Literary Transmission Beliefs and Manners of Palestine in the 1 Century B.C.E.—IV Century C.E* (New York: Jewish Theological Seminary of America, 1950; and his *Greek in Jewish Palestine: Studies in the Life and Manners of Jewish Palestine in the II-IV Centuries C.E.* (2nd ed.; New York: Philipp Feldheim, 1965); and his "How Much Greek in Jewish Palestine?" in *Essays in Greco-Roman and Related Talmudic Literature* (New York: KTAV Publishing House, 1977) 325-43; Henry Fischel, "Story and History: Observations on Greco-Roman Rhetoric and Pharisaism," in *Essays in Greco-Roman and Related Talmudic Literature*, 443-73; Morton Smith, "Palestinian Judaism in the First Century," *Essays in Greco-Roman and Related Talmudic Literature*, 183-97; J. N. Sevenster, *Do You Know Greek? How Much Greek Could the First Jewish Christians Have Known?* (Leiden: E. J. Brill, 1968).

[36]David Daube, "Rabbinic Methods of Interpretation and Hellenistic Rhetoric," *HUCA* 22 (1949) 240. Daube makes an interesting argument concerning "Hillel's seven norms of interpretation and Alexandria, a centre of Hellenistic scholarship" (241), which were the oldest rules according to which the Scripture is to be 'interpreted.' These rules or norms reflect some rhetorical principles, such as antithesis, analogical

Boaz Cohen writes that "Paul was eminently imbued with the culture of his day, and was undoubtedly familiar with the current doctrines of Greek rhetoric and Roman law, which was natural for a man raised in Tarsus, the seat of a university where Stoic philosophy and Roman law were taught."[37] It is natural to surmise that there was some fertile cross-pollination between Hellenism and the Jews of the Diaspora in the practical matters of life in the *polis*, that is, in most things except for the worship of the city gods. While the Jews maintained their own *politeuma*, namely that of the Mosaic Law, yet exposure to a culturally dominant society necessitated some amount of syncretism and social identification in those areas which would make the Jews more acculturated and less insulated. After all, no one is brought up and educated in a vacuum. Even the Jews in the explication and application of the Law to themselves and its appeal to others proceeded from a cultural interpretation provided by then current educational models.

Whether one accepts Lieberman's quote from Gamaliel the Elder's son, R. Simeon ben Gamaliel, who speaks of "a thousand young men in my father's

---

reasoning, *a fortiori* or *a minori ad maius* argument, and the rule of the general and the specific (reminiscent of the τόπος of the "more and less" to be discussed in the last chapter). Daube's point is that Hillel, a contemporary of Cicero and student of Shemaiah and Abtalion who were "the first Rabbis to be called *darshanim*, 'interpreters of Scripture'" and who at least studied and taught in Alexandria, a great rhetorical center, was influenced by Greek methods of reasoning. One can plausibly surmise then that if the great Hillel opened himself up to this influence, Paul likewise had no problem in receiving training in rhetorical and philosophical skills.

[37]Boaz Cohen, *Jewish and Roman Law: A Comparative Study* (New York: Jewish Theological Seminary of America, 1966) 56.

house, five hundred of them studied Torah while the other five hundred studied

Greek wisdom,"[38] the fact is that such a situation is plausible. One wonders

which group (or was it both?) Paul was in as a student of Gamaliel? Though

he says in Acts 22:3 that he "was educated strictly in the law of our fathers" at

the feet of Gamaliel, this statement does not preclude Paul's exposure to Greek

thought and Greek rhetorical skills needed for oral persuasion, or at least his

acquaintance with learning the methods of one's opponents if for no other reason

than to use these skills against them.

The internal evidence for Paul's knowledge and assimilation of Greek

patterns of thought and rhetorical skills comes from Paul himself in his few

reference to classical literature (Acts 17:28, if one does not consider this

specifically Lukan; 1 Cor 15:33;) and in the artful manner in which he imitates

the models and τόποι of classical rhetoric to exhort or dissuade, accuse or

defend, praise or blame.[39] Schüssler-Fiorenza, following Michael Bünker's

---

[38]Saul Lieberman, *Hellenism in Jewish Palestine*, 104. He says further: "We have no reason to disbelieve this statement. Nobody would have invented this kind of tradition." Lieberman says this in a chapter devoted to the alleged ban on Greek Wisdom among the Rabbis, in which he writes (101-02) that "there is no hint of a ban on the *study* of Greek Wisdom or the Greek Language; the injunction involves only the *teaching of children.*"

[39]Roberts (*Demetrius "On Style,"* 278-79) writes: "In his Greek epistles, St. Paul can quote Epimenides and Menander; at Athens, where he quotes Aratus, he can deliver a Greek speech to a critical audience. As a great letter-writer and one who fully understood that a good letter should be one of the two sides of an imaginary dialogue (*Style*, 223), St. Paul was in the true Peripatetic tradition. Even in the minutiae of self-expression, he will be found to be in accord with that same tradition as preserved and developed in the work on *Style*. The famous thirteenth chapter in the First Epistle to the Corinthians exemplifies the ἀσύνδετα and the διλογίαι which, when used in season, are praised in *Style*, 267-269, 103."

analysis of 1 Cor 1:10-4:21 and 1 Corinthians 15, says that Paul's "distinction between ἐν πειθοῖ σοφίας and ἐν ἀποδείξει πνεύματος indicates that he knew the rhetorical distinction between oratory as mere persuasion and speech as a process of forming one's opinion on the basis of arguments and proofs."[40]

Paul was a man of his time who, first as a Jew and then as a Christian, actively sought the information which could make him more effective in reaching the educated Hellenistic circles both of Palestine and of the surrounding Mediterranean region. Paul knew the Corinthians were "rich . . . in discourse" (2 Cor 8:7); so he knew he had to meet them on their own ground, as he does in his letters to them. As the authors of the *Assembly Annotations* of 1688 said:

> Though the Apostle made little use of Oratory in his ordinary Discourses and Epistles, yet he knew how to use it to the Ends which he aimed at, *viz.* the Glory of God, and the good of Souls that were under his care. He did not turn Divinity into mere words and Rhetorical flourishes; yet he made use of these sometimes, as a waiting Maid to Divinity.

Hugo Grotius in his *Annotationes in Novum Testamentum* had remarked at that same time: "Paul was not ignorant of the art of rhetoric, to move people by praising them."[41] The skill of eloquence and persuasion that Paul manifests in 2 Corinthians 10-13 in the use of the three classical methods of proof and in the manipulation of many Hellenistic rhetorical τόποι and τρόποι reflects formal schooling in Greek-Roman rhetoric.

---

[40]Schüssler-Fiorenza, "Rhetorical Situation and Historical Reconstruction in 1 Corinthians," 392. For Michael Bünker's quote see his *Briefformular*, 49.

[41]Betz gives both quotations in *2 Corinthians 8 and 9*, 8.

C. The Integrity of 2 Corinthians 10-13

The integrity of 2 Corinthians is a longstanding, complicated, and essentially moot question. Since the time of Johann Semler's 1776 commentary on 2 Corinthians, wherein he proposed for the first time several distinct fragments in this Letter, the debate on partition theories of 2 Corinthians, as in 1 Corinthians, has hotly continued.[42]

Various partition hypotheses have argued for the division of 2 Corinthians into chapters 1-7, 8, 9, and 10-13 as separate letters. Other scholars, on the other hand, have maintained the literary unity of the Letter, in spite of the alleged harsh transition between chapters 9 and 10, sometimes from the question-begging argument of the authority of tradition (W. Kümmel); sometimes from a naively psychologizing argument as to the shifting moods of Paul (Lietzmann) or as "an interruption in the dictation of the letter" (the *Diktatpause* of J. D. Michaelis); sometimes from thematic reasons (Nils Dahl) or from the underlying structure of thought (H. J. Holtzmann); sometimes from the simple "we don't know" hypothesis (the *ars nesciendi*) of C. F. G. Heinrici; and sometimes, more successfully, from the study of rhetoric (Frederick Danker) and from form-critical and compositional analysis (Niels Hyldahl). As Betz has aptly remarked, the unity of 2 Corinthians is also an hypothesis and,

---

[42]This brief summary of partition theories of 2 Corinthians is indebted to H. D. Betz, *2 Corinthians 8 and 9*, 3-36.

in any case, the lack of methodological reflection on both sides is a serious handicap to the resolution of the problem, for the arguments oftentimes operate "on hypothetical constructions lying behind the text" and not "on the level of the text itself."[43]

In light of the arguments and counterarguments for the unity of 2 Corinthians from notable scholars, it is difficult to venture an opinion as to the continuity of 2 Corinthians 10-13 with the preceding chapters 1-9. To summarize the history of research in this area and then to suggest and demonstrate a new approach pro or con would be a study in itself. This investigation is not concerned whether 10-13 was the "letter of tears" or some other letter to settle some disobedience nor with the chapters' relationship to 1-9. This study treats chapters 10-13 as a separate and distinct compositional unit for the sake of rhetorical analysis. The aim is to see the rhetorical effectiveness of chapters 10-13 to determine how Paul uses the three classical methods of proof to answer and quell a potential revolt against his authority and to claim superiority over the false apostles and thus to force the Corinthian community to come to terms with itself vis-à-vis leadership and its continued existence as a Pauline church. This approach, isolating 2 Corinthians 10-13 as a self-contained textual unit and examining its argumentative structures and rhetorical techniques for its exegetical understanding, is a legitimate literary task that does

---

[43]Betz, *2 Corinthians 8 and 9*, 26. In this work Betz, following Hans Windisch, argues that chaps. 8-9 are independent of the rest of 2 Corinthians. He bases his conclusions on rhetorical and epistolary grounds in their use of administrative language.

not compromise the integrity of the entire letter nor disturb the meaning of the passage. Whether or not there was redactional activity in 2 Corinthians does not preclude the advantage of viewing chapters 10-13 as a rhetorical whole that has a beginning, middle, and end and thus a unit for analysis.

D. Greco-Roman Epistolography and Rhetoric

Since all we know of Paul's rhetorical ability is from his letters, it is important to make some brief comments on the relation of rhetoric to Greek epistolary theory and Greek letter-writing and Roman letter models.[44] While this field of inquiry is still in its infant investigatory stages due to a paucity of epistolary handbooks and actual letter models that have survived,[45] one can

---

[44]See the following selected literature on this growing field: Stanley Stowers, *Letter Writing in Greco-Roman Antiquity* (LEC; Philadelphia: Westminster Press, 1986); Francis Xavier J. Exler, *The Form of the Ancient Greek Letter of the Epistolary Papyri (3rd c. B.C.-3rd c. A.D.): A Study in Greek Epistolography* (Chicago: Ares Publishers, 1976); John L. White, *Light from Ancient Letters* (Philadelphia: Fortress, 1986) and "Ancient Greek Letters," in *Greco-Roman Literature and the New Testament: Selected Forms and Genre* (ed. David Aune; SBLSBS 21; Atlanta: Scholars Press, 1988) 85-105; and his "New Testament Epistolary Literature in the Framework of Ancient Epistolography," *ANRW* 25, 2 (1984) 1730-56; William Doty, *Letters in Primitive Christianity* (Philadelphia: Fortress, 1973); for Greco-Roman rhetoric, epistolography, and Paul's letters, see H. D. Betz, *Galatians* (Hermeneia; Philadelphia: Fortress, 1979) 14-25.

[45]The two extant major epistolary handbooks are *Epistolary Types* attributed to Demetrius of Phalerum and *Epistolary Kinds* by either Libanius or Proclus. As for letters, only those of Plato and a few survive from the Greek tradition; those of Aristotle, Theophrastus and others are lost. There are those, however, of Cicero from the Roman tradition (931 were written between 68 and 43 B.C.E.) and a few of Seneca. See Stanley Stowers, "Greek and Latin Letters," in *Anchor Bible Dictionary* (ed. David Noel Freedman; New York: Doubleday, 1992) 4, 291-92, See also Abraham J. Malherbe, *Ancient Epistolary Theorists* (SBLSBS 19; Atlanta: Scholars Press, 1988).

make some general remarks relative to the thesis of this paper.

First, according to ancient epistolary theory, letters were regarded as a substitute for one's physical presence and as "one of the two sides of a dialogue," yet "a little more studied than the dialogue."[46] The physical separation of friends or clients necessitated a style of writing that imagined the two people were in intimate or professional oral communication. As Stowers writes: "The letter 'fictionalizes' the personal presence of the sender and receiver. The authorial voice is constructed as if speaking directly to the audience."[47]

Nice and convenient as this may sound, the letter nevertheless simply lacked one important ingredient that gave impact and greater meaning to the words, namely oral delivery. The sender was unable to take advantage of all those aspects of oral communication that gave distinct coloration to the message. It is possible, though not demonstrable, that Paul trained his letter-carrier on how to express his words with the correct inflections, pauses, tone, and gestures to convey his argument and full range of emotions. Not much has been written on this aspect of Paul's circular letters to the churches. It is difficult to imagine that his most personal and emotionally filled letters, for example, the so-called "letter of tears," would have been randomly left to someone in the congregation to read in the same monotone one finds his letters still being read in church

---

[46]Demetr. *Eloc.* 223.

[47]Stowers, "Greek and Latin Letters," 290.

services to this day. Although there is no strict evidence for this, Paul plausibly took some provisions to ensure that his half of the dialogue was delivered the way he himself would have delivered it were he there in person.[48]

Another general consideration is the occasionality of the letter, its historical context, social status, place and time, and interactions that call forth the letter and contribute to its meaning. In the case of 2 Corinthians 10-13, what was the rhetorical situation that called forth Paul's response? And equally important, why did it call forth the type of response it took, namely a persuasive one?[49] All we know of the situation is what we can infer from Paul's remarks and the direction his persuasive discourse took. We reconstruct the other half of the dialogue based on his answer which gives insight into the rhetorical situation. It would be interesting, for example, to have more details about the "different gospel" and "other Jesus" (2 Cor 11:4) Paul says his opponents were preaching.

A third consideration is the ability of the letter writing to incorporate and absorb other forms of literature, theoretical frameworks, genres, and styles of writing. How much of rhetorical theory could a letter adapt to simulate, for example, a deliberative argument? In the case of 2 Corinthians 10-13, is it legitimate to suggest that Paul adopted and adapted the three methods of proof

---

[48]More will be said on the issues of oral delivery and Paul's letters later in the paper.

[49]Lloyd F. Bitzer ("The Rhetorical Situation," *PhRh* 1 [1986] 6) defines the rhetorical situation "as a complex of persons, events, objects, and relations presenting an actual or potential exigence which can be completely or partially removed if discourse, introduced into the situation, can so constrain human decision or action as to bring about the significant modification of the exigence."

to serve his purposes in responding to the situation in 2 Corinthians? This study claims that he knew these methods of proof from his exposure to rhetorical theory and practice and used them quite consciously to modify the beliefs and attitudes of the Corinthians.

Another general remark related to the last one is the integration of the knowledge and devices of professional rhetoric to the exigencies of letter-writing. According to Stowers, the epistolary handbooks show "a knowledge of rhetoric." In other words, there was some degree of appropriation of rhetorical theory and practices to letter-writing, especially by the literary letter-writer who was able to adapt the principles and practices of rhetoric to the "real" situation between individuals imagined by a letter. In the case of Paul, who Stowers says reflects "a handbook knowledge of letter writing style and theory,"[50] the situation at Corinth called forth in 2 Corinthians 10-13 a response that incorporated in letter form a virtual speech-act that was calculated to resolve, to the same degree as oral delivery, the exigence at hand.

All of this is to say that the possibilities were there for a creative literary mind such as Paul's to test the limits of letter-writing by acting in 2 Corinthians 10-13 as if he were standing in front of the Corinthians and declaiming, reflecting on his good character, playing upon their emotions and sense of values, and convincing them through his rhetorical arguments. There is no doubt that Paul's letters have a very individual stamp so that it will be difficult

---

[50]Stowers, "Greek and Latin Letters," 291.

to find parallel literary works reflecting this kind of epistolographic rhetoric. Nevertheless, the following chapters demonstrate Paul's attempt to adapt the three classical methods of proof as a way of bringing positive resolution to the serious challenges to his gospel and authority at Corinth.

CHAPTER TWO

'ΗΘΟΣ : PROOF THROUGH CHARACTER AND MORAL APPEAL

A. The Definition and Nature of ἦθος

The first of the artificial proofs (πίστεις) which Aristotle said the speaker

must furnish through the speech itself is ἦθος. This proof consists in effecting

persuasion in an audience through a presentation of the genuinely good moral

character of the speaker. It is the ἦθος ἐν τῷ λέγοντι or τοῦ λέγοντος which

Aristotle speaks about in *Rh.* 1.2.3. The orator must be a person who comes

across in the speech itself as one who is competent and intelligent in regard to

the facts of a case, credible and honorable in presenting them, and well-disposed

to the audience. As Aristotle writes: "The orator persuades by moral character

when the speech is delivered in such a manner as to render the speaker worthy

of confidence."[51] An audience listens more carefully and believes more readily

when it perceives the speaker to be a person of superior moral integrity. Since

the function of rhetoric, as Aristotle often mentions, is to discover the *available*

means of persuasion and its end is a judgment, the speaker must take great pains

to dispose the audience towards belief and action in what is proposed by

---

[51]Arist. *Rh.* 1.2.4.

demonstrating qualities that inspire confidence in the reasonableness and trustworthiness of one's statements.

The speaker engenders this confidence by means of the speech itself (δεῖ δὲ καὶ τοῦτο συμβαίνειν διὰ τὸν λόγον) and not through any preconceived idea of the speaker's character (μὴ διὰ τὸ προδεδοξάσθαι ποιόν τινα εἶναι τὸν λέγοντα).[52] Aristotle says that the speech itself must carry the weight of the persuasion; the speech must project the speaker's ability, truthfulness, and congenial disposition toward the audience. Of course, it helps greatly if the speaker has a reputation for these positive qualities but swaying an audience toward πίστις is a function of how well the speaker demonstrates these evidences of intellectual and moral superiority διὰ τὸν λόγον.

The moral character of the speaker, as Aristotle continues, constitutes κυριωτάτη πίστις. Aristotle exaggerates here to make a serious point. It is not enough to be convincing through enthymemes and examples, sources of more direct logical proofs appealing to the reason, which will be discussed in chapter four. Something equally important must prevail in order to persuade, that is, to move people into belief and action:

> Since the object of rhetoric is judgement . . . it is not only necessary to consider how to make the speech itself demonstrative and convincing, but also that the speaker should show himself to be of a certain character and should know how to put the judge into a certain frame of mind. For it makes a great difference with regard to producing conviction . . . that the speaker should show himself to be possessed of certain qualities

---

[52]Ibid.

> and that the hearers should think that the speaker is disposed in
> a certain way towards them; and further, that they themselves
> should be disposed in a certain way towards him.[53]

Aristotle displays his psychological wisdom in emphasizing the crucial part $\mathring{\eta}\theta o\varsigma$

plays in a speech by pointing out that the way one comes across to an audience

and the way an audience is disposed to a speaker can make or break a speech.

Aristotle makes it clear that an audience's opinions vary and that it sees things

altogether different or at least different to a degree according to the emotions

it entertains toward a speaker, "for when a man is favorably disposed toward

another on whom he is passing judgment, he either thinks that the accused has

committed no wrong at all or that his offense is trifling; but if he hates him, the

reverse is the case."[54]

What are those qualities which the speaker needs in his or her character to

carry the audience persuasively toward a determinate judgment? Aristotle says

they are three: $\phi\rho\acute{o}\nu\eta\sigma\iota\varsigma$, $\dot{\alpha}\rho\epsilon\tau\acute{\eta}$, and $\epsilon\H{v}\nu o\iota\alpha$.[55] As Cope explains, $\phi\rho\acute{o}\nu\eta\sigma\iota\varsigma$

enables the speaker "to judge the expediency of the policy he recommends, or

the inexpediency of that from which he would dissuade the people." Further,

$\dot{\alpha}\rho\epsilon\tau\acute{\eta}$ lends "weight and dignity to his words to obviate all suspicions of

passion, prejudice, self-interest or any evil motive." And $\epsilon\H{v}\nu o\iota\alpha$ refers to the

"friendly intentions to, or regard for the interests of, the assembly he is

---

[53]Arist. *Rh.* 2.1.3.

[54]Arist. *Rh.* 2.1.4.

[55]Arist. *Rh.* 2.1.5.

addressing."[56] Lacking one or, worse, all of these, a speaker will not be able to induce belief. On the other hand, a speaker who, as Aristotle says, "appears to possess all three will necessarily convince his hearers."[57] The means whereby a speaker may appear to have φρόνησις and ἀρετή flow from a classification of the virtues which Aristotle had earlier discussed in 1.9. Εὔνοια, on the other hand, is a result of the correct handling of the emotions which Aristotle at this point proceeds to analyze at great length, a discussion that overlaps on the issue of the πάθος of a speech, another proof source, which will be treated in the next chapter.

The analysis of ἦθος so far has examined the favorable impression created in and by the speech of the speaker's own character. This is only part of the meaning of ἦθος. Aristotle discusses two other kinds of ἦθος of which a speaker needs to be aware of for effective persuasion.[58] He speaks of the second meaning as ἤθη τῶν πολιτειῶν in 1.8.6, or "the characters of each form

---

[56]E. M. Cope, *An Introduction to Aristotle's Rhetoric: With Analysis Notes and Appendices* (London: Macmillan and Co., 1867) 245-6.

[57]*Rh.* 2.1.6.

[58]Cope (*Introduction to Aristotle's Rhetoric*, 108-113) was the first to suggest other meanings for ἦθος based on Aristotle's "plainly enough marked" distinction. He critiques Spengel's confounding of the first two meanings of ἦθος. William M. A. Grimaldi, S.J. (*Aristotle, Rhetoric II: A Commentary* [New York: Fordham University Press, 1988] 5-6; 183-89) debates Cope on Aristotle's meaning of ἦθος in certain passages but concludes, like Cope, with an understanding of ἦθος that means more than just the character of the speaker. Grimaldi writes: "On this matter I would have to conclude that if any distinction on ἦθος as entechnic proof were to be made, I would say that A. thinks of ἦθος primarily as that of the speaker . . ., and secondarily but equally as that of the auditors" (186).

of government." Aristotle proceeds to name and discuss these various forms of

government in 2.12-17, together with the different periods of life from youth to

old age and the different classes of society to show that the speaker must

accommodate his or her language to fit the audience's political, temperamental,

cultural, and social condition in order not only to be relevant but also to avoid

any sentiment that would alienate the audience. The speech must conform to

these various characters as Aristotle sums up in 2.18.1. Thus a speaker, to be

effective, would not elaborate on the virtues of democratic ideals to an audience

imbued with a taste for the monarchy, nor use feelings, motives, or principles

toward the old which appeal only to the young, nor conciliate the rich and

powerful with words and images that are more suited to a lower social class.

The reason for this adaptation to the audience is very clear:

> Since all are willing to listen to speeches which harmonize with
> their own character and to speakers who resemble them [or
> speeches which resemble or reflect their character], it is easy to
> see what language we must employ so that both ourselves and
> our speeches may appear to be of such and such a character.[59]

The speaker, in short, must take on the nature of the audience, as it were, and

endeavor to impart a feeling of positive transference and rapport for the sake of

rendering it friendly and receptive. One could consider this second meaning of

$\mathring{\eta}\theta o\varsigma$ as an aspect of the speaker's $\epsilon\mathring{v}\nu o\iota\alpha$ toward an audience, which was one

of the three essential qualities cited above to express the speaker's own

character; but there is a difference, according to Cope, "both in the object

---

[59]Arist. *Rh*. 2.13.16.

aimed at and the kind of character that has to be assumed."[60] I would agree
that this second meaning of ἦθος is not merely the ἦθος ἐν τῷ λέγοντι, but is
the character of the audience itself. The two are not identical, even though
there is a reciprocal relationship of subject to object. Cope cites Cicero as
making the same distinction:

> Moreover the orator must have an eye to propriety not only in
> thought but in language. For the same style and the same
> thoughts must not be used in portraying every condition in life,
> or every rank, position or age, and in fact a similar distinction
> must be made in respect of place, time and audience (*aut auditor
> omnis*). The universal rule, in oratory as in life, is to consider
> propriety. This depends on the subject under discussion, and on
> the character of both the speaker and the audience (*eorum qui
> audiunt*).[61]

This is not merely an academic distinction but an important task, of which
Aristotle was aware. The speaker in creating the speech must be concerned not
only for effectively projecting one's own character but also for appropriating the
character or ethical condition of the audience, all with the intent of using the
available means of persuasion.[62]

---

[60]Cope, *Introduction to Aristotle's Rhetoric*, 111. Wilhelm Süss, *ETHOS: Studien
zur älteren griechischen Rhetorik* (Leipzig: B. G. Teubner, 1910) 1-2, reflects this
distinction within ἦθος as that between the subjective-dynamic aspect of the speaker and
the objective-psychological condition of the listener.

[61]Cic. *Orat.* 21.71. The Latin insertions are italicized in Cope's quotation from
Cicero's Latin original. Cope calls Cicero's "eorum qui audiunt" the ἦθος ἐν τοῖς
ἀκρωμένοις, apparently to distinguish this ἦθος from the ἦθος ἐν τῷ λέγοντι. See
Cope, *Introduction to Aristotle's Rhetoric* 111, n. 2.

[62]Grimaldi (*Aristotle, Rhetoric II*, 6) also emphasizes the importance of the
audience's ἦθος: "But essential to what he [Aristotle] has to say of it is the fact that the
speaker must know the ἦθη of the varied kinds of government, in which concept
government is viewed as a *moral person*. . . . It is obvious from this that even when

There is yet a third variety of ἦθος which Cope says may be introduced into the speech to express character. This has to do with the *style* of the speech and is fitting for the narrative (διήγησις) section, as Aristotle says:

> And the narrative should be of a moral character, and in fact it will be so, if we know what effects this. One thing is to make clear our moral purpose; for as is the moral purpose, so is the character, and as is the end, so is the moral purpose.[63]

Aristotle goes on to say that Socratic dialogues have moral character, whereas mathematical treatises do not; for the latter have no moral purpose. He goes on immediately to add that "other ethical indications are the accompanying peculiarities of each individual character." Cope's commentary on this meaning of ἦθος designates it as a kind of word-painting which "aids the proof in some slight degree by imparting to the speech an air of truthfulness and fidelity." The speaker, in other words, should be so acquainted with the general characteristics of the age, sex, nationality, and other qualities of the person being described that the speaker will be able by the speech to paint that person with words that make that person come to life for the audience. Aristotle expresses this third meaning of ἦθος in the following words:

> Character also may be expressed by the proof from signs,

---

the terms ἦθος is used of the speaker more than his own ἦθος is at issue. Relative and important to it is the speaker's understanding of the ἦθος of those addressed. . . . Aware, as we should be, of the importance of action on the part of the auditors to the rhetorical art, one can dismiss only with difficulty the speaker's need for such knowledge of ἦθος τῶν ἀκροατῶν in presenting his own ἦθος." The speaker's ἦθος, therefore, is not the only part of this entechnic proof. The ἦθος of the auditors in the rhetorical situation must also be known.

[63]Arist. *Rh.* 3.16.8.

because to each class and habit there is an appropriate style. I mean class in reference to age—child, man, or old man; to sex—man or woman; to country—Lacedaemonian or Thessalian. I call habits those moral states which form a man's character in life; for not all habits do this. If then anyone uses the language appropriate to each habit, he will represent the character; for the uneducated man will not say the same things in the same way as the educated.[64]

In this way, as Cope says, "the narrative will gain in liveliness, our portrait or description in faithfulness, and our accuracy in these minutiae will convey a favourable impression to the audience of our trustworthiness in general."[65]

Ἦθος is drawn for the audience if the language isolates and illustrates the special peculiarity of a person, whether that one is the speaker or the speaker's friend or adversary. For instance, in several examples afforded by Aristotle:

"He was talking and walking on at the same time," which indicates effrontery and boorishness. Nor should we speak as if from the intellect, after the manner of present-day orators, but from moral purpose: "But I wished it, and I preferred it; and even if I profited nothing, it is better." The first statement indicates prudence, the second virtue; for prudence consists in the pursuit of what is useful, virtue in that of what is honourable.[66]

The choice and arrangement of words give ethical coloring to any trait of the individual portrayed and are indicators of a person's values, habits, or principles. Thus a speaker can show in and by the speech one's own ἦθος or that of another and thereby produce a positive or negative attitude that can affect the outcome of the persuasion.

---

[64]Arist. *Rh.* 3.7.6.

[65]Cope, *Introduction to Aristotle's Rhetoric*, 113.

[66]Arist. *Rh.* 3.16.9.

The importance of ἦθος in Aristotle's model of rhetoric as persuasion is clearly evident from the foregoing analysis. He says in a variety of ways that proofs are not only established by demonstrative arguments but by ethical ones as well, "for we have confidence in an orator who exhibits certain qualities, such as goodness, goodwill, or both."[67] The speaker should make it a point in the course of a speech to "narrate anything that tends to show your own virtue" and by contrast, "the wickedness of your opponent."[68] In fact, Aristotle goes so far as to say that if the speaker does not have any enthymemes for proofs, the ethical will do, for "it is more fitting that a virtuous person should show oneself good than that one's speech should be painfully exact."[69]

Cicero in his various rhetorical works has much to say on the ἦθος of a speech. In the immature work of his youth, *De Inventione*, of which he later spoke disparagingly,[70] Cicero was already concerned with certain aspects of ἦθος, namely that of making the auditor "well-disposed, attentive, and receptive" in the exordium.[71] The goodwill (*benevolentia*) of an audience, he goes on to say, springs from four quarters: "from our own person, from the

---

[67]Arist. *Rh.* 1.8.6.

[68]Arist. *Rh.* 3.16.5.

[69]Arist. *Rh.* 3.17.13.

[70]Cic. *De Or.* 1.5.

[71]Cic. *Inv. Rhet.* 1.14.20. Cicero (*Part. Or.* 8.28) gives the three aims of the exordium as *ut amice, ut intelligenter, ut attente audiamur.*

person of the opponents, from the persons of the jury, and from the case itself."[72] He briefly describes each source of goodwill, each of which, as will later be seen, has much to offer in understanding Paul's method of securing the attention of his Corinthian listeners and of projecting his own ἦθος as a technique of persuasion. First,

> We shall win goodwill from our own person if we refer to our own acts and services without arrogance; if we weaken the charges that have been preferred, or of some suspicion of less honourable dealing which has been cast upon us; if we dilate on the misfortunes which have befallen us or the difficulties which still beset us; if we use prayers and entreaties with a humble and submissive spirit.

Next,

> Goodwill is acquired from the person of the opponents if we can bring them into hatred, unpopularity, or contempt. They will be hated if some act of theirs is presented which is base, haughty, cruel, or malicious; they will become unpopular if we present their power, political influence, wealth, family connections, and their arrogant and intolerable use of these advantages, so that they seem to rely on these rather than on the justice of their case.

Aristotle had earlier anticipated Cicero's reflections on acquiring goodwill paradoxically from one's opponents. Aristotle suggested that some methods of removing prejudice or disagreeable suspicion against the speaker are for the speaker to counter-attack the accuser, to attack slander because it raises false issues and does not rely on the real facts of the case, to bring out the wickedness of one's opponents, to arouse indignation by disparaging what

---

[72]Aristotle (*Rh.* 3.14.7) cites the same four methods to secure goodwill. *Rhet. Her.* 1.4.8 also mentions the same four.

opponents consider important.[73] Furthermore,

> Goodwill will be sought from the persons of the auditors if an account is given of acts which they have performed with courage, wisdom, and mercy, but so as not to show excessive flattery: and if it is shown in what honourable esteem they are held and how eagerly their judgement and opinion are awaited.

And lastly,

> Goodwill may come from the circumstances themselves if we praise and exalt our own case, and depreciate our opponent's with contemptuous allusions.[74]

In addition to securing the goodwill of the audience, the speaker must make the listeners attentive if they are to be receptive to the message. The speaker accomplishes this, among other ways, "if we show that the matters which we are about to discuss are important . . . or that they concern all humanity or those in the audience. . . ." Likewise, Cicero gives guidelines on how to handle insinuations when the audience is hostile. Hostility arises from the audience if there is something scandalous in the case or "if those who have spoken first seem to have convinced the auditor on some point." One way the speaker handles this prejudiced atmosphere is to show one's listeners that one's opponents do not shake the speaker who is ready to reply with confidence and assurance. This method of defense generally leaves the audience thinking it has assented too readily rather than that the speaker has been overconfident.[75]

---

[73]Arist. *Rh.* 3.15.2-10.

[74]Cic. *Inv. Rhet.* 1.16.22.

[75]Cic. *Inv. Rhet.* 1.17.24-25.

Some of the situations Cicero discusses and the solutions he proposes have an uncanny relevance to Paul's crisis in Corinth, to the responses he makes and the manner in which he handles them, as the ensuing discussion illustrates.

In this same work Cicero echoes Aristotle's second meaning to ἦθος, in which a speaker adapts to an audience's character. He discusses this meaning, however, in an indirect way by describing various arguments in which the speaker, without regard for an audience's sensibilities or experiences, alienates it to the detriment of persuasion. For instance, "if anyone speaking before the Roman *equites* who desire the privilege of serving on the jury should praise Caepio's law regulating jury service," this would be considered an offensive argument, since Caepio's *lex Servilia iudiciaria* sought to deprive the *equites* of their exclusive right to serve as *judices*. Another example would be "if a person speaking before Alexander of Macedon against someone who had stormed a city should say that nothing is more cruel than to destroy cities, when Alexander himself had destroyed Thebes," this would be considered a "contrary" argument. Still another example would be someone who "might say that he is helping his friend out of kindness, but expects to get some profit from it," this would make an argument inconsistent since "conflicting statements are made by the same speaker on the same subject." Last, "if a general in exhorting his soldiers to fight should magnify the strength, forces and good fortune of the enemy," this would give rise to an "adverse" argument which is one "which does harm to one's own case in some respect."[76] In all of these and many more examples Cicero cites, there is a great lack of sensitivity toward the audience on the part of the speaker which will produce a less than favorable impression on the listeners. Immature as this early work of Cicero's might seem, it shows significant understanding of the ethical and moral character necessary in a speech to win the sympathy of an audience.

In his more mature work, *De Oratore*, cast in the form of a conversation to convey the *ars rhetorica* of Aristotle and Isocrates, Cicero shows quite explicitly the value of ἦθος, that psychology is sometimes more important to persuasion than logical demonstration, that to paint the characters of one's clients "in words, as being upright, stainless, conscientious, modest and long-suffering under pressure, has a really wonderful effect; and this topic . . . is so compelling, when agreeably and feelingly handled, as often to be worth more than the merits of the case." He goes on to say:

> Now nothing in oratory, Catulus, is more important than to win for the orator the favor of his hearer, and to have the latter so affected as to be swayed by something resembling a mental impulse or emotion, rather than by judgements or deliberation. For men decide far more problems by hate, or love, or lust, or rage, or sorrow, or joy, or hope, or fear, or illusion, or some other inward emotion, than by reality, or authority, or any legal standard, or judicial precedent, or statute.

He then proceeds to delineate what qualities are powerful in winning the goodwill of the audience. The speaker should "display the tokens of good-

---

[76]Cic. *Inv. Rhet.* 1.50.92-93. *Rhet. Her.* 1.5.9 has a briefer discussion without examples.

nature, kindness, calmness, loyalty and a disposition that is pleasing and not grasping or covetous, and all the qualities belonging to persons who are upright, unassuming and not given to haste, stubbornness, strife, or harshness." Cicero concludes his observations by saying:

> A potent factor in success, then, is for the characters, principles, conduct and life, both of those who are to plead cases and of their clients, to be approved and conversely those of their opponents condemned; and for the feelings of the tribunal to be won over, as far as possible, to goodwill towards the advocate and the advocate's client as well. Now feelings are won over by a man's merit, achievements, or reputable life, qualifications easier to embellish, if only they are real, than to fabricate where non-existent.[77]

Cicero reflects his previous thinking on the importance of $\mathring{\eta}\theta o\varsigma$ in a speech in his short work on the art of oratory designed for the instruction of his son entitled, *De Partitione Oratoria*. All the familiar themes of securing an audience's goodwill, understanding, and attention through the promotion of one's character and the demotion of the character of one's opponents receive emphasis once again. The speaker must come across to the audience from the outset of the speech in a friendly, intelligent, and interesting manner. These qualities help to make the audience attentive to the thoughts, receptive to the message, and susceptible to the persuasive power of the speaker. Cicero writes in regard to eliciting a friendly hearing:

> The first of these topics consists in our own personality and those of the judges and of our opponents: from which the first steps to secure goodwill are achieved by extolling our own merits or

---

[77]Cic. *De Or.* 2.43.178-184.

worth or virtue of some kind, particularly generosity, sense of duty, justice and good faith, and by assigning the opposite qualities to our opponents, and by indicating some reason for or expectation of agreement with the persons deciding the case; and by removing or diminishing any odium or unpopularity that has been directed against ourselves, either by doing away with it or diminishing it or by diluting it or by weakening it or by setting something against it or by making an apology.[78]

In his theory of ἦθος as an important method of proof, Cicero follows the lead of Aristotle. He also accepts Aristotle's tripartite meaning of ἦθος: as reflected in the character of the speaker, the audience, and the style of language. There is an interplay between speaker and audience through the medium of language. Cicero is one with Aristotle in underscoring the point that ἦθος issues from the very act of the speech itself. The speaker paints character, whether one's own or another's, before the very eyes of the audience through the action of words and their effective arrangement so as to influence the listeners' mind, induce belief, and promote action. The orator's ἦθος is, as it were, a fiction created for the moment by linguistic skills to effect a willing suspension of disbelief in one reality in order to embrace another.

This power of the speech to create ἦθος does not find resonance in the rhetorical theory of Quintilian. In his eyes, it is essential that an orator must be a good and virtuous person to begin with in order to deserve the title of orator. This is Quintilian's definition of ἦθος, which becomes a pre-requisite condition even before any word is uttered: "The first essential for [an orator]

---

[78]Cic. *Part. Or.* 8.28.

is that he should be a good man, and consequently we demand of him not merely the possession of exceptional gifts of speech, but of all the excellence of character as well."[79] He restricts the name of orator and the art itself to those who are good.[80] Quintilian's ideal orator has genuine title to the name of philosopher, that is, one in whom a blameless character and the mastery of the science and art of speaking well are perfectly paired.[81] After analyzing and rejecting many definitions of rhetoric from previous Greek and Roman theorists, Quintilian concludes that the one most suited to his understanding is one he slightly paraphrases from Chrysippus who derived it from Cleanthes: rhetoric is *bene dicendi scientia*, a definition which "includes all the virtues of oratory and the character of the orator as well, since no man can speak well who is not good himself."[82] Quintilian cites Aristotle (*Rh.* 1.2.4) in defense of his statement that "the strongest argument in support of a speaker is that he is a good man."[83]

In his brief discussion Quintilian seems uncertain how to define ἦθος. He

---

[79]Quint. *Inst.* 1.Pr.9.

[80]Quint. *Inst.* 2.15.2.

[81]Quint. *Inst.* 1.Pr.18.

[82]Quint. *Inst.* 2.15.34

[83]Quint. *Inst.* 5.12.9. Quintilian stretches Aristotle's definition to fit his theory that an orator must *a priori* be a morally good person. Aristotle had connected the ἦθος of the speaker with the act of speaking, a creation of the speech act from which confidence in the speaker arises, "not to any preconceived idea of the speaker's character." These are the words of Aristotle from the very same passage Quintilian selectively quotes.

states that Latin has no verbal equivalent for ἦθος. At one point he states that

ἦθος and πάθος (the use of emotions in a speech) are of the same nature with

only a difference in degree. He has difficulty establishing the usefulness of

ἦθος in the speech itself, since he has already located the source of persuasion

outside the oration in the good character of the orator. Finally, after an

unsuccessful analysis, he concludes:

> Ἦθος in all its forms requires the speaker to be a man of good
> character and courtesy. For it is most important that he should
> himself possess or be thought to possess those virtues for the
> possession of which it is his duty, if possible, to commend his
> client as well, while the excellence of his own character will
> make his pleading all the more convincing and will be of the
> utmost service to the cases which he undertakes.

In this rather idealistic situation, Quintilian has to conclude that an immoral

person could never be an orator:

> For the orator who gives the impression of being a bad man
> while he is speaking, is actually speaking badly, since his words
> seem to be insincere owing to the absence of ἦθος which would
> otherwise have revealed itself.[84]

Since the good character of the speaker is one of the sources of persuasion,

it is usually counterproductive, according to Quintilian, to boast. He considers

it a mistake for an orator to praise one's own eloquence, since it might make the

audience feel small. However, it is not out of place for Cicero, Quintilian's

idol, to boast; for he says that Cicero does not boast of his oratory but of his

political achievements.[85]   In spite of this reticence to boast, Quintilian

---

[84]Quint. *Inst.* 6.2.18-19.

[85]Quint. *Inst.* 11.1.18-19.

nevertheless has to admit "that there are occasions when an orator may speak
of his own achievements, as Demosthenes himself does in his defense of
Ctesiphon"; or, as Cicero modestly displays in attributing his success in putting
down the Catalinian conspiracy "to the courage shown by the senate or to the
providence of the immortal gods."[86].

It is relevant at this point to backtrack historically and discuss the rhetorical
theory of Isocrates, the contemporary and competitor of Aristotle, since he
anticipates Quintilian's ideal orator as one who has intrinsic goodness. In his
famous speech, *Antidosis*, Isocrates defines what he means by ἦθος:

> The man who wishes to persuade people will not be negligent as
> to the matter of character; no, on the contrary, he will apply
> himself above all to establish a most honourable name among his
> fellow-citizens; for who does not know that words carry greater
> conviction when spoken by men of good repute than when spoken
> by men who live under a cloud, and that the argument which is
> made by a man's life is of more weight than that which is
> furnished by words? Therefore, the stronger a man's desire to
> persuade his hearers, the more zealously will he strive to be
> honourable and to have the esteem of his fellow-citizens.[87]

---

[86]Quint. *Inst.* 11.1.22-23.

[87]Isoc. *Ant.* 278. Cf. Arist. *Rh.* 1.2.4: κυριωτάτη πίστις τὸ ἦθος. Wealthy
Athenians paid for the public services or "liturgies," such as fitting out a warship (a
trierarchy) or picking up the expenses of a drama or simply a chorus in a drama. As
George Norlin (*Isocrates II* [LCL; Cambridge, MA: Harvard Press, 1982] 181) in his
Introduction to this speech writes: "Anyone allotted to such a duty might challenge
another to accept the alternative of either undertaking this burden in his stead or of
exchanging property with him. Such a challenge was called an 'antidosis.' If the
challenged party objected, the issue was adjudicated by a court." Isocrates had
undergone such a trial and lost. The plaintiff had misrepresented Isocrates' wealth and
slandered both his character and the influence of his teaching. This oration is Isocrates'
written reply in which he gives "a true image of his thought and of his whole life"
(*Ant.* 7).

He goes on to say that philosophers like him are not blind to the power of good will but appreciate it even more than others. While probabilities and proofs have their value, "an honourable reputation not only lends greater persuasiveness to the words of the man who possesses it, but adds greater luster to his deeds, and is, therefore, more zealously to be sought after by men of intelligence than anything else in the world."[88]

Isocrates is painfully aware that he is the victim of gross calumny and that his audience is prone to give credence to this "our greatest bane," for "it causes liars to be looked on with respect, innocent men to be regarded as criminals, and judges to violate their oaths; in a word, it smothers truth, and pouring false ideas into our ears, it leaves no man among our citizens secure from an unjust death."[89] At the same time, he realizes that to attempt a eulogy of himself under conditions like these would only result "in arousing the displeasure or even the envy of his hearers."[90] But he is determined to review his life and actions for which he feels he deserves approbation. However, a fictional voice in the oration reminds him of the ἦθος of his audience and cautions against self-recommendation. The voice of his friend warns:

> "Some men . . . have been so brutalized by envy and want and are so hostile that they wage war, not on depravity, but on prosperity; they hate not only the best men but the noblest pursuits; and, in addition to their other faults, they take sides

---

[88]Isoc. *Ant.* 280.

[89]Isoc. *Ant.* 18-19.

[90]Isoc. *Ant.* 8.

with wrong-doers and are in sympathy with them, while they destroy, whenever they have the power, those whom they have cause to envy. . . . For as things are, what judgment can you expect such men to reach when you tell them of your life and your conduct, which are not in the least degree like their own, but such as you are attempting to describe to me?"

The friend goes on to say that it doesn't matter how eloquently and truthfully Isocrates shows his listeners what an upright citizen he has been, how his students have all been of benefit to the state as a result of their education under him, or even how generous he has been in bearing the costs for many public services, his auditors will be resentful because of their own ill-fortune. In a situation like this, the friend advises Isocrates in words that anticipate those of Plutarch on self-praise discussed below: "Knowing, then, that such will be the attitude of your audience, consider well what you had better say and what you have better leave unsaid."[91] Isocrates finds this advise "amazing in the extreme" but has to agree ultimately that it is "utter folly to seek to justify myself to those who are not minded like other men but are harder on the innocent than on the guilty." So he addresses his remarks to the other half of the jury that is more fair-minded.

It is clear from this example that no matter how sterling the ἦθος of Isocrates was, the ἦθος of the audience was such so as to preclude the effectiveness of persuasion through the good character of the speaker. The power of slander and prejudice against his teaching methods on the art of

---

[91]Isoc. *Ant.* 144-49.

speaking well is too pervasive in this context for Isocrates' words to have any persuasive effect in spite of his attempts to employ emotional appeals and reasoned views. There are times when $\mathring{\eta}\theta o\varsigma$ is of no advantage to the speaker and to insist on it is to cause one's listeners to become hardened, even more so when it is combined with a sharp attack on their uncritical acceptance of rival teaching and their narrowness in appreciating the speaker's philosophy.

The establishment of $\mathring{\eta}\theta o\varsigma$ is close to encomium, since praise and self-praise are intimately connected with the projection of $\mathring{\eta}\theta o\varsigma$, which strives to present the virtues and moral character of the speaker. To this end, praise becomes part of the means of proof. Aristotle connects both virtue and praise, when he writes: "Praise is language that sets forth the greatness of virtue."[92] Praise brings to the light of day a person's virtuous actions and noble achievements which are signs of moral habit: "We pronounce an encomium upon those who have achieved something."[93] Praise recognizes the worth of an individual, gives honor where it is due, and pronounces the person a model of trustworthiness and imitation.[94] Praise is an expression of moral approbation of a virtuous character. Praising oneself or another is a matter of

---

[92] Arist. *Rh.* 1.9.33.

[93] Ibid.

[94] James T. Fitzgerald (*Cracks in an Earthen Vessel* 107-114) gives an excellent discussion of this topic with numerous citations from classical authors on the nature and practice of praise. He mentions but does not discuss the important idea "that praise and the recognition of achievement [are] a social obligation basic to the existence of a community," a notion that is of significant value in the thinking of rhetorical theorists and in the practice of the great orators.

reputation, strategy, and appropriateness. The value of praise depends, first of

all, on the source. This can become a persuasive circle, since there is an

assumption of the trustworthiness of the encomiast—which is precisely the issue

in establishing ἦθος. Aristotle is somewhat enigmatic and circular himself when

he writes on this topic:

> We will next speak of virtue and vice, of the noble and the
> disgraceful, since they constitute the aim of one who praises and
> of one who blames; for, when speaking of these, we shall
> incidentally bring to light the means of making us appear of such
> and such a character, which, as we have said, is a second method
> of proof; for it is by the same means that we shall be able to
> inspire confidence in ourselves or others in regard to virtue.[95]

Thus the value of praise depends on the source, so that the speaker, especially

if talking about oneself, must create the conditions of plausibility from

recognized qualities of honor, good repute, and trustworthiness. Similarly,

praise must be bestowed strategically and appropriately, that is, when and how

much in order to win persuasion, so as not to seem as though one were

boasting.[96] Too much boasting that is not done with the Ciceronian virtue of

---

[95]Arist. *Rh.* 1.9.1.

[96]The practice of writing encomia was an important part of the *progymnasmata* of
Greco-Roman education on the secondary level. They were exercises, based on accepted
models, in highlighting the good qualities of someone or something, whether they were
factual or not. A person's virtues were the usual topics for commendation but they
could also encompass such items as noble birth, health, education (Arist. *Rh.* 1.9.33).
Exercises in vituperation and invective were the counterparts to encomia. While the
practice of encomia was usually associated with epideictic oratory, the element of praise
was useful in establishing ἦθος in a deliberative speech. See H. I. Marrou, *A History
of Education in Antiquity* (Mentor Books; New York: The New American Library,
1964) 272-73; also Donald L. Clark, *Rhetoric in Greco-Roman Education* (New York:
Columbia University Press, 1957) 194-198.

58

propriety becomes offensive self-praise.

The practice of self-laudation or περιαυτολογία was an accepted Greco-Roman rhetorical technique. Such a practice, however, had to be used with discretion and with an awareness both of the occasions when self-praise was called for and of the so-called φάρμακα to its negative impact on an audience. Otherwise, overblown self-praise, from a rhetorical point of view, could diminish one's ἦθος, causing one to look ridiculous and rendering one's listeners antagonistic. In addition to being a hindrance to persuasion, self-praise also created religious and ethical problems with disastrous results in the minds of the listeners. Plutarch incisively investigated the offensiveness of περιαυτολογία and how self-praise can be used, if at all, inoffensively in the essay from his *Moralia* entitled, Περὶ τοῦ ἑαυτὸν ἐπαινεῖν ἀνεπιφθόνως.[97] In general, Plutarch finds self-praise distasteful and the mark of an ill-bred individual but as he comments rather wryly in the opening lines of the essay,

---

[97]For other discussions, see Quin. *Inst.* 11.1.15-28; Alex. *Rh.* (3.4.9-14 Spengel); Ps-Aristides, *Concerning Civil and Simple Speech* 12.2.7 (2.506.8-20 Spengel); and Ps-Hermogenes, *On Aids for a Vigorous Style* 25 (441, 15-442, 21 Rabe). Aristotle does not discuss self-praise *per se* but does talk in his *Eth. Nic.* 4.7, of the ἀλαζών (the boastful person) and the εἴρων (the mockingly self-deprecating person). However, these figures become simply embodiments of their true or false claims upon reality. As Philip H. De Lacy and Benedict Einarson ("On Praising Oneself Inoffensively" in Plut. *Mor.* [LCL; Harvard Press, 1984] 110) explain in their Introduction, Plutarch "supposes his statesman virtuous and truthful and deals with the ends that justify him in praising himself and the devices that by making the self-praise palatable enable him to use it so as to achieve those ends." Thus Plutarch looks at a rhetorical technique as a moralist. The word περιαυτολογία probably was suggested by the less loaded expression "to speak about myself" which Demosthenes used in his *De Cor.*, which then became a *topos* of the rhetoricians. Danker (*II Corinthians* and "Paul's Debt to the *De Corona* of Demosthenes," in *Persuasive Artistry*, 263-80) makes use of Plutarch's essay and Demosthenes' famous oration to cite rhetorical parallels in Paul.

even though many condemn the practice of speaking to others of one's own importance, yet not many even of these people "avoid the odium of it."[98] Plutarch admits, however, that there are times and reasons when circumstances demand the use of self-praise and render it ethically acceptable. The use of self-commendation is particularly apppropriate when the speaker has to establish one's ἦθος with the audience for various reasons.[99]

The first circumstance that pre-eminently qualifies for self-praise is when one faces slander or unjust accusations. In this case, self-praise becomes part of an *apologia* that the audience accepts as a matter of justice and does not resent. In fact, as Plutarch writes, self-glorification at a moment like this not only does not appear "puffed up, vainglorious, or proud . . . but it displays as well a lofty spirit and greatness of character, which by refusing to be humbled humbles and overpowers envy."[100] A second circumstance when it is permissible to use self-laudation is when misfortune casts a person down and the person boasts in order "to pass from a humbled and piteous state to an attitude

---

[98]Plut. *Mor.* (*On Praising Oneself Inoffensively*) 539A. The odium arises for various reasons. First, self-praisers are "shameless, since they should be embarrassed even by praise from others." Second, they are ἄδικοι, since "they arrogate to themselves what it is for others to bestow"; and third, the listener, if silent, appears "disgruntled and envious," and, if compelled to join in, is forced into κολακεία (539D-E).

[99]H. D. Betz in "De laude ipsius (Plut. *Mor.* 539A-547F)" (*Plutarch's Ethical Writings and Early Christian Literature* [Studia ad Corpus Hellenisticum Novi Testamenti 4; Leiden: Brill, 1978] 367-393) has given a bibliography and an excellent analysis of this essay and its points of contact with the New Testament.

[100]Plut. *Mor.* 540D.

of triumph and pride." In so doing the person appears "great and indomitable," which is a far cry from appearing to be full of "whining and self-abasement in adversity."[101] A third permissible circumstance is when one experiences an affront and exercises freedom of speech with boldness and boasts out of a sense of justice. This would be self-defense.[102]

When the situations mentioned occasion the use of self-praise, the speaker can effectively employ several techniques to avoid reproach from the audience. One irreproachable technique is the use of *antithesis* whereby, by way of contrast, one "admits" to a charge but goes on to show "that the opposite of what one is charged with would have been shameful and base."[103] Another

---

[101]Plut. *Mor.* 541A-B. Self-praise over one's hardships is a quite common topos to enhance one's ἦθος. Fitzgerald (*Cracks in an Earthen Vessel*, 110, n. 181) offers some classical citations: "for example, in regard to working day and night (Cic. *Sen.* 23.82; cf. 1 Thess 2:9), the meagerness of one's diet (Sen. *Ep.* 18.9), the simplicity of one's life (Ps-Diog. *Ep.* 27=118,16-17 Malherbe), and one's patient endurance, be it *patientia* (Cic. *Tusc.* 2.14.33), *constantia* under torture, pain, and death (Lactant. *Div. Inst.* 5.14) or *hypomonē* under frightful circumstances (Ps-Diog. *Ep.* 27 (118,17-18 Malherbe). For boasting in regard to poverty, cf. esp. Apul. *Apol.* 17-23. . . . On exile and boasting, cf. Dio Chrys. *Or.* 45.1-2."

[102]Plut. *Mor.* 541C-D. "It was this, for example, that allowed Demosthenes to speak with full freedom and made palatable the self-praise with which he fills nearly the whole oration *On the Crown*, as he glories in the very charges brought against him: his conduct as ambassador and statesman in the war" (541E-F).

[103]Plut. *Mor.* 541F. An example would be the charge of Metellus against Cicero that the latter's "testimony had killed more men than his pleading had saved" and Cicero reply: "'Who denies that I am more honest than eloquent?'" The contrast is between the charge and what would truly be shameful. Fitzgerald (*Cracks in an Earthen Vessel*, 109) associates this with boasting "from necessity and not for glory" and documents in footnote 179 the notion of ἀνάγκη as the justification for self-praise: "Gorgias B lla.28,32 (2.301.12; 302.15 Diels-Kranz), where it forms an *inclusio* for the self-laudation; Dem. *Or.* 18.4; Quint. *Inst.* 11.1.18, 22-23; Ps-Aristides, *Concerning Civil and Simple Speech* 12.2.7 (2.506.10-12 Spengel); and Ps-Hermogenes, *On Aids for a Vigorous Style* 25 (441,27; 442,6-11 Rabe). Cf. also Plut.

method to remove the offensiveness of self-praise, no matter what situations may give rise to it, is to blend the praises of the speaker's audience with one's own. The speaker should especially laud others "whose aims and acts are the same as [one's] own and whose general character is similar." A third method is for the speaker to temper one's brilliance by throwing in "certain minor shortcomings failures, or faults, thus obviating any effect of displeasure or disapproval." A last technique is for the speaker to disburden one's self of all the honor by "letting part of it rest with chance, and part with God."[104]

These are the "outward φάρμακα," according to Plutarch, to dilute and defuse the inherent offensiveness in self-praise. They are the remedies to recommend one's ἦθος in a speech of persuasion so that the audience does not turn away in disgust or inattentiveness. There are, in addition, "inherent φάρμακα" in the very content of the praise. First, if a speaker is thought to have acquired his reputation or character at no cost or trouble, then the speaker must speak out on the enormous hardships one has experienced. People ironically envy those who have acquired their honor and fame "with much hardship and peril."[105] Second, it is not enough for self-praise merely to

---

Comp. Dem. et Cic. 2.1."

[104]Plut. *Mor.* 542B-543F. Cf. Quint. *Inst.* 11.1.23 and Cic. *Fam.* 15.5.2 regarding giving glory to God; and Cic. *Inv. Rhet.* 1.16.22; Plut. *Mor.* 82D; and Hermogenes in his *On Issues* (345-52 Rabe) for the advantage of modestly expressing one's deficiencies.

[105]Isocrates (*Ant.* 142-149) learned from his fictional friend that merely to recount one's good fortune and successes can cause envy in one's listeners because they see the unworthiness of their own lives. One must show that it has been by hard work that one

avoid offense and envy. It should be used with some further end in view. This end is to see others inspired with emulation and ambition, to awaken ardor and purpose, to afford hope to the despairing. Likewise self-praise should be used with a view to humbling the headstrong and chastening the overbold and also to rousing "the spirits of the terrified and timorous by a seasonable recourse to self-praise." Last, it is not offensive to praise oneself if it means counteracting mistaken praise to or by another which "injures and corrupts by arousing emulation of evil and inducing the adoption of an unsound policy where important issues are at stake;" nor is true self-praise to be avoided if it means diverting "the hearer's purpose to a better course by pointing out the difference." In this way, evil praise is shown up for what it is, as a tragic foil, when true praise is set beside it.[106]

In conclusion, Plutarch advises avoiding the treacherous καιροί and λόγοι "that make us blunder into περιαυτολογία on the slightest occasion." One such

---

has achieved such benefits from life and even then the explanation may not work, as the word "possibly" in the following quotation reveals: "For possibly if they had seen that it is through hard work and sacrifice that you provide yourself with the means wherewith to discharge your public duties and to maintain your affairs in general, they would not have felt the same about it. But in fact they think that these fees which come to you from your foreign pupils are much greater than they actually are, and they consider that you live in greater ease and comfort than not only the people in general but also those who cultivate philosophy and are of the same profession as yourself."

[106]Plut. *Mor.* 544C-546A. For Epictetus and others, proper self-glorification receives its justification if it is for the benefit of others. Braggarts only want to glorify themselves. Cynics, on the other hand, point out their excellent example to others in order to offer them the same remedies which they themselves used to attain health. See his *Diss.* 4.8. Dio Chrys. (*Or.* 57.4-5) says that "it is the mark of a foolish person to be ashamed to praise himself when by praise he is likely to confer the greatest benefits." For these passages, cf. Fitzgerald, *Cracks in an Earthen Vessel*, 110-11.

trap is being seized with jealousy at the praise of others which sends us into an uncontrollable urge for self-praise. Another such pitfall is to be so enamored of ourselves because of some exploit which turned out well that we drift unconsciously into vain boasting. A third snare, especially common in older people, is to magnify ourselves in censuring other people, as if we "in the like circumstances have been prodigies of wisdom." For, as Plutarch says, "when a man intermingles praise of himself with censure of another, and uses another's disgrace to secure glory for himself, he is altogether odious and vulgar, as one who would win applause from the humiliation of another." The last insidious καιρός is to lead others on to compliment us, to run on with our own praises, and to allow flattery to bait us into asking for more praise.[107] The overall concluding advice Plutarch gives is to "avoid talking about ourselves unless we have in prospect some great advantage to our hearers or to ourselves."[108] Fraught though it is with rhetorical perils, self-praise is a major aspect in the consideration of ἦθος as a rhetorical proof in a speech of persuasion and figures in prominently in the rhetorical strategy of Paul in 2 Corinthians 10-13.

The foregoing analysis of ἦθος has shown how the recommendation of

---

[107]Plut. *Mor.* 546C-547C. In the last pitfall, the individual is victimized by an insatiable hunger so that praise becomes an addiction. "You should restrain those who mention some great merit of yours, not find fault with them for doing you scant justice, as most do, going on themselves to recall and gorge themselves on other actions and feats of prowess until by thus commending themselves they undo the commendation of others" (547B). The admonition is not to get too close to the fire, lest you burn yourself irremediably.

[108]Plut. *Mor.* 547F.

one's self is essential for the purposes of persuasion.[109] To paint one's own character in words that convey one's stainless life, conscientious fulfillment of duty, generous spirit, loyal concern, and long-suffering attitude and behavior makes for a powerful effect in a persuasive speech. The speaker seeks agreement from the audience, in many respects, precisely on the fact that the speaker comes across as a trustworthy, admirable, and respectable individual. In fact, the power of one's personality may be stronger and more effective than the actual λόγος of a speech. Aristotle, Cicero, Quintilian and others recognized the psychological dynamic operative in a great orator: one must move, impress, and delight (*ut et concilientur animi . . . et moveantur*, Cic. *De Or* 2.28.121) before one can instruct an audience. The orator does this through a judicious use of self-recommendation, personal encomium, and appreciative self-reference without degenerating into sophistic περιαυτολογία and *synkrisis*. Ἦθος is one of the major proofs in a speech.

B. The Use of ἦθος in Ancient Sources

The purpose of this section is to illustrate the theory of ἦθος from actual speeches, letters, and other writings antecedent to and contemporaneous with

---

[109]Cic. *De Or.*, 2.26.114: "As soon then as I have received my instructions and classed the case and taken the matter in hand, the very first thing I determine is that point to which I must devote all such part of my speech as belongs peculiarly to the issue and the verdict. Next I contemplate with the utmost care those other two essentials, the one involving the recommendation of myself or my clients, the other designed to sway the feelings of the tribunal in the desired direction."

Paul's letters to show rhetorical practice and literary influence. There are more examples than one has space to cite but the following will sufficiently demonstrate that speakers necessarily had to sell themselves (i.e., their character) if they hoped to sell their thoughts and to influence the judgments they wanted their listeners to make. The presentation of ἦθος became a major mode of argumentation in the writings of many orators of antiquity who used self-commendation judiciously and artfully to defend themselves against slander, to project themselves as worthy of others' trust, and to commend their conclusions as the only expedient and just ones.

One thinks immediately of Demosthenes, considered even by other great speakers, such as Cicero, as the greatest orator of antiquity.[110] His famous speech, *De Corona*, which became a model for imitation in succeeding centuries, is a veritable manual of the rhetorical practice of the times. In this work, Demosthenes demonstrates time and again the studied use of ἦθος, made more urgent in his case since he and his friend Ctesiphon, to whose defense he came, were being indicted for an unconstitutional action which could have brought severe penalties. Proof from ἦθος was extremely critical in this particular case, since the prosecution, conducted by the famous orator Aeschines, had contended among other charges that the decree to give a crown to Demosthenes as a reward for public services contained false statements as to Demosthenes' public merits and financial integrity. With such charges on the

---

[110]See Cic. *Orat.* 2.6.26.

66

docket, it was necessary for Demosthenes to vindicate his public actions, as it was necessary for Aeschines as the prosecutor to attack Demosthenes' entire political career. Thus it was incumbent on Demosthenes to justify his public actions by citing time and again his political integrity and his good deeds on behalf of the nation. In so doing, he intended to come across as the benefactor of the state who defended the public policy approved by the jury itself. If the jury condemned Demosthenes, it would condemn itself.[111]

With this background in mind, it is enlightening to see how Demosthenes employs ἦθος as a deliberate argument to clear his name and win his case. In the opening lines of his oration, he is aware of the impression constant self-reference might make and so he prepares his audience for the use of ἦθος:

> . . . There is the natural disposition of mankind to listen readily to obloquy and invective, and to resent self-laudation. To him [Aeschines] the agreeable duty has been assigned; that part that is almost always offensive remains for me. If, as a safeguard against such offense, I avoid the relation of my own achievements, I shall seem to be unable to refute the charges alleged against me, or to establish my claim to any public distinction. Yet, if I address myself to what I have done, and to

---

[111]Demosthenes and Aeschines were at the beginning colleagues and friends in the first embassy from Athens to Philip of Macedon to negotiate for peace. However, their association dissolved after the second embassy when Demosthenes, for reasons that are moot, brought a charge of treason against Aeschines. The hatred between the two statesmen became implacable. Aeschines saw his chance for revenge in indicting Ctesiphon, a friend of Demosthenes, who had recommended a crown for the great orator for his services to the state. Aechines (*Against Ctesiphon*) countered by calling the action illegal. Demosthenes (*On the Crown*) responded and won the case. Both speeches display a barrage of invectives and personal attacks. Since Aeschines' speech was first and had already filled the minds of the jurors with slander against Demosthenes, the latter had to indulge in an extraordinary amount of ἦθος to paint himself in a better light. The verdict was a complete victory for Demosthenes and Ctesiphon.

> the part I have taken in politics, I shall often be obliged to speak about myself. Well, I will endeavor to do so with all possible modesty (ὡς μετριώτατα); and let the man who has initiated this controversy (ἀγῶν) bear the blame of the egoism which the conditions (τὸ πρᾶγμα) force (ἀναγκάζῃ) upon me.[112]

Demosthenes cleverly points out to the jurors the dilemma he faces because of Aeschines' attacks on his character. To say nothing in answer would give credence to the slanders; to answer them involved talking about his achievements. He defuses the possible alienation of his audience by pointing out to them the necessity of the defense of his character through self-recommendation, but he makes it clear he will talk about himself and his good works within the canons of moderation and propriety.[113] Later, as we shall see, Paul uses derivatives of the same language cited in Greek above to say that the Corinthians forced him (με ἠναγκάσατε) to boast (2 Cor 12:11)) but that he will boast οὐκ εἰς τὰ ἄμετρα (2 Cor 10:13). Demosthenes above all is interested in maintaining their goodwill, which, as has been noted, is essential to persuasion:

> Any loss, especially if inflicted by private animosity, is hard to bear; but to lose your goodwill and kindness is the most painful of all losses, as to gain them is the best of all acquisitions. Such being the issues at stake, I implore you all alike to listen to my

---

[112]Dem. *De Cor.* 4.

[113]See footnote 103 for remarks on ἀνάγκη as a basis for self-praise. Twice Demosthenes uses the verb ἀναγκάζω to show that his self-praise is coming out of him unwillingly: ἀναγκασθήσομαι and ἀναγκάζῃ. Demosthenes' audience is able to absorb a good deal of his raw boasting because he is addressing the outlandish charges of Aeschines. The Athenian audience delighted in the exchange between invective and display of character in a speech.

defense against the accusations laid, in a spirit of justice.[114]

In many places, Demosthenes reminds his listeners of his outstanding character mainly through his service to the nation. He cites his public acts as showing that he has done his best for the state.[115] These benefits to the state mainly derived from his intense opposition to Philip and his policy of aggrandizement. Before Demosthenes entered into public office and began to speak in the assembly, he reminds the Athenians that Philip had many successes, but "his enterprises were thwarted after the day on which I entered public life."[116] He recounts his measures to strengthen the Athenian navy by radically changing public policy: "I also claim credit for the very fact that all the measures I adopted brought renown and strength to the city, and that no measure of mine was invidious or vexatious, or spiteful or shabby and unworthy of Athens."[117] He tells his audience that it was his decrees, his defense of the Byzantines against the encroachments of Philip of Macedon, his prevention of the estrangement of the Hellespont, and many other public actions which benefitted the city: "Who advised ($\lambda\acute{\epsilon}\gamma\omega\nu$) the city, moved ($\gamma\rho\acute{\alpha}\phi\omega\nu$) the resolutions, took action ($\pi\rho\acute{\alpha}\tau\tau\omega\nu$), devoted himself whole-heartedly ($\acute{\alpha}\pi\lambda\hat{\omega}\varsigma\ \delta o\acute{\upsilon}\varsigma$) and without stint to that business? I did; and I need not argue how profitable my policy

---

[114]Dem. *De Cor.* 5-6.

[115]See Dem. *De Cor.* 57, 86, 87, 173.

[116]Dem. *De Cor.* 60. Note Demosthenes' use of *praeteritio*.

[117]Dem. *De Cor.* 108.

was."[118] Demosthenes' simple use of ἐγώ and his audience's experience

(ἔργῳ) of his public service display his ἦθος.

He tells his listeners of his private financial gifts to the city, especially his

outfitting of ships to fight against Philip. He becomes highly incensed that

Aeschines wants an audit of his free donations:

> Is there any law so compact of iniquity and illiberality that, when
> a man out of sheer generosity has given away his money, it
> defrauds him of the gratitude he has earned, drags him before a
> set of prying informers, and gives them authority to hold an audit
> of his free donations?[119]

He also talks of his gifts in the private sector, particularly to the distressed, the

dowries he has arranged, the captives he has ransomed and other such acts of

charity.[120] He scores a major point when he modestly deprecates such

benefactions but in doing so subtly reminds his audience the need for gratitude

to those who are benefactors:

> My view is that the recipient of a benefit ought to remember it
> all his life, but that the benefactor ought to put it out of his mind
> at once, if the one is to behave decently, and the other with
> magnanimity. To remind a man of the good turns you have done
> to him is very much like a reproach. Nothing shall induce me to
> do anything of the sort; but whatever be my reputation in that
> respect, I am content.[121]

In his peroration (297-323), coming after his arguments against Aeschines

---

[118]Dem. *De Cor.* 88.

[119]Dem. *De Cor.* 112.

[120]Dem. *De Cor.* 268-269.

[121]Dem. *De Cor.* 269.

in 126-226, Demosthenes sums up his moral probity and ethical behavior while in office in order to leave one last good impression with his listeners: "At the very outset of my career I had chosen once and for all the path of political uprightness and integrity, and resolved to support, to magnify, and to associate myself with the honor, the power, and the glory of my native land."[122] When the navy was going to pieces, he passed a statute which compelled the wealthy to take their fair share of the expenses to relieve the oppression of the poor. The rich offered him enormous sums as bribes not to propose the measure. He uses his refusal in the face of these attractive offers as a sign of his good character:

> Do you think it was a trifling relief I gave to the poor, or a trifling sum that the rich would have spent to escape their obligations? I pride myself not only on my refusal of compromise and on my acquittal, but also on my having enacted a beneficial law and proved it such by experience.[123]

And likewise: "At home I never preferred the gratitude of the rich to the claims of the poor; in foreign affairs I never coveted the gifts and the friendship of Philip rather than the common interests of all Greece."[124] By magnifying his character in this way, Demosthenes implies that Aeschines's behavior, which he has detailed in previous remarks, has not been so upright. In his peroration (298-323), Demosthenes talks of his honesty in all of his dealings:

---

[122]Dem. *De Cor.* 322.

[123]Dem. *De Cor.* 107.

[124]Dem. *De Cor.* 109.

> With a soul upright, honest and incorruptible, appointed to the control of more momentous transactions than any statesman of my time, I have administered them throughout in all purity and righteousness. On these grounds I claim this distinction [namely, the crown].[125]

For all of this service, Demosthenes says that the Athenians should show him the gratitude due to a benefactor (268-69 and 316, as well as 153, 108, 285). For his help in momentarily checking the expansionist policies of Philip, he says that "for that relief, men of Athens, you have first and chiefly to thank the kindness of some friendly god, but in a secondary degree, and so far as one man could help, you have to thank me."[126] He later aligns himself with the venerated Athenians of antiquity who rendered enormous service to their country and concludes that the same gratitude and commendation should be given to those in the present who have achieved something equally as great for their country:

> Consider this question: is it more decent and patriotic that for the sake of services (εὐεργεσίας) of men of old times, enormous as they were, nay, great beyond expression, the services that are now being rendered to the present age should be treated with ingratitude and vituperation, or that every man who achieves anything in a spirit of loyalty should receive some share of the respect and consideration of his fellow-citizens?[127]

In a final accolade to his ἦθος, Demosthenes writes:

> There are two traits, men of Athens, that mark the disposition of

---

[125]Dem. *De Cor.* 298. See all 320-323.

[126]Dem. *De Cor.* 153. Demosthenes shares his success with the gods, which, as Plutarch would later say, is a way of rendering the self-praise palatable to the audience.

[127]Dem. *De Cor.* 316.

the well-meaning citizen;—that is a description I may apply to myself without offense. When in power, the constant aim of his policy should be the honour and the ascendancy of his country; and on every occasion and in all business he should preserve his loyalty. That virtue depends on his natural disposition: ability and success depend on other considerations. Such, you will find, has been my disposition, abidingly and without alloy.[128]

Cicero also uses $\mathring{\eta}\theta o\varsigma$ to foster his arguments and to elicit the goodwill of his audience.[129] In his famous orations against Cataline, he frequently cites his own noble deeds on behalf of Rome. In the opening lines of his *In Catalinam III*, Cicero writes what appears to be a rather pompous and arrogant claim. After saying quite without modesty that the Republic of Rome was snatched from the very jaws of destruction by his toil and vigilance, he continues:

The day on which we are saved is, I believe, as bright and joyous as that on which we are born, because delight at our salvation is assured while at birth our future is uncertain, and because we are not conscious of our birth but feel pleasure at our preservation. If I am right, then surely when we have out of gratitude and by our praises raised to the immortal gods the man who founded this city, you and your descendants should hold in honor the man who has saved this same city after its foundation and growth to greatness. It is I who have quenched the fires which were on the point of being set to the whole city, to its temples, its shrines, its houses and its walls and which were about to engulf them. It is I who have thrust back the swords drawn against the Republic and have dashed the daggers they held at your throats. It is through my efforts that these plots have been detected and displayed to the Senate. . . .[130]

---

[128]Dem. *De Cor.* 321.

[129]Some would say too much so. Cicero had a reputation for overpraising himself. Quintilian (*Inst.* 11.1.18) and Plutarch (*Mor.* 540F) make references to this.

[130]Cic. *Cat.* 3.2.

Time and again in this speech Cicero talks about his courage, his prudence, his foresight in freeing the Republic from dire peril: ". . . citizens, my actions have secured the salvation of you all. . . . I have preserved both city and citizens safe and sound."[131]

The self-praise which is many respects seems overblown is somewhat mitigated in its immodesty by Cicero in several passages attributing some of the outcome for the safety of the Republic to the immortal gods and particularly to Jupiter.[132] In *In Catalinam IV*, after acknowledging the fame, valor, and bravery of such Roman giants as Scipio, Africanus, Marius, and Pompeius, Cicero says that "there will certainly be some place for my fame amid the praise of these men," for a victory at home against a civil war is just as important as those won abroad. Cicero asks nothing in return "for my exceptional devotion to your cause and for the painstaking efforts with which, as you can see, I have preserved the Republic," except to be remembered for this occasion and for the whole of his consulship.[133]

In his oration *Pro Sulla*, Cicero once again uses the powerful advocacy of his devotion to the cause of Rome to argue his case:

> . . . but I, as consul, by my decisions, by my efforts and at the risk of my life, but without any state of emergency, without a levy, without use of arms, without an army, by the arrest and confession of five men, I rescued the city from burning, the

---

[131]Cic. *Cat.* 3.25.

[132]Cic. *Cat.* 3.18,22.

[133]Cic. *Cat.* 4.21-22.

citizens from slaughter, Italy from devastation and the Republic from destruction. By the punishment of five demented deperadoes I saved the lives of all the citizens, the peace of the world, this city, the home of each of us, the defense of foreign kings and peoples, the glory of all nations and the heart of the empire.[134]

In his eloquent speech delivered before the college of pontiffs entitled *De Domo sua,* wherein he attempts to recover his property which Clodius, who had engineered his exile, had razed and cleverly consecrated to Liberty so as to place it beyond recovery, Cicero speaks of the necessity of his boasting to his arch enemy in a passage that is full of mordant wit:

You go so far as to bid me cease from boasting; you declare that the assertions I am in the habit of making concerning myself are intolerable, and, with a pretty turn of wit, you come forward with an elegant and humorous jest to the effect that I am accustomed to call myself Jupiter, and also to assert that Minerva is my sister. My insolence in calling myself Jupiter is not so great as my ignorance in thinking that Minerva is Jupiter's sister. But I at least do claim virginity for my sister; you have not permitted your sister to be a virgin. But I would warn you against the practice of applying the name of Jupiter to yourself, since in your case, as in his, you may use the term of sister and that of wife with regard to the same lady. And since you blame me for being too boastful in sounding my own praises, who, I would ask you, has ever heard me speak of myself, save under the constraint of an inevitable necessity? For if, when crimes of theft, corruption, and passion are imputed to me, I am in the habit of replying that it was by my forethought, at my own risk, and through my exertions that my country was saved, it must be considered that I am not so much boasting of my own exploits, as stating facts in answer to charges.[135]

In this same speech, Cicero calls himself the light of Rome's salvation (27.75),

---

[134]Cic. *Sull.* 33.

[135]Cic. *Dom.* 34.92-35.93.

the one "whose existence was the only thing that prevented the state from falling utterly under the power of slaves" (43.111), who "by his labors had preserved the city at the risk of his life" (53.137). Cicero accommodates himself to the ἦθος of his audience, the body of pontiffs who made the decisions in matters of public religion, by constant references to the gods, religion, holiness, and sacred space, to argue, in a cogent analogy, for the rebuilding of his home:

> What is more sacred, what more inviolably hedged about by every kind of sanctity, than the home of every individual citizen? Within its circle are his altars, his hearths, his household gods, his religion, his observances, his ritual; it is a sanctuary so holy in the eyes of all, that it were a sacrilege to tear an owner therefrom.[136]

In another of his speeches upon his return from exile, *De Haruspicum Responsis*, this one to the official Soothsayers of Rome, Cicero answers Clodius' accusations that an alleged sacrilege had occurred at the site of Cicero's returned property. Cicero refutes the charges by saying that the site was not his property but someone else's whom Clodius had murdered. Cicero likewise accuses Clodius of sacrilege and polluting the sacrifices of the Bona Dea. In his rebuttal, Cicero draws for his audience negative images of the kind of character Clodius is in order to devaluate his slanders:

> But for Clodius my hatred is no greater today than it was on that day when I discovered that he had burnt his fingers in the fires of awful rites, and had been dismissed in his woman's garb from the house of the supreme Pontiff which he had made the scene of vile adultery. It was then, then I say, that I marked and anticipated long before its arrival the fierce hurricane that was

---

[136]Cic. *Dom.* 41.109.

being roused, the furious tempest that was brewing to imperil the state. I saw that criminality so savage and effrontery so monstrous, displayed by a maddened and exasperated young nobleman, could not be kept within the limits of a peaceful existence; but that one day, if it were allowed to go unchecked, the plague would break forth, fraught with ruin to the community.[137]

In an unusual letter to M. Cato in 50 B.C.E., Cicero petitions this powerful

Roman for his support for a triumph and for his election as augur in recognition

of his exemplary service as governor of Cilicia. Cicero says that his

achievement in this province had not been meager or contemptible but was of

such quality and extent that persons with lesser exploits have received the

highest honors from the Senate. It is basically a letter of self-recommendation

in which Cicero hails his ἦθος as an able administrator and as one who has

safeguarded the peace and security of Rome against the threat of a most serious

war. He hints in the same letter that this honor would help to heal the wound

of injustice he suffered as a result of his exile and would be a recognition of

himself as of the most distinguished character. He pleads the cause of his

triumph by saying that he governed his province both by the excellence of his

moral character as well as by military exploits, a combination that enhances his

argument.[138]

Both in theory and in practice, the argument from ἦθος was an essential

---

[137]Cic. *Har. Resp.* 3.4.

[138]Cic. *Fam.* 15.4. Cicero's application for a triumph was opposed by Cato, who gives his reasons in a letter (*Fam.* 15.5) that is as sarcastic as it is elaborate in its compliments. Cicero's reply to Cato is gracious in the extreme but perhaps not without a touch of irony.

ingredient in any act of persuasion. Orators used this proof to advantage to establish their intellectual competency, cultural credentials, and moral and spiritual character in order to gain the goodwill and credence of their listeners. At the same time, they used the lack of ἦθος in their opponents to undermine the credibility and trust of those who wished to sway an audience's allegiance in some other direction. The ἦθος or ethically good nature of the speaker, whether created by the speech or intrinsic to the individual, was usually projected in the exordium to create immediate credibility and recapitulated in the peroration to leave the audience with a good lasting impression.[139] Used in conjunction with arousing the emotions of an audience and establishing reasonable proofs, ἦθος was a most effective method for helping one's listeners to make the association of assent from one's character to one's judgments. Given the fact that ἦθος was a standard and studied technique in any persuasive discourse in classical antiquity, we now turn to an examination of how Paul used proof from ἦθος as a major argument in 2 Corinthians 10-13 to establish his legitimacy as a true apostle, to regain the confidence of the Corinthians in himself, and to secure their adherence to his interpretation of the Gospel.

C. The Use of ἦθος in 2 Corinthians 10-13

Paul had a serious task before him in composing his response to the

---

[139]See Arist. *Rh.* 3.14; 3.19

Corinthians. Itinerant apostles who opposed Paul entered the Corinthian community and leveled many accusations and objections against his character, his apostolic leadership, his theology, his style of preaching, and his missionary practices. They were persuasive in convincing the Corinthians that Paul was a γόης, an imposter, thus effectively denying his legitimacy as an apostle and questioning his interpretation of the Gospel. In light of his commission from Christ and for the sake of his Corinthian church, Paul sought to clear his good name against these charges and expose the character of those who were slandering him. To do this, he needed to establish his ἦθος in 2 Corinthians 10-13 and so dispose his listeners to accept him as a legitimate apostle. One mode of doing this was to show he had done them no wrong but rather had their best interests at heart. Before Paul could expose the "different spirit and gospel" (2 Cor 11:4) and the false claims (11:12) of his detractors, he had to convey his ἦθος in a way that convinced his congregation that he was a man of φρόνησις, ἀρετή, and εὔνοια, the sources from which ἦθος arose.[140]

Paul does this by securing for himself the goodwill and the intelligent and receptive hearing of his audience from the four quarters discussed by Aristotle, Cicero, and other rhetorical theorists: from his own person, from the person of his opponents, from the persons of his audience, and from the case itself.[141] From his own person, Paul captures the good will of the Corinthians by

---

[140]Arist. *Rh.* 2.1.5.

[141]Arist. *Rh.* 3.14.7f; Cic. *Inv. Rhet.* 1.16.22; *Rhet. Her.* 1.4.8; Cic. *Part. Or.* 8.28. See pp. 44-46 for previous discussion of this.

boasting of his own acts and services without arrogance, as we shall presently see. From the person of his opponents, Paul brings the Corinthians to his viewpoint by presenting a very negative picture of his detractors as arrogant in their claims, self-seeking in their motives, and intolerable in their use of advantages. He gains his auditors' respect and attention by showing them what honorable esteem he has for them, how perceptive he believes they are in detecting frauds, and how eagerly he awaits their sensible judgment in a matter of great importance. Finally, from the case at hand, Paul gets an intelligent hearing by arguing for his interpretation of the Gospel as the authentic teaching about Christ and by disparaging the gospel of his opponents as full of "sophistries and proud pretension" (10:5). Throughout his response, Paul weaves together these four types of argument to project an $\mathring{\eta}\theta o\varsigma$ of trustworthiness, competence, and concern which operates as a powerful rhetorical proof for the genuineness of his message.

To establish his $\mathring{\eta}\theta o\varsigma$ Paul is forced to defend himself, both to refute the charges against him and to secure the *benevolentia* ($\epsilon\mathring{v}\nu o\iota\alpha$) of the Corinthians, as Demosthenes had done before him.[142] Although he deeply dislikes it and calls it "folly" ($\mathring{\alpha}\phi\rho o\sigma\mathring{v}\nu\eta$, 11:1,17) and "useless" ($o\mathring{v}\ \sigma v\mu\phi\acute{\epsilon}\rho o\nu$, 12:1), he is realistic enough to know that he has no choice in the matter ($\kappa\alpha v\chi\mathring{\alpha}\sigma\theta\alpha\iota\ \delta\epsilon\mathring{\iota}$, 12:1; cf. 11:18) but to accommodate himself temporarily to the demands of the occasion and speak on a level that appealed to the sensibilities of his listeners.

---

[142]Dem. *De Cor.* 4.

He has to create an atmosphere in which, as Cicero said, *ut amice . . .*

audiamur.[143] Before he does this, however, he cannot hold back an ironic

rejoinder which simultaneously contextualizes his response and chastises the

Corinthians that the best kind of praise, as Plutarch had observed, is the kind

that comes from others: "It is not the person who recommends one's self who

is approved but the one whom the Lord recommends" (10:17).[144] Paul's

persuasive power in 2 Corinthians 10-13 comes in great measure from the $\dot{\eta}\theta o\varsigma$

he projects to the Corinthians, even though created reluctantly out of boasting.

Paul's boasting, however, is not rooted in a vain desire to create a

pretentious presence but arises from some identifiably legitimate reasons which

accord with the Greco-Roman world's acceptance of non-offensive self-

recommendation: out of necessity,[145] as an *apologia*,[146] for the sake of

calling the Corinthians to their senses,[147] in praise of God,[148] and as a

---

[143]Cic. *Part. Or.* 8.28.

[144]Plut. *Mor.* 539C-D: ". . . even the winners of the crown at the games are proclaimed victors by others, who thus remove the odium of self-praise. . . . For while praise from others, as Xenophon said, is the most pleasant of recitals, praise of ourselves is for others most distressing." There is a double barb in Paul's rejection of self-praise. The first has its roots in the Old Testament. Self-praise amounts to self-deification and blasphemy (Betz, *Plutarch's Ethical Writings*, 373) and so is contrary to all decency and is ἄδικος (*Mor.* 539D). Secondly, praise of one's self cannot begin qualitatively or quantitatively to match the kind God can give to one.

[145]See 2 Cor 12:11; 18; Plut. *Mor.* 540F, 542E. See also Dem. *De Cor.* 4; Quint. *Inst.* 11.1.18-19.

[146]See 2 Cor 11:12; 11:22-28; 12:1-6; Dem. *De Cor.* 8 and *passim*; Quint. *Inst.* 11.1.22-23.

[147]See 2 Cor 11:1-3; 13:1-10); Plut. *Mor.* 539F, 544E, 545D-546A.

criticism of his detractors.[149]   It is thus that Paul uses his ἦθος in 2 Corinthians 10-13 as perhaps his most powerful defensive weapon, a major source of proof.

He was duty bound, first of all, to his own calling as an emissary of Christ to tell the truth about himself in the face of the demeaning and slanderous remarks made about him. Paul realized well that his detractors were using the effective oratorical technique of painting an adversary in the bleakest of colors in order to derogate from the latter's case or authority. Paul did it himself toward his detractors, as we shall later see, to diminish their ἦθος.[150] Among the accusations against Paul, inferred from his response, were the following:

1. He is ταπεινός (10:1).

2. He is ἀσθενής (10:10; he lacks the σχῆμα, the powerful physical presence (παρουσία) of an apostle.

3. His λόγος is ἐξουθενημένος (10:10).

4. He is ἰδιώτης τῷ λόγῳ (11:6).

5. He is πανοῦργος (12:16).

---

[148]See 2 Cor 10:17; Plut. *Mor.* 542E-543A.

[149]See 2 Cor 10:12-18; 11:12, 18-21; Plut. *Mor.* 543A-F, 544F-545A.

[150]*Mutatis mutandis*, Isocrates (*Ant.* 5) refers to this technique: ". . . for, although my opponent made no argument whatever on the merits of the case, and did nothing but decry my 'cleverness' of speech and indulge in extravagant nonsense about my wealth and the number of my pupils, they [the lay public] imposed the trierarchy upon me." Norlin (*Isocrates II*, 187 n.c) writes that a favorite device of the orators in the Athenian Courts was "to warn the jury against the adversary as δεινὸς λέγειν." Cf. Pl. *Ap.* 17B.

6. He is θάρρος from the safe distance of letters (10:2).

7. He walks κατὰ σάρκα (10:2).

8. He is ὑστερηκέναι τῶν ὑπερλίαν ἀποστόλων (11:5).

9. He is [οὐ] Χριστοῦ εἶναι (10:7).

10. He does not have δοκιμή . . . τοῦ ἐν [αὐτῷ] λαλοῦντος Χριστοῦ (13:3).

11. He does not show τὰ σημεῖα (καὶ τέρατα καὶ δυνάμεις) τοῦ ἀποστόλου (12:12).

These charges are deliberately calculated to impugn Paul's reputation and his message. Who these opponents were, what their theological beliefs and rhetorical training were, and what their purpose was are all moot points.[151] The fact is they have attacked Paul's good sense and practical wisdom in guiding the Corinthians (10:10-11), his virtue and integrity as an apostle (11:12), and his goodwill and sincerity toward the best interests of the Corinthians (12:14-17), which in effect amount to denying Paul the three fundamental qualities inherent in ἦθος. To persuade the Corinthians to a revaluation of their assumptions both about himself and about his Gospel, Paul, in the face of such attacks, must argue from the same three qualities to show

---

[151]See the following works for a discussion of the identity, theology, and purpose of these opponents: Victor Furnish, *II Corinthians* (Anchor Bible; New York: Doubleday, 1986) 500-502; Dieter Georgi, *The Opponents of Paul in Second Corinthians* (Philadelphia: Fortress, 1986); C. K. Barrett, "Paul's Opponents in II Corinthians," *NTS* 17 (1971) 233-254; Gerhard Friedrich, "Die Gegner des Paulus im 2 Korintherbrlef," in *Abraham unser Vater: Juden und Christen im Gespräch über die Bibel* (Michel Festschrift, eds. O. Betz, M. Hengel and P. Schmidt; AGJU 5; Leiden: Brill, 1963) 181-215.

that he is just the opposite of what his detractors say he is. He must make his case more convincing than his opponents' to win back the good esteem of the Corinthians toward him, their respect for his manner of apostleship, and their confidence in his Gospel. It is a situation in which ἦθος, the projection of one's character, becomes a crucial form of proof. A parallel contest can be found in the debate between Aeschines and Demosthenes in which both orators mutually attack the character of the other while building up their own. The significant factor here is that Paul was not present personally to declaim his response to his attackers. His letter form had to create the virtual experience of the rhetorical occasion where the speaker attempts to capture the goodwill of the auditors in order to produce conviction in them.[152]

---

[152]It is not too farfetched to suggest that Paul probably trained Titus or some other letter carrier to declaim his response with the proper emphases, intonations, and gestures to underscore his proofs. Delivery or declamation were at the very heart of a successful oration. Aristotle (*Rh.* 3.1.2) writes that "it is not sufficient to know what one ought to say, but one must also know how to say it." The "how to" refers both to style and to delivery, "which is of the greatest importance." He goes on to say: "Now delivery is a matter of voice, as to the mode in which it should be used for each particular emotion; when it should be loud, when low, when intermediate; and how the tones, that is, shrill, deep, and intermediate, should be used; and what rhythms are adapted to each subject. For there are three qualities that are considered,—volume, harmony, rhythm. Those who use these properly nearly always carry off the prizes in dramatic contests. . . . But since the whole business of rhetoric is to influence opinion, we must pay attention to it, not as being right, but necessary" (3.1.4-5). See also Cic. *De Or.* 1.31.143 ("deliver . . . with charm and effect"); Cic. *Or.* 17.55-60 for some convincing comments on the importance of delivery ("Demosthenes was right, therefore, in considering delivery to be the first, second and third in importance."); Cic. *Brut.* 142 for the use of the voice and gestures to win confidence and to stir compassion; *Rhet. Her.* 3.11.20 and *passim*; Quint. *Inst.* 2.10.2-15 and *passim*. For letter-carriers in Christian antiquity and the practice of reading aloud, see Martin R. P. McGuire, "Letters and Letter Carriers in Christian Antiquity" *CW* 53 (1960) 148-53;184-86;199-200; J. Balogh, "Voces paginarum. Beiträge zur Geschichte des lauten Lesens und Schreibens," *Philol.* 82 (1927) 202-240.

To refute the charges and at the same time to project a persuasive ἦθος, Paul does "a little boasting" (11:16). He is forced (δεῖ, 12:1) because of the slander to make two rhetorically significant personal acknowledgments which reveal a fullness in apostolic integrity and divine commission. Both of these claims (11:21) operate concomitantly on a literal and on an ironic level. On the literal level, they are used in an unabashedly forthright way to claim a superior ἦθος and therefore to project himself as a person with a more credible witness and message: "What anyone else dares to claim . . . I, too, will dare" (11:21). On the ironic level, they are used to show the absolutely spurious claim of any ἦθος that does not acknowledge a reversal of human values and an admission of divine favor: "I speak with absolute foolishness" (11:21). In that way Paul questions his opponents' criteria! His argument for the superiority of his character and witness over that of his opponents is that the source of his ἦθος goes beyond impotent "human resources" (10:3) and resides in the power of God.

Paul advances two claims for the quality of his ἦθος: his περιστάσεις, the hardships he endured on behalf of the Gospel (11:23-29), and the singular gift of his rapture into the third heaven where he enjoyed extraordinary revelations (12:1-6).[153] Paul makes these disclosures as a result of the atmosphere of prejudice that has bred suspicion in the Corinthians. As Aristotle said about the

---

[153]Using the convention of modern secondary literature, we shall refer to this list of hardships in the body of our text as a *peristasis* catalogue or by the Bultmanian term *Peristasenkatalog*.

topos of removing prejudice, a person must "make use of the arguments by which one may clear oneself from disagreeable suspicion."[154] Paul's argument in this case is that he has performed among the Corinthians "with great patience [with unflagging endurance] the signs that show the apostle, signs and wonders and deeds of power" (12:12). He has been forced to make these revelations: "You have driven me to it" (12:11). At the same time he offers them as an apologetic: "I am in no way inferior to the super-apostles" (11:5; 12:11). He reveals these personal details for their sake to reassure the Corinthians that God's power is at work in him for their benefit and that they are in no way inferior to the rest of the churches (12:13): "Do you think throughout this recital that I am defending myself to you? Before God I tell you, in Christ, I have done everything to build you up, my dear ones" (12:19).

Paul has another motive in mind in making his disclosures, one that is mainly a critique of his opponents but also a lesson for the Corinthians. In spite of the extraordinary quality of his endurance of sufferings and gifts from God, they are really nothing to boast about. They prove nothing if they are *self-commending*, if they are occasions for vaunting one's ministry (11:12) and usurping divine recommendation (10:17). Paul's reproach is that his opponents' criticism of what he lacks in physical appearance, bold preaching, and rhetorical sophistication are "weaknesses" that allow full range for the power of God to work in him. If that is so, Paul says, then "I willingly boast of my weaknesses

---

[154]Arist. *Rh.* 3.15.1.

instead, that the power of Christ may rest upon me" (12:9). That, he says to his opponents and to the Corinthians, is true strength (12:10), for then we live with the dead and living Christ by God's power in us (13:4). In tandem with this point, Paul last of all boasts of his achievements in order to give credit to God, who is the source of such extraordinary signs and the real object of boasting: "If I find that I must make a few further claims about the power the Lord has given us for your upbuilding and not for your destruction, this will not embarrass me in the least" (10:8). Paul will not boast beyond moderation ($o\dot{v}\kappa$ $\epsilon\dot{\iota}\varsigma$ $\tau\dot{\alpha}$ $\ddot{\alpha}\mu\epsilon\tau\rho\alpha$, 10:15a) in contrast to the false apostles who break every rule and measure of propriety.

Thus with the *peristasis* catalogue and his experience of paradise, Paul demonstrates the quality of his $\ddot{\eta}\theta o\varsigma$ against the fraudulent claims of his opponents (10:5), assertions which the Corinthians have superficially taken to be the power of the Spirit (10:7). He has assumed this posture of self-praise for one purpose, to awe them to such an extent so as to reclaim their allegiance in and acclamation of him as their spiritual leader who can direct them to God "with the Gospel of Christ" (10:14). Paul's rhetorical purpose in revealing these aspects of his character is to do precisely what the rhetorical theorists and orators of his times said must be done in any act of persuasion, namely, use the argument from one's life, which Aristotle had said was the most powerful means of persuasion, to bring one's listeners to an indisputable judgment. The following discussion will show how Paul uses these two self-revealing passages as crucial arguments for his defense against slander and for his recommendation to the Corinthians.

The *peristasis* catalogue was a respectable technique in the ancient world to reveal character and to win the confidence of an audience. As James Fitzgerald has written in an excellent study of catalogues of hardships in the Corinthian correspondence: "*Peristasis* catalogues serve to legitimate the claims made about a person and show him to be virtuous because *peristaseis* have a revelatory and probative function in regard to character."[155] According to the cultural mentality of the Greco-Roman world prevalent at the time of Paul, especially in Stoic circles, adversity best revealed one's character and times of hardship tested the authenticity of one's virtue. The words of Epictetus, "It is difficulties that show what men are," summed up the function of *peristaseis* in the writings of many classical writers.[156] Suffering and virtue were inextricably bound together, the one revealing the other and demonstrating the good character of an individual. Seneca wrote that "to triumph over the calamities and terrors of mortal life is the part of a great man only." No one could know if a person was great if fortune did not give that person an

---

[155]James T. Fitzgerald, *Cracks in an Earthen Vessel*, 203. The discussion that follows in the text is heavily indebted to his research into classical authors on hardship catalogues. See also Anton Fridrichsen, "Peristasenkataloge und Res Gestae," *SO* 8 (1929) 78-82; "Zum Stil des paulinischen Peristasenkatalogs 2 Cor.11:23ff," *SO* 7 (1928) 25-29; Robert Hodgson, "Paul the Apostle and First Century Tribulation Lists," *ZNW* 74 (1983) 59-80; Josef Zmijewski, *Der Stil der paulinischen "Narrenrede,"* (BBB 52; Köln/Berlin: Hanstein, 1978) 232-322.

[156]Epict. *Diss.* 1.24.1; also 1.6.36. Jewish and Christian circles had like ideas about adversities but for different reasons, such as love for the Torah, God, Christ.

opportunity of showing one's worth. He concluded that "Disaster is Virtue's opportunity."[157] The individual who bore patiently and courageously with adversity received glory and praise because people saw with their own eyes the evidences of that person's virtue.

In the Greco-Roman world hardship was a sign of God's love, as well as a sign of God's approval and esteem.[158] Seneca in *De Providentia* writes: "God hardens, reviews, and disciplines those whom he approves, whom he loves."[159] At the same time, God endows the individual graced with adversity, according to Epictetus, with the requisite strength "to enable us to bear all that happens without being degraded or crushed thereby."[160] This being the case, it is a sign both of humility and genuine wisdom to acknowledge that "the attainment of virtue is ultimately the result of the divine, who has provided both the means and the assistance that are indispensable for this

---

[157]Sen. *Prov.* 4.1-2, 6.

[158]Fitzgerald, *Cracks in an Earthen Vessel*, 76-82.

[159]Sen. *Prov.* 4.7. His words surrounding this quotation eloquently convey the worth of an individual marked by God for adversity: "God, I say, is showing favour to those whom he desires to achieve the highest possible virtue whenever he gives them the means of doing a courageous and brave deed, and to this end they must encounter some difficulty in life. . . . Why is it that God afflicts the best men with ill health, or sorrow, or some other misfortune? For the same reason that in the army the bravest men are assigned to the hazardous tasks; it is the picked soldier that a general sends to surprise the enemy by a night attack, or to reconnoitre the road, or to dislodge a garrison. Not a man of these will say as he goes, 'My commander has done me an ill turn,' but instead, 'He has paid me a compliment.' In like manner, all those who are called to suffer what would make cowards and poltroons weep may say, 'God has deemed us worthy instruments of his purpose to discover how much human nature can endure'."

[160]Epict. *Diss.* 1.6.40; also 1.6.28; 2.16.13-14; 3.8.6.

accomplishment."[161]   The individual then renders praise to God for the

victory, not to oneself.   If self-praise is deemed appropriate because of

circumstances discussed earlier, the individual always glorifies God through

whose love and benevolence the person has achieved such triumphs.

There are many examples of comparative trial lists similar to Paul's,

mostly from the Greco-Roman world, but also from Josephus, the Nag

Hammadi Library, and the Mishnah.[162]   Of particular relevance are the ones

that appear in Plutarch's biography of Alexander, one of which has a great deal

in common with Paul's tribulations catalogue.   Plutarch's Alexander boasts:

> But my body bears many a token of an opposing Fortune and no
> ally of mine. First, among the Illyrians, my head was *wounded
> by a stone* and my neck by a *cudgel*. Then at the Granicus my
> head was *cut open by an enemy's dagger*, at Issus my *thigh was
> pierced by the sword*. Next at Gaza my *ankle was wounded by
> an arrow*, my *shoulder was dislocated*, and I whirled heavily
> round and round. Then at Marathon the bone of my *leg was split
> open by an arrow*. There awaited me towards the last also the
> *buffetings* I received among the Indians and the violence of
> *famines*. Among the Aspasians my *shoulder was wounded by an*

---

[161]Fitzgerald, *Cracks in an Earthen Vessel*, 85. The following words of Seneca in
an essay entitled "On the God Within Us" (*Ep.* 41.4-5) eloquently express the idea that
endurance is possible only through divine help: "God is near you, he is with you, he
is within you. This is what I mean, Lucilius: a holy spirit indwells within us, one who
marks our good and bad deeds, and is our guardian. . . . Indeed, no man can be good
without the help of God. Can one rise superior to fortune unless God helps him to
rise?. . . If you see a man who is unterrified in the midst of dangers, untouched by
desires, happy in adversity, peaceful amid the storm, . . . will not a feeling of
reverence for him steal over you? Will you not say: 'This quality is too great and too
lofty to be regarded as resembling this petty body in which it dwells? A divine power
has descended upon that man'. . . . A thing like this cannot stand upright unless it be
propped by the divine."

[162]See Robert Hodgson, "Paul the Apostle and First Century Tribulation Lists,"
ZNW 74 (1983) 59-80, for many examples from these sources.

arrow, and among the Granridae my leg. Among the Mallians, the shaft of an *arrow sank deep into my breast and buried its steel;* and I was struck in the *neck by a cudgel.* . . . Moreover, there were the trials of the campaign itself: *storms, droughts, deep rivers, the heights of the Birdless Rock, the monstrous shapes of savage beasts, an uncivilized manner of life,* the constant succession of *petty kings* and their repeated *treachery.*

Another of Alexander's biographers, by the name of Arrian, likewise uses the

topos of the tribulation list in recounting the great general's labors on behalf of

his Macedonian soldiers on the verge of rebellion:

I have no part of my body, in front at least, that is left without *scars*; there is no *weapon*, used at close quarters, or hurled from afar, of which I do not carry the mark. Nay, I have been *wounded by the sword*, hand to hand; I have been *shot with arrows*, I have been *struck from a catapult, smitten many a time* with stones and clubs, for you, for your glory, for your wealth; I lead [sic] you conquerors through *every land, every sea, every river, mountain, plain.*[163]

What these two quotations have in common with Paul, as Hodgson points out,

is the fact of "Paul and Alexander's boasting vis-à-vis mounting opposition" and

"tribulation as the path to deification." He goes on to single out the

mythological hero Heracles as the model for this second motif of tribulation

leading to deification. Hodgson concludes in reference to Paul:

But it is perhaps those lists in which Paul is "boasting" of his tribulations as the substance of his διακονία "ministry" that are best served by the comparison with the theme of Heracles' labors, especially 2 Cor 11:23-29. Formally and materially Paul's list stands close to those of Plutarch and Arrian, while functionally it both substantiates Paul's claim to be a true apostle

---

[163]These citations are quoted from Hodgson, "Paul and First Century Tribulation Lists," 77-78. The italics are his.

and implies the transcendental origin of his office and gospel.[164]

These examples illuminate the prevalence of these catalogues of hardships at the time of Paul, although Paul's use of them is unique to his theological purposes.

It is against this Greco-Roman backdrop of adversity as a gift from God which tests and proves the virtue of an individual's character that we best interpret Paul's *peristasis* catalogue in 2 Cor 11:21-29. His striking disclosure of his endurance of hardships for the sake of the Gospel has several purposes in the text which, when taken together, serve as an unassailable testimony to his character. The *peristasis* catalogue, first of all, acts as a proof of the reality of his divine calling and of his virtue. Only an individual called by God could undergo such an overwhelming number of perilous experiences and come through them all. Though his understanding of God is different than that of the Stoic moralists, yet Paul has the same conviction as they that he has been divinely chosen because of his hardships to act as a witness to God's message. These trials are necessary, as Epictetus wrote, "because He is training me, and making use of me as a witness to the rest of men."[165] Paul has been physically exercised and humbled in these hardships by God who now sends him to the Corinthians as a guide and a model (2 Cor 12:19). The recognition of his shortcomings in 12:7 is a good recommendation of his authentic character, for he refers his accomplishments to the divine power outside of himself. Paul

---

[164]Hodgson, "Paul and First Century Tribulation Lists," 80.

[165]Epict. *Diss.* 3.24.113.

mentions his numerous tribulations in order to convince the Corinthians that he is more of a minister of Christ than his opponents (11:23), simply because he has been tried by God more and survived. His critics had said he was not of Christ. In answer Paul points to his *peristaseis* and says these are the "proof of the Christ who speaks in me" (13:3). Because of these weaknesses, mistreatment, distress, persecutions, and difficulties (12:10), Paul argues he has the approval of God and that is what really counts (10:17). Paul's scars are his best recommendation and a powerful testimonial to the genuineness of his character.

Secondly, in conjunction with the above, the *peristasis* catalogue acts as a counterbalance to the self-appraising claims of Paul's opponents to show that their boasting is far off the mark for more than one reason. They boast immoderately, that is, they are full of personal achievement and self-glorification; they engage both in self-recommendation and self-comparison; and they fail to acknowledge their debt to God as the source of their achievements (10:12-18). Just as they engage in the ancient practice of *synkrisis* or comparison to lend an air of superiority to their boasts, Paul likewise does the same but with an entirely different norm. Paul argues he is not so bold as to compare himself with people who are their own appraisers (10:12). The implication is that if he did, he would certainly lose out. In a very subtle and indirect way, in contrast to the behavior of his opponents, Paul does not depend on his own recognizance but claims for himself a recommendation from the very person of God, which is certainly superior. When he says in 11:5 before his catalogue of hardships and in 12:11 after it that he is "not at all inferior to the super-apostles, even though I am nothing," Paul creates an ironic *inclusio* which is meant to deprecate the human endorsement involved in the boastful claims of his opponents, while underscoring his own superiority. The paradoxical argument is that although he is "nothing" in his own eyes, he is in actuality far superior to his opponents because he is being recommended by the Lord (10:17). As Fitzgerald remarks apropos of another passage but highly relevant here: "By claiming that God approves his actions Paul is appealing to the only one who is truly qualified to judge and whose judgment is the only one that really matters (1 Cor 4:4-5). It functions here like the testimony of the 'expert' in Hellenistic tradition."[166] Paul's ironic *synkrisis* becomes a very powerful argument for the establishment of his ἦθος to the Corinthians.

In the *peristasis* catalogue and later in the gift of his rapture into paradise, it is interesting to note how Paul solves the dilemma of self-praise. He vacillates between restraint and openness. At one moment he criticizes his opponents for "bragging about their human distinctions" (11:18) and in the next moment he is indulging in it himself. He castigates his opponents for their "much-vaunted ministry" (11:12) while at the same time he mocks himself for his "self-assured boasting" (11:17). Paul seems uneasy with talking about his unusual gifts, mainly because he does not want "to boast immoderately"

---

[166]Fitzgerald, *Cracks in an Earthen Vessel*, 183, n.180.

(10:15), that is, usurp God's place as the source and object of boasting. Throughout his argument, however, in spite of his fluctuating feelings, Paul has no doubts that his boasting is totally different from that of his opponents. He manifests this syntactically, leaving no doubt in the auditors' ears of his sarcastic judgment of the emptiness of his opponents' claims. He makes a distinction between *self*-commendation which he denounces and *self-commendation* which he approves by the placement of the pronouns respectively before and after the verb. When Paul speaks negatively about self-commendation, he places the pronoun before the verb (10:12,18); but when he speaks positively about his own, he places it after the verb (10:12).[167] This is a way of rhetorically indicating that his *peristaseis* stand in obvious superior contrast to those of his opponents, thus stressing from yet another angle the excellence of his character in whom the Corinthians can have absolute confidence.

Paul's last purpose in publishing his *peristasis* catalogue is directed toward the ἦθος inherent in the Corinthian community. As explained quite early in the chapter, a speaker in order to persuade must be concerned to fit one's remarks

---

[167]This observation is taken from Fitzgerald (*Cracks in an Earthen Vessel*, 187) who gives credit on the placement of the reflexive pronoun to H. Alford, *The Greek New Testament* (4 vols; rev.ed.; 1871-75; repr., Grand Rapids: Baker, 1980) 2.688. Although the examples in 2 Cor 10-13 are not numerous, there are other places in the same letter where the pronoun is before the verb συνιστάνομεν (3:1; 5:12; compare 4:5: ἑαυτοὺς κηρύσσομεν) and where the pronoun is after the verb (4:2; 6:4). It is plausible that Paul for rhetorical effect may have coached the speaker to inflect for the congregation this stylistic artifice to convey meaning and value through appeal to hearing. If so, Paul's auditors would have been further amazed at yet another example of his rhetorical skill.

to the particular social and cultural temperament of the audience in order to effect rapport and a receptive hearing. The speaker must reflect the character of the audience in its tastes, motives, and feelings and adapt the speech's words, images, and thought to the ethical condition of the audience. Paul is aware that both his catalogue of hardships and his rapture experience would appeal to the tastes of the Corinthian community for "signs and wonders and deeds of power" (12:12), especially since these were the very things his opponents were telling the Corinthians he was lacking. In catering to their need to hear such achievements, Paul uses the *peristasis* catalogue both as a pedagogical device for instructing them in the recognition of true self-commendation as that which comes from God and also as a parenetic means, in Plutarch's sense, to instill confidence and to exhort to emulation. Paul alludes to the educational value of his experiences both for himself and for the Corinthians when he writes that just as "it is true that [Christ] was crucified out of weakness but lives by the power of God," so "we too are weak in him but we live with him by God's power in us" (13:4).

The other side of the coin of his catalogue of sufferings is the catalogue of God's power.[168] This is precisely his boast and the only letter of recommendation he needs. Paul furthermore uses his catalogue of hardships as a parenetic device to encourage the Corinthians to live up to the challenge of their faith. He tells them that Christ is "not weak in dealing with you but is

---

[168]Fitzgerald, *Cracks in an Earthen Vessel*, 171.

powerful in you" (13:3). He asks them to test and examine themselves to see

if they are living by this Pauline Gospel: "Perhaps you yourselves do not realize

that Christ Jesus is in you—unless, of course, you have failed the challenge"

(13:5). Paul boasts of his hardships not only for his sake but for theirs as well.

He boasts of his endurance through God's δύναμις in order to demonstrate the

power of his ἦθος to commend his trustworthiness to them and to elicit their

allegiance. But he also boasts in order to implant this same ἦθος in them,

which the false apostles have countermanded by preaching "another Jesus than

the one we have preached . . . a different spirit than the one you have received

. . . a gospel other than the gospel you accepted (11:4)."

There is a great deal of irony in the use Paul makes of this catalogue with

the Corinthians. Paul comes across to them as being surprised that they were

not offended by the crass way his opponents praised themselves which exceeded

all decency. Paul ironically rebukes them for viewing things superficially (10:7)

and for being dazzled with human distinctions (11:18). Their "wisdom"

consists in enduring mistreatment at the hands of fools who have created for

them a catalogue of hardships which is a caricature of the one Paul receives at

the hands of God. Their *peristasis* catalogue consists in putting up "with those

who exploit you, who impose upon you and put on airs, with those who slap

you in the face" (11:20)![169] It is a mock catalogue of unflattering acts which

---

[169]Fitzgerald (*Cracks in an Earthen Vessel*, 206-207) points out the ironic use of *sophos*-imagery in 11:19-20, where the endurance of the Corinthians of the abuses at the hands of the pseudo-apostles is presented as that of the φρόνιμοι. "The catalogue here serves the dual function of castigating his opponents by describing their abusive

unmasks their basic lack of maturity and discrimination. The Corinthians put up with fools (11:19) and thus demonstrate the impoverished extent of their φρόνησις. The irony is embedded in the kind of behavior and self-commendation they will accept as constitutive of authentic apostolic character and in the definitions they give to weakness and wisdom. The Corinthians look at things τὰ κατὰ πρόσωπον (10:7) and have criticized Paul for being ἀσθενής (10:10). In 11:21 he ironically apologizes κατὰ ἀτιμίαν that he has been "too weak to do such things" to the Corinthians. In admitting this "dishonorable fault," Paul forces the Corinthians to re-examine their definition of "weakness" and of his character. Paul makes a fundamental revaluation of Corinthian interests, weakness and boldness, foolishness and wisdom, God-recommendation and self-commendation, powerlessness and strength in his *peristasis* catalogue, to bring the Corinthians to a reassessment of his slandered character and to an acceptance of his leadership. After seeing the proof of the Christ who speaks in Paul (13:3), the Corinthians should no longer entertain doubts about his looks, his speaking ability, his alleged inferiority to the super-apostles, or anything else that would sway them from their "sincere and complete devotion to Christ" (11:3), as proclaimed through his Gospel. They should be the ones henceforth to commend him so that he is not forced to engage, like the fools they have allowed to charm them, in his own self-boasting.

---

acts and of shaming the Corinthians by mock praise." One way of showing one's ἦθος is by pointing out the ψόγοι (faults) of one's opponents

The περισσοτέρως and πολλάκις quality of the περιστάσεις serves Paul's interest in allowing the sheer preponderance to persuade. One of Paul's purposes is to secure the goodwill of the Corinthians by extolling his own merits and actions, particularly the virtue and bravery shown in enduring them for the sake of the Gospel and, as he says to correct one of the criticisms against him, as a minister of Christ (11:23). The volume is calculated to show that he is *more* (ὑπὲρ ἐγώ, 11:23)) Christ's minister than his opponents in order to contrast his credentials with theirs and to remove any prejudice against him.[170] The copious evidences of his trials expressed by the *epanaphora* of κινδύνοις,[171] his *daily* pressures, his care for *all* the churches are rhetorical techniques Paul employs to express a fullness of suffering and divine power and

---

[170]As Oda Wischmeyer (*Der höchste Weg* [SNT 13; Gütersloh: Mohn, 1981] 85-86, esp. n. 218-220) has suggested, the opponents of Paul also boasted of their hardships as ministers of Christ and their letters of recommendation must have contained such catalogues of hardships. Fitzgerald (*Cracks in an Earthen Vessel* 25, n. 95) writes in this regard: "The shift from κἀγώ to ὑπὲρ ἐγώ in 2 Cor 11:23, followed by adverbs indicating excess, clearly implies that Paul is comparing his own sufferings to those of his opponents and using his greater number of hardships to declare himself superior to them. The logic is crude and *deliberately* so. Since he had suffered *more* than his opponents, he is *more* a messenger of Christ than they." Fitzgerald rightly takes Georgi (*Gegner*) to task for denying that the superapostles boasted of their sufferings for Christ or that Paul is doing an ironic imitation of their self-depiction. More likely "Paul differed from them in his *interpretation* of his hardships, not in the fact that he suffered and they did not. . . . Paul is clearly responding to items the opponents boasted of, their Jewishness (11:22), their status as *diakonoi* of Christ (11:23), their 'visions and revelations' (12:1), and their miracles (12:12)." M. L. Barre ("Paul as 'Eschatologic Person': A New Look at 2 Cor 11:29," *CBQ* 37 [1975] 500-26, esp. 518) also indicates that Paul's opponents boasted of their struggles.

[171]The figure of speech known as *epanaphora*, as *Rhet. Her.* 4.13.19 says, "occurs when one and the same word forms successive beginnings for phrases expressing like and different ideas. . . . This figure has not only much charm, but also impressiveness and vigour in highest degree."

so to project an ἦθος of incomparable superiority, all with the serious intent to

persuade the Corinthians that he is their true emissary from God to preach the

gospel of Christ.

Paul's rapture into paradise (12:1-6) functions as the second major

example of his argument from ἦθος.[172] He clearly intends the disclosure of

this significant experience in his life to neutralize the boasts of his opponents

who parade their "visions and revelations" (12:1), their miracles (12:12), and

their vaunted status as διάκονοι of Christ (11:23) in contrast to Paul's alleged

deficiencies. The "little boasting" he ironically promised in 11:16 now

seemingly bursts the bounds of propriety to include a heavenly ascent and a

mystical revelation which is anything but small! When he produced this

incredible piece of evidence to argue that he was God's only apostle to the

Corinthians, did Paul have in the back of his mind the idea, associated with such

an experience, that a heavenly ascent conferred superhuman status on the person

---

[172]See the following for discussion: Russell P. Spittler, "The Limits of Ecstasy: An Exegesis of 2 Corinthians 12:1-10," in *Current Issues in Biblical and Patristic Interpretation: Studies in Honor of Merrill C. Tenney* (ed. Gerald F. Hawthorne; Grand Rapids: Eerdmans, 1975) 259-66; A. T. Lincoln, "'Paul the Visionary': The Setting and Significance of the Rapture to Paradise in II Corinthians XII, 1-10," *NTS* 25 (1979) 204-220; Robert M. Price, "Punished in Paradise: An Exegetical Theory on II Corinthians 12:1-10," *JSNT* 7 (1980) 33-40; William Baird, "Visions, Revelation, and Ministry: Reflections on 2 Cor 12:1-5 and Gal 1:11-17," *JBL* 104 (1985) 651-62; Alan F. Segal, "Paul and Ecstasy," in *SBLSP* (ed. Kent Harold Richards; Atlanta: Scholars Press) 25 (1986) 555-80; David L. Halperin, "Heavenly Ascension in Ancient Judaism: The Nature of the Experience," in *SBLSP* (ed. Kent Harold Richards; Atlanta: Scholars Press) 26 (1987) 218-32; Martha Himmelfarb, "Apocalyptic Ascent and the Heavenly Temple," in *SBLSP* (ed. Kent H. Richards; Atlanta: Scholars Press) 26 (1987) 210-17. J. D. Tabor, *Things Unutterable: Paul's Ascent to Paradise in Its Greco-Roman, Judaic, and Early Christian Contexts* (Studies in Judaism; Lanham, MD: University Press of America, 1986). These works give further bibliography.

privileged to undertake it?[173] It is possible to conclude that Paul, in order to

make his persuasive argument from character a clinching one, intimates through

citing this heavenly journey that he is an angel or messenger of God who, like

Isaiah, was privileged to participate in the proceedings of God's court. Paul

says that he "was snatched up to Paradise to hear words which cannot be

uttered, words which no one may speak" (12:4). This grandiose claim on

Paul's part, never made explicit, is based on the well-known technique of

emphasis. According to *Rhet. Her.* (4.53.67), emphasis is a "figure which

leaves more to be suspected than has been actually asserted. It is produced

through Hyperbole, Ambiguity, Logical Consequence, Aposiopesis, and

Analogy."[174]   Paul's demur a sentence later highlights the effect he has

---

[173]Martha Himmelfarb ("Apocalyptic Ascent and the Heavenly Temple," 212-213) argues this point: "In gnostic texts ascent means the reunification of the spirit with the divine from which it comes. In the magical papyri the purpose of the ascent is often divinization, taking on the power of a god. In the apocalypses the visionary usually achieves equality with the angels in the course of the ascent. This equality is expressed through service in the heavenly temple." Paul must have been acquainted with the Merkabah ("throne") mysticism of his day in which the mystic hoped to repeat the vision of Ezekiel (1:4-2:14) as well as the motif of a visionary journey to heaven in contemporary apocalyptic texts featuring patriarchs and prophets like Enoch, Ezra, Baruch, Moses, and Levi. The divinization or angelic transformation of these personages is a major motif.

[174]It is most instructive to explore the definitions *Rhet. Her.* 4.53.67 gives to each of these figures because they seem to be quite relevant to the rhetorical effect Paul attempts to produce in the recounting of his rapture experience: "Emphasis is produced through Hyperbole [*exsuperatio/superlatio;* see also 4.33.44] when more is said than the truth warrants, so as to give greater force to the suspicion." Paul knows the matter of angelic status is really not thinkable in his own mind but he leaves the seed of doubt in the minds of the Corinthians who are dazzled by such pretensions. "Emphasis is produced through Ambiguity when a word can be taken in two or more senses, but yet is taken in the sense which the speaker intends." This has to do with the double and multiple meanings in words. One of them is the use of an objective *persona* for the vision which in reality is Paul himself and the matter of boasting. Paul says he can

created in the Corinthians: "But I refrain, lest anyone think more of me than what he sees in me or hears from my lips" (12:7)! The associations he has created in the minds of the Corinthians about "a man in Christ" (12:2) who was admitted into the heavenly temple around God's throne to hear unutterable secrets stand in ironic juxtaposition to his earlier critique of his opponents who are merely in the guise of apostles of Christ (11:13) and who are really satans disguised as angels of light (11:14). These harsh designations of his opponents are echoed in the "angel of Satan" (12:7) given to Paul to beat him and keep him from getting proud as a result of his "extraordinary revelations." The implications of these connections portray Paul as God's messenger plagued by adversaries from hell. Paul's rhetorical strategy, based on well-known techniques related to the projection of character to an audience, is to sway the minds of the Corinthians through amplification of his own qualifications to enhance his credibility as a legitimate apostle and at the same time to bring his

---

boast about that person but he cannot boast about himself! The ambiguity accentuates his double use of boasting in his argument. "Emphasis is produced through Analogy, when we cite some analogue and do not amplify it, but by its means intimate what we are thinking." Paul's listeners would catch the connection being made between the "person snatched up to Paradise" and Paul. Lastly, "emphasis is produced through Aposiopesis if we begin to say something and then stop short, and what we have already said leaves enough to arouse suspicion." This is quite evidently the case when Paul abruptly breaks off his description of the heavenly ascent by saying paradoxically that he heard "words which cannot be uttered, words which no one may speak." It's as if he were saying: "I can't begin to describe it further," or "I dare not say any more." No further details are given, leaving the Corinthians hanging in suspense. *Rhet. Her.* 4.30.41 says further of aposiopesis: "Here a suspicion, unexpressed, becomes more telling than a detailed explanation would have been." As an example, Demosthenes (*De Cor.* 129) begins talking of the low profession of Aeschines' mother and suddenly breaks off with these sarcastic words: "But I protest that, however well the story becomes you, I am afraid that I may be thought to have chosen topics unbecoming to myself."

opponents into disrepute.

There are several other points in Paul's rapture experience which serve to add more luster to his character. These are the small, almost adventitious, remarks Paul makes in the course of recounting his heavenly journey which depict a man long experienced in such visions. In what might be considered casual asides, Paul mentions that he had his rapture experience "fourteen years ago" (12:2), that during that time he had an "excess ($\dot{\upsilon}\pi\epsilon\rho\beta o\lambda\hat{\eta}$) of revelations" (12:7); also "visions and revelations," (12:1), and that he talked to the Lord regularly (12:8). Their cumulative effect counteracts the damaging slander that he is inferior in spiritual gifts or that he lacks "the signs that show the apostle" (12:12). More positively, the effect is an unexpressed boast, one certainly not lost on the Corinthians, that he, Paul, is more of a veteran at these religious experiences than his opponents. The incidental way Paul incorporates these facts into his account takes any resentment out of his self-praise and allows the realization that his character is approved by God slowly to dawn on the Corinthians and become their conviction. This subtle approach conveys a feeling to the Corinthians that perhaps they rushed into their negative judgments of Paul too quickly and need to reassess his character. In any event, Paul has scored a major point about his character with an economy of words that reveal a longstanding friendship with the Lord.

In concluding his incredible rapture experience with the humiliating thorn-in-the-flesh incident, Paul is following a device recommended by Plutarch when dealing with an audience which is fair-minded, such as Paul believes the Corinthians to be. This device is known as *amending the praise*.[175] It is a subtle transfer of self-praise from meritorious actions justly recognized to better reasons and behaviors for praise. The object is to draw the attention of the audience away from superficial points and get them to acknowledge accomplishments that are more noteworthy. As Plutarch writes: "This precedent allows the orator, if meritorious, when praised for eloquence, to transfer the praise to his life and character, and the commander admired for skill or success in war to speak freely of his clemency and justice."

Paul uses this technique as a pedagogical tool to educate the Corinthians away from superficial fascination (10:7) with "human distinctions" (11:18) and toward a theology of "weak human behavior" (10:2) in which the power of Christ resides (12:9-10). After having regaled the Corinthians with a disclosure of his ineffable journey to the third heaven and his admission that he has had many such experiences, he draws their attention away from extolling him for these honors which exalt his character to those behaviors in him which truly call for praise, namely his weaknesses. In so many words, Paul is saying that their praise, whether directed toward the self-recommended false apostles or toward him, is being bestowed for the wrong reasons which have nothing to do with real character. Paul is displeased with the Corinthians for praising those things which are unbecoming, just as he is displeased ultimately with his own use of

---

[175]Plut. *Mor.* 543A-E.

boasting about his adversities and his visions. By disclosing a personal affliction, Paul undercuts his previous arguments to bolster his character by external claims from his *peristasis* catalogue and his rapture experiences and tells the Corinthians that they are passing over his greatest and noblest encomium, namely his weaknesses, which truly show that "he belongs to Christ" (10:7). And so by a transvaluation of terms and a transfer of praise, Paul can say that he now boasts of his weaknesses, which is real power (12:9), rather than of his gifts, however extraordinary, which cannot eliminate the weakness he suffers (12:7). The Corinthians should recognize that what gives Paul his legitimacy as their apostle and his claim on their allegiance is an ἦθος founded not on self-recommendation but on the power of weakness, in which there is the "the proof of the Christ who speaks in me" (13:3). With this maneuver of ironically sabotaging his own carefully rendered proof based on persuasive ἦθος, Paul brings down the entire structure of Corinthian wisdom and declares that nothing else matters except the power of God as expressed in the weakness of the crucified Christ: "We demolish sophistries and every proud pretension that raises itself against the knowledge of God" (10:5).

There are several other factors at work in this pericope that are calculated to highlight the ἦθος of Paul and thus to determine the outcome of the argument. This is done mainly through the use of style to express character. As discussed early in the section on ἦθος, the speaker can give ethical coloring to his own character or that of his friend or adversary through the adroit use of language. A speaker can isolate and illustrate the special peculiarity of a person

and indicate one's values and status through the choice and arrangement of

words. In so doing the speaker can produce a positive or negative effect in the

audience toward the goal of persuasion. Paul very effectively uses language in

conjunction with his other arguments to project his ἦθος. Through the use of

recurring images and dynamic words, Paul succeeds in developing the

perception that he is to be reckoned with as one full of authoritativeness

(power), trustworthiness (wisdom and competence), and generosity.

His power and authority are conveyed right at the beginning of the passage

when he claims to act with "God's power" (10:4,8). This image pervades

Paul's entire persuasive speech. In military terms, Paul portrays himself as one

who will courageously wage battle to destroy strongholds, demolish sophistries,

bring thoughts into captivity, and punish the disobedient (10:4-6).[176]   In

---

[176]Abraham Malherbe ("Antithenes and Odysseus, and Paul at War," *HTR* 76:2
[1983] 143-173) discusses the use of military imagery in 2 Cor 10:3-6 in terms of "two
military images which were popular in the first century [which] were derived from
Antithenes. He applied the image of a city fortified against a siege to the wise man's
rational faculties with which he fortifies himself, and he applied the image of a soldier's
personal armor to the garb of Odysseus the proto-Cynic, who through his versatility and
self-humiliation adapted himself to circumstances in order to gain the good of his
associates and save them." Malherbe argues that the Stoics, in their attempts at self-
understanding, appropriated the imagery of the fortified city and used it in their
description of the sage who turns his reason into a citadel, while the Cynics adapted the
imagery of the philosopher's garb as their armor to describe their personal security.
Both schools of philosophy, in various degrees, used Odysseus as their model.
Malherbe claims that Paul uses both images in 10:3-6 but he is at a loss to determine
the precise relationship of 10:1-6 to the rest of the chapters 10-13. Both images are in
tension, for when Paul describes his own armament, he makes use of the
Cynics'tradition of self-understanding.   On the other hand, when he describes the
objects of his attack, the false apostles, he does so in terms of the self-sufficient, self-
confident Stoics secure in the fortification of their own reason. Paul uses the Cynics
armor, namely his life as dependent on the outside power of God, to attack his

contrast to the criticism of "weak human behavior" leveled against him, Paul

immediately establishes his character as one identified with the divine, whose

power he possesses ("The weapons of our warfare . . . possess God's power")

to act against those who proudly rise up in rebellion "against the knowledge of

God" (10:4-5).

Aligned as he is with God, Paul portrays his $\H\eta\theta o\varsigma$ as one totally informed,

qualified, and sensible who can tell the Corinthians that they "things

superficially" (10:7). His identification here with the wisdom of God, just as

he had previously argued with his being filled with the power of God, portrays

his character as a major determining factor in his message. Through these

images associating himself with divine power and wisdom, Paul intends to sway

the minds of the Corinthians in order to instill in them confidence in his

message.

The element of trustworthiness is a further persuasive attribute in Paul's

rhetorical use of $\H\eta\theta o\varsigma$. He says he will be in action among them what he is by

word in his letters (10:11). His $\dot\alpha\rho\epsilon\tau\H\eta$ is already a matter of record with the

Corinthians. As with his authoritative and divinely inspired power and wisdom,

his trustworthiness is associated with God's competence. Paul says he comes

approved and recommended by God (10:18). By contrast, the ones who have

brought a new kind of gospel, another Jesus and a different spirit from the one

---

opponents whose citadels are elevated against the knowledge of God. Our discussion
in the text makes different use of the warfare imagery.

Paul preached (11:4), must be false, deceitful ministers of Satan, untrustworthy apostles who go around disguised as angels of light (11:13-15). Their ἦθος corresponds to their deeds. The consistent contrast in chapter 10 between the knowledge of God and sophistries (10:5), obedience and disobedience (10:6), God's power and human weapons (10:4), upbuilding and destruction (10:8), boasting in the Lord and self-recommendation (10:12,18) and other such dualities immediately establishes, through the arrangement of images, the moral excellence of Paul and the validity of his message.

The last element of ἦθος conveyed by the language and imagery of the text is that of generosity and gratitude. Paul reminds the Corinthians that he is their benefactor who "will gladly spend myself and be spent for your sakes" (12:15). Like Demosthenes and Cicero and so many before him, Paul cites his labors and sufferings on their behalf: "I have done everything to build you up, my dear ones" (12:19). He was no burden to them (12:13); he did not take advantage of them (12:17); he performed the signs and wonders and deeds of power of an apostle among them (12:12); he preached the Gospel to them (11:4); he now prays for their spiritual completion (13:9). Consequently, he expects their gratitude: "You are the ones who should have been commending me" (12:11). By emphasizing his role as a selfless benefactor, Paul develops a context, in virtue of his ἦθος, where the goodness of his person is inseparable from the goodness of his message. Paul's ἦθος, under this aspect, functions as a source of influence for the correct judgment he wants the Corinthians to make by reason of patron-client reciprocity.

The obligation of gratitude in the Greco-Roman world was a very serious duty.[177] "Not to return gratitude for benefits is a disgrace," Seneca wrote, "and the whole world counts it as such."[178] He called the practice of benefits, the act of giving and receiving, as something that constituted the chief bond of human society:

> We need to be taught to give willingly, to receive willingly, to return willingly, and to set before us the high aim of striving, not merely to equal, but to surpass in deed and spirit those who have placed us under obligation, for he who has a debt of gratitude to pay never catches up with the favour unless he outstrips it; the one should be taught to make no record of the amount, the other to feel indebted for more than the amount.[179]

The reciprocal character of benefits was the overriding feature of this bond and imposed an equal obligation of continued giving and receiving on both parties. A benefit, according to Seneca, "is the act of a well-wisher who bestows joy and derives joy from the bestowal of it, and is inclined to do what he does from

---

[177]See Paul Veyne, *Bread and Circuses* (tr. Brian Pearce; New York: Viking Penguin, 1990); Richard P. Soller, *Personal Patronage in the Early Empire* (Cambridge: Cambridge University Press, 1982); Stephen Charles Mott, "The Power of Giving and Receiving: Reciprocity in Hellenistic Benevolence," in *Current Issues in Biblical and Patristic Interpretation: Studies in Honor of Merrill C. Tenney* (ed. Gerald F. Hawthorne; Grand Rapids: Eerdmans, 1975) 60-72. The classic work in this area is Frederick Danker, *Benefactor: Epigraphic Study of a Graeco-Roman and New Testament Semantic Field* (St. Louis: Clayton Publishing House, 1982). Danker ("Paul's Debt to Demosthenes' *De Corona*," 278, n. 2) writes further: "Hellenes consider ingratitude one of the most heinous of crimes. It would be carrying owls to Athens to cite even 1% of the decrees that contain the phrase: 'so that all may know that our city knows how to render thanks . . . .'."

[178]Sen. *Ben.* 3.1.1.

[179]Sen. *Ben.* 1.4.3.

the promptings of his own will." What counts is not what is done or given but the spirit and intention of the giver or doer.[180]   Once given and received, a benefit placed the beneficiary under the obligation to respond with gratitude. The recipient's gratitude in turn placed the benefactor under further obligation to do more.   Reciprocity was at the heart of Greco-Roman benevolence and controlled societal conduct and interpersonal relations on every level.   Such a practice influenced both benefactor and recipient in their mutual choices of to whom to give and from whom to receive.   The most serious offense in this relationship was ingratitude, not returning thanks or honor or giving credit to the benefactor.

Reciprocity included more than just the patron-client relationship.   It also incorporated the responsibilities of friendship, parental respect and filial affection, service to one's country in war and peace, the teacher-student relationship, and a whole host of other exchanges that contributed to the well-being of society.   At the base of all this was gratitude.   Cicero gives a magnificent praise of gratitude in these various situations in his defense of his friend, Plancius:

> For indeed, gentlemen, while I would fain have some tincture of
> all the virtues, there is no quality I would sooner have, and be
> thought to have, than gratitude. For gratitude not merely stands
> alone at the head of all the virtues, but is even mother of all the
> rest. . . . Take friendship away, and what joy can life continue
> to hold? More, how can friendship exist at all between those
> who are devoid of gratitude? . . . Who is there, who has there

---

[180]Sen. *Ben.* 1.5.1

> ever been, so rich in material wealth as to be independent of the good offices of many friends? And assuredly these good offices themselves cannot exist independently of memory and gratitude.[181]

To be grateful was at the heart of Greco-Roman ethics and the source of many blessings.

Paul's proof from ἦθος recalls his benefits to the Corinthians. The greatest gift he gave them was acting as marriage broker between Christ and them (11:2). He has furthermore been their architect in the faith (10:8; 12:19). He has loved and served them with extraordinary self-giving (12:15). He refers to all these benefactions in order to show the Corinthians what εὔνοια he has towards them in contrast to the super apostles whose benefits to the Corinthians consist in demeaning exploitation (11:20). He can say truthfully that neither he nor Titus ever took advantage of them (12:18). Several times he insists that he has not been a burden to them (11:9; 12:14,16), although they might have a different view of his refusal to accept support from them. In light of all this Paul vehemently denies that his opponents work on these same terms or that they have the same unselfish love for the Corinthians (11:12). In fact, Paul warns the Corinthians that his opponents cannot be trusted. The Satan-masquerade imagery suggests that the false apostles are anti-benefactors. They are not the kind of servant-benefactor Paul is who will gladly "spend myself and

---

[181]Cic. *Planc.* 33.80-81.

be spent for your sakes" (12:14).[182]

It is clear from Paul's defense of his ἦθος to the Corinthians that far from deserving their disloyalty because of the slanders made against him, he should rather be the recipient of their undying gratitude. They are the beneficiaries of his sufferings and his special gifts from God. If the obligations between benefactor and beneficiary are so important in social and political life, they are even more important in the spiritual life he has given them. The relation Paul has with Christ in God, the Benefactor *par excellence*, has repercussions in the life of the Corinthians. They can expect numerous more benefactions from God through Paul in a degree the super apostles can never match. They are obliged to him for this service.[183] He now says that the moment has come for him to call in their gratitude (12:11) which is to be expressed through their allegiance

---

[182]Danker ("Paul's Debt to Demosthenes' *De Corona*," 267, n. 2) suggests a similar thought by paraphrasing a passage from Aeschin. *In Ctes*. 247-48 about being on one's guard "against those who claim title to being public benefactors, but cannot be trusted." Aeschines' words need to be quoted in full here since they put the finger right on the mark of Paul's indignant reaction to the suggestion that the false apostles work on the same terms as he does. Aeschines asks the jury how they hope to escape the disgrace they will surely feel if they give a crown to Demosthenes and he answers for them: "By guarding against those who arrogate to themselves the name of 'patriot' and 'benefactor,' but are untrustworthy in character. For loyalty and the name of friend of the people are prizes which are offered to us all, but for the most part those persons are the first to take refuge in them in speech who are farthest from them in conduct."

[183]Once again Danker ("Paul's Debt to Demosthenes' *De Corona*," 278) puts the matter in a way that opens up worlds of insight for our argument from ἦθος: "God is the Supreme Benefactor, Jesus is the Great Benefactor. Paul is an envoy of both and his way of life will pass divine audit. As the Corinthians' benefactor, with a record of loyal service, in their behalf, he is entitled to their appreciation." Not to say thanks to Paul is not only to violate a "basic cultural code" but also "their responsibility to God and Jesus Christ." Any ingratitude on the Corinthians' part, therefore, by their lack of submission to his gospel and his authority, can result in the dire consequence of having their spiritual gifts cut off.

to his apostleship (12:14) so that they can put him under further obligations to them (12:15). In summary, Paul's basic argument here is that he has an ἦθος which is filled with unmatched benevolence toward the Corinthians, a giving that is generous and selfless. This should be recommendation enough for their loyalty to him, their patron, who can secure even more and greater benefits from his benefactor, namely God. To rupture this bond through ingratitude and the dishonor of disobedience is to disrespect the past and to jeopardize their future. This is a powerful argument from ἦθος based on the hallowed societal bond of reciprocity.

This concludes our discussion of Paul's use of the proof from ἦθος to establish his trustworthiness, to demonstrate his virtue, and to garner the goodwill of the Corinthians. There are further elements in the passage which are related in some fashion to Paul's argument from his character, such as his εὐγένεια (11:22), the layers of irony and the frequent word-plays on καύχησις and ἀσθένεια, the serious yet self-mocking thrust of his argument, the use of antitheses in his *synkrisis*, the sarcastic resort to *paronomasia* (10:5-6, 12; 12:5), the pungent use of *litotes* (10:12; 11:6), the emphatic function of *anaphora* in his hardship catalogue, and so many other rhetorical techniques which function throughout the passage to reveal Paul, contrary to all prejudices on the part of the Corinthians, as a master of all that they admired in the pseudo-apostles.

CHAPTER THREE

ΠΑΘΟΣ : THE USE OF EMOTIONS

A. The Definition and Nature of Πάθος.

The second set of proofs which Aristotle cites as a principal ingredient in persuasion comes from πάθος, which refers to "putting the hearer into a certain frame of mind."[184] If the orator persuades by the moral force of character, as we have seen, the orator likewise persuades "by means of his hearers, when they are roused to emotion by his speech; for the judgements we deliver are not the same when we are influenced by joy or sorrow, love or hate."[185] In other words, a listener can be swayed to an entirely different conclusion while under the powerful effects of different emotions. An audience has different emotional states invested in a variety of issues and logical arguments will not change an opinion. A rhetor therefore must be acquainted with these emotions in order to use them appropriately and strategically to move an audience toward the judgment the rhetor wishes them to make or the beliefs to accept. As Aristotle writes, a person "must be capable of . . . study in . . . the emotions—the nature

---

[184]Arist. *Rh.* 1.2.3.

[185]Arist. *Rh.* 1.2.5.

113

and character of each, its origins, and the manner in which it is produced."[186]

In any act of persuasion, a speaker must either eliminate or considerably diminish all obstacles to a positive acceptance of the speaker's viewpoint or issue so that the purpose of the rhetorical act may be fulfilled. The speaker must induce the audience to identify with oneself to such an extent that differences are minimized, beliefs converge, values are shared, and judgments are mutually affirmed. Aristotle says explicitly that the speaker must put the hearer into a certain frame of mind. To put it colloquially, this is taken to mean that the speaker must massage the audience towards acceptance of the speaker's goal. Since rhetoric is the use of the available means of persuasion, the speaker must have knowledge of what emotions drive an audience, what precise emotions one seeks to engender, and how and when to enact them to arouse the audience to a satisfactory judgment.

Aristotle defines the emotions as

> . . . all those affections which cause men to change their opinion in regard to their judgements, and are accompanied by pleasure and pain; such are anger, pity, fear, and all similar emotions and their contraries. And each of them must be divided under three heads; for instance in regard to anger, the disposition of the mind which makes men angry, the persons with whom they are usually angry, and the occasions which give rise to anger.[187]

The speaker must know all three conditions; otherwise, Aristotle says, it is impossible to arouse that emotion. He proceeds then to define and analyze the

---

[186]Arist. *Rh.* 1.2.7.

[187]Arist. *Rh.* 2.1.8-9.

various emotions: anger, with its subsets of slight, disdain, insults, dishonor, slander, and ungratefulness; next love and friendship and their contraries, enmity and hatred; fear and its contrary, confidence; shame and shamelessness; benevolence; pity and indignation; envy and self-conceit, and emulation. Aristotle discusses with unusual psychological precision the frame of mind, the reasons, and the objects of each emotion in a person. In words which are applicable to the other emotions, Aristotle concludes his discussion of anger with the following remark:

> It is evident then that it will be necessary for the speaker, by his eloquence, to put the hearers into the frame of mind of those who are inclined to anger, and to show that his opponents are responsible for things which rouse men to anger and are people of the kind with whom men are angry.[188]

He also writes, still in reference to anger but relevant to the rest of the moral πάθη:

> It is evident, then, that men must have recourse to these topics when they desire to appease their audience, putting them into the frame of mind required and representing those with whom they are angry as either formidable or deserving of respect, or as having rendered them great services, or acted involuntarily, or as exceedingly grieved at what they have done.[189]

As in most things he says, Aristotle's observation seems very modern: the speaker must know the audience and adapt the words of one's speech, if one hopes to effect not only communication but persuasion as well. The speaker must know the audience's make-up, its basic shared assumptions, common

---

[188]Arist. *Rh.* 2.2.27.

[189]Arist. *Rh.* 2.3.17.

experiences and values, its biases, educational level, the extent and depth of its emotional attachments, and so many other variables to be able to have the audience internalize one's message and act on it.

It is in precisely in this area where ἦθος and πάθος overlap in Aristotle. In the last chapter we had discussed the ἤθη τῶν πολιτειῶν (*Rh.* 1.8.6.) as the second meaning Aristotle gives to ἦθος, "the characters of each form of government," indicating that the speaker most likely to project one's own goodness and win the goodwill of the audience is the one who adapts to the characteristic qualities inherent in the audience; or as Aristotle says, "the character most likely to persuade must be that which is characteristic of it [each form of government]." Likewise, if the speaker wants to put the audience into a certain frame of mind, then the speaker must know the *feelings* and passions which ordinarily influence the preponderant element in the audience. In *Rh.* 2.12-17, Aristotle discusses in detail these characters and connects these ἤθη "according to their emotions" (τὰ δὲ ἤθη ποῖοί τινες κατὰ τὰ πάθη, *Rh.* 2.12.1).

It is important to understand this connection and to realize that ἦθος and πάθος coalesce throughout the persuasive argument in their respective appeals to the ever changing variety of qualities and feelings in an audience. Aristotle gives a very apt example at the end of his discussion on this point. He says that both the old and young are inclined to the emotion of pity but not for the same reason. The old show it out of weakness, whereas the young show it for humanity's sake. Consequently, the speaker who knows this bit of the psychology of the audience will make emotional appeals most likely to be serviceable. Arousing emotions, targeting and redirecting feelings, creating new experiences and suggesting new thought processes for the audience through playing on its passions will do more for the speech than logical proofs.

Friedrich Solmsen argues that Aristotle was breaking new ground when he cut himself off completely from the previous traditional rhetoric of connecting the emotions to particular parts of the speech, to the so-called μόρια λόγου consisting of προοίμιον (*exordium*), διήγησις (*narratio*), πίστεις (*probationes*), and ἐπίλογος (*peroratio*).[190] Those who advocated this system dealt with the emotions mainly as a quality of the proem to capture the goodwill of the audience and in the epilogue to move the audience to anger or pity as a lasting impression, but they did not conceive of πάθη as integral to the proof as such. It was Aristotle who established the theory of πάθη "in its own right as one of the primary subjects of the rhetorical system" and subjected it to a careful analysis as a crucial form of rhetorical proof.[191] Solmsen goes on to show

---

[190]Friedrich Solmsen, "Aristotle and Cicero on the Orators's Playing Upon the Feelings," in *CP* 33 (1938) 390-404.

[191]Solmsen, "The Orator's Playing Upon the Feelings," 394. In another article ("The Aristotelian Tradition in Ancient Rhetoric," in *Rhetorika: Schriften zur aristotelischen und hellenistischen Rhetorik* [ed. Rudolf Stark; Hildesheim: Georg Olms, 1968] 315) Solmsen writes: "Thus, in opposition to the old τέχνη where the material was arranged under 'proem,' 'narration,' 'proofs,' 'epilogue,' or even more parts, a new type comes into existence, consisting of three main parts: Proofs (or material content), Style, and Disposition. The 'proofs' have not much more than the name in common with the 'proofs' in the alternative system; 'proofs' are no longer a part but a function of the speech." He writes further (319): "Aristotle's innovation consists not

how Aristotle in his system of rhetoric was influenced by Plato's *Phaedrus* to

include this element of ψυχαγωγία, which George Kennedy defines as the art

of enchanting the soul through emotional appeals.[192] Later τέχναι (handbooks

of rhetoric), especially among the Hellenistic rhetoricians, did not continue the

Aristotelian theory of πάθη but reproduced the "parts of the speech"

approach.[193]

Cicero over two centuries later emphasized Aristotle's theory of πάθος

in his rhetorical treatises and practiced it quite extensively in his orations, as we

shall later demonstrate.[194] In his very early treatise, *De Inventione*, he

studiously repeated the Hellenistic textbook approach of confining the use of

---

only in his granting to πάθη and ἤθη a status on a par with the arguments and thereby elevating them to first-rate factors but also in his careful analysis of the nature of the various emotions and of the conditions under which they may be either aroused or allayed."

[192]George Kennedy, *The Art of Persuasion in Greece* (Princeton, NJ: Princeton University Press, 1963) 95.

[193]Solmsen ("Aristotelian Tradition in Rhetoric," 337) says that "our evidence for the Hellenistic centuries (which is more definite and explicit than usual) suggests that the inclusion of ἤθος and πάθος—the speaker's character and the art of playing upon the feelings—was abandoned by the Hellenistic rhetoricians. How soon after Aristotle this happened it is difficult to say, but one of the usual taunts of the philosophers against the rhetoricians in the late Hellenistic centuries seems to have been this very point—that the rhetoricians had given up the analysis *more Aristoteleo* of character and emotions." The Stoic bias against emotions played a part in this but still rhetoricians continued to give practical suggestions for the use of emotions in the proem and the epilogue. Solmsen ("The Orator's Playing Upon the Feelings," 395-96) gives evidence for his conclusions.

[194]Cicero (*De Or.* 2.36.152) refers to Aristotle as "my own most particular admiration" and "that godlike genius." In 2.38.160 of the same book Cicero says he read the book of Aristotle which set forth "the rhetorical theories of all his forerunners, and those other works containing sundry observations of his own on the same art."

emotions to the proem and the epilogue,[195] but by the time he came to write his *De Oratore*, after years of actual experience in oratory, he realized that emotional appeals were as important as any rhetorical argument and should be used throughout the speech for effective control of the feelings of the audience. He wrote in this regard:

> And because (as I have repeatedly said already) there are three methods of bringing people to hold our opinion, instruction or persuasion or appeal to their emotions, one of these three methods we must openly display, so as to appear to wish solely to impart instruction, whereas the two remaining methods should be interfused throughout the whole of the structure of our speeches like the blood in our bodies. . . . but in regard to the portions of a speech that in spite of proving no point by means of argument, nevertheless have a very great effect in persuading and arousing emotion, although the most appropriate place for them is in the introduction and conclusion, nevertheless it is often useful to digress from the subject one has put forward and is dealing with, for the purpose of arousing emotion; and accordingly very often either a place is given to a digression devoted to exciting emotion, or this can rightly be done after we have established our own arguments or refuted those of our opponents, or in both places, or in all the parts of the speech, if the case is one of this importance and extent; and the cases that are the weightiest and fullest for amplification and embellishment are those that give the greatest number of openings for a digression of this kind, so allowing the employment of the topics which either stimulate or curb the emotions of the audience.[196]

Cicero came to see Aristotelian πάθος as one of his major *probationes* in his art of persuasion. To express this task of the orator, he used a variety of verbs for πάθος: *movere* and its cognates *permovere* and *commovere, concitare,* and

---

[195]See *Inv. Rhet.* 1.15-18; 1.52-56. In discussing the peroration, Cicero includes the fifteen methods of *indignatio*, the arousing of indignation or ill-will, and the sixteen methods of *conquestio*, the arousing of pity and sympathy.

[196]Cic. *De Or.* 2.77.310-12.

flectare.[197]

It is principally in his *De Oratore* that Cicero made his convictions felt about *movere audientium animos*. He writes that nothing is more important in oratory than to have the hearer "so affected as to be swayed by something resembling a mental impulse or emotion, rather than by judgement." People decide more problems by inward emotions, such as love, hate, lust, rage, sorrow, or fear "than by reality, or authority, or any legal standard, or judicial precedent, or statute."[198] In another passage closely related to the preceding one, he talks about a style of speaking which

> excites and urges the feelings of the tribunal towards hatred and love, ill-will or well-wishing, fear or hope, desire or aversion, joy or sorrow, compassion or the wish to punish, or by it they are prompted to whatever emotions are nearly allied and similar to these passions of the soul, and to such as these.[199]

In a slightly different vein, Cicero writes that it is advantageous for the speaker if the members of the tribunal "carry within them to Court some mental emotion that is in harmony with what the advocate's interest will suggest." In other words, the speaker will have an easier time of it if there are already some pre-existing emotions the speaker can play upon. Cicero writes on this point:

> This indeed is the reason why, when setting about a hazardous and important case, in order to explore the feelings of the tribunal, I engage wholeheartedly in a consideration so careful,

---

[197]See Cic. *De Or.* 2.27.115; 2.29.128; 2.77.310; 3.27.104; *Orat.* 21.69; *Brut.* 49.185; 80.276.

[198]Cic. *De Or.* 2.42.178.

[199]Cic. *De Or.* 2.44.185.

that I scent out with all possible keenness their thoughts, judgements, anticipations and wishes, and the direction in which they seem likely to be led away most easily by eloquence.[200]

By eloquence in this context he undoubtedly means the power of words to capitalize on the audience's character and feelings "to take the course in which I am urging them on," which will allow him to "set sail for that quarter which promises something of a breeze." If he can detect no predispositions, he claims his task of persuasion is harder because he has no help from the listener's character but must call everything forth through the speech itself. In any event, eloquence is so potent, according to Cicero, that he eulogizes it in the words of the poet Pacuvius as the "soulbending sovereign of all things," which "can not only support the sinking and bend the upstanding, but, like a good and brave commander, can even make prisoner a resisting antagonist."[201] A great deal of this power Cicero attributes to the use of emotions in a speech.

In dealing with the use of emotions in the art of persuasion, Cicero makes one of the most innovative guidelines for success: the necessity for the orator to feel the emotions one is trying to arouse in others. He says:

> It is impossible for the listener to feel indignation, hatred or ill-will, to be terrified of anything, or reduced to tears of compassion, unless all those emotions, which the advocate would inspire in the arbitrator, are visibly stamped or rather branded on the advocate himself.

Cicero insists these feelings should not be counterfeit—nor were they ever

---

[200]Cic. *De Or.* 2.44.186-7.

[201]Cic. *De Or.* 2.44.187.

actually feigned in any of his speeches—as he goes on to say through his

protagonist:

> I give you my word that I never tried, by means of a speech, to
> arouse either indignation or compassion, either ill-will or hatred,
> in the minds of a tribunal, without being really stirred myself, as
> I worked upon their minds, by the very feelings to which I was
> seeking to prompt them. For it is not easy to succeed in making
> the arbitrator angry with the right party, if you yourself seem to
> treat the affair with indifference; or in making him hate the right
> party, unless he first sees you on fire with hatred yourself; nor
> will he be prompted to compassion, unless you have shown him
> the tokens of your own grief by word, sentiment, tone of voice,
> look and even loud lamentation. For just as there is no substance
> so ready to take fire, as to be capable of generating flame
> without the application of a spark, so also there is no mind so
> ready to absorb an orator's influence, as to be inflammable when
> the assailing speaker is not himself aglow with passion.[202]

Cicero illustrates this point of authenticity with the example of the actor and the

poet who feel the emotions they are projecting. As a illustration of his

oratorical use of personally felt emotions, Cicero, through Antonius, the

protagonist in this part of his *De Oratore*, describes the trial of Manius Aquilus,

in which he was trying to excite compassion in the audience for the fallen hero

who was being prosecuted for extortion. Antonius says that on seeing "him cast

down, crippled, sorrowing and brought to the risk of all he held dear, I was

myself overcome by compassion before I tried to excite it in others." Antonius

goes on dramatically to tear open his client's tunic and expose his scars while

repeatedly naming him and calling upon his colleagues to support him and

invoking the gods, all in loud lamentation and "accompanied by tears and vast

---

[202]Cic. *De Or.* 2.55.189-90.

indignation on my part."[203] Antonius was able to move the souls of his listeners because he conveyed to them the righteous indignation which he felt deeply within his own soul. Antonius relates his successful defense of Aquilius to Sulpicius, his fellow conversationalist, "in order to help you to be wrathful, indignant and tearful in your speech-making."

Continuing the discussion on emotions, Antonius goes on to compliment Sulpicius on his prosecution of a friend of Antonius, Gaius Norbanus, "not by eloquence only, but far more by vehemence, indignation and fiery enthusiasm, that I hardly ventured to draw near and put it out." But Antonius describes his own approach to the defense of Norbanus (who had proceeded against the notorious Servilius Caepio eventually exiled for treason and embezzlement), beginning slowly with an historical and academic treatment of civil discords to lay the rational groundwork and then blending in a more emotional plea filled with loyal love and justifiable grief for his comrade. Antonius concludes by saying to Sulpicius that "it was rather by working upon, than by informing, the minds of the tribunal, that I beat your prosecution on that occasion." Sulpicius responds in admiration for Antonius' successful defense in words that dramatize the approach of a successful orator:

> For when (as you told us) I had left you with a conflagration rather than a case to dispose of,—ye Gods!—what an opening you made! How nervous, how irresolute you seemed! How stammering and halting was your delivery! How you clung at the outset to the solitary excuse everyone was making for you—that

---

[203]Cic. De Or. 2.47.195-96.

you were defending your own familiar friend and quaestor! So, in the first place, did you prepare the way towards getting a hearing! Then, just as I was deciding that you had merely succeeded in making people think intimate relationship a possible excuse for your defending a wicked citizen,—lo and behold!— so far unsuspected by other people, but already to my own serious alarm, you began to wriggle imperceptibly into your famous defense, of no factious Norbanus, but of an incensed Roman People, whose wrath, you urged, was not wrongful, but just and well-deserved. After that what point against Caepio did you miss? How you leavened every word with hatred, malice and pathos!

Antonius continues his discussion of the emotions with Sulpicius by going over some of the rules for emotional oratory. He lays particular emphasis upon those feelings eloquence has to excite in the minds of the audience: love, hate, wrath, jealousy, compassion, hope, joy, fear and vexation. A good speech, he says, is a blend of the mild and the emotional style, the first winning the goodwill of people and the other inflaming them, the one adapted to the recommendation of the speaker's life and manners (related to $\mathring{\eta}\theta o\varsigma$) and the other demanding passion and strife, one appealing to the mental capacities of the audience, the other reaching out to their emotional side rather than to their understanding. This latter side "can only be reached by diction that is rich, diversified and copious with animated delivery to match. Thus concise or quiet speakers may inform an arbitrator, but cannot excite him, on which excitement everything depends."[204]

Cicero says much the same things in the *Orator*. He makes mention of

---

[204]This entire discussion was taken from Cic. *De Or.* 2.47.194-53.214.

the two topics of character and emotion which, "if well handled by the orator arouse admiration for his eloquence." After citing the topic which is expressive of character, he writes:

> . . . the other, which [the Greeks] call παθητικόν or "relating to the emotions," arouses and excites the emotions: in this part alone oratory reigns supreme. The former [character] is courteous and agreeable, adapted to win goodwill; the latter is violent, hot and impassioned, and by this cases are wrested from our opponents; when it rushes along in full career it is quite irresistible.[205]

Cicero cites his own orations with their vigorous style and genuine expressions of feeling, sometimes accompanied by high theatricality, which were instrumental in dislodging his opponents. He writes in relation to appeals to pity for clients:

> I owe my reputation for excellence on such occasions, not to any natural gift, but to a genuine sympathy. . . . Nor is the appeal for sympathy the only way of arousing the emotions of the jury—though we are wont to use it so piteously that we have even a babe in our arms during the peroration, and in another plea for a noble defendant we told him to stand up, and raising his small son we filled the forum with wailing and lamentation—but the juror must be made to be angry or appeased, to feel ill will or to be well disposed, he must be made to feel scorn or admiration, hatred or love, desire or loathing, hope or fear, joy or sorrow. . . . [It is] a vigorous spirit which inflames me to such an extent that I am beside myself; and I am sure that the audience would never be set on fire unless the words that reached him were fiery.[206]

In the *Brutus*, Cicero gives the interesting story of the orator Galba as a reflection on the power of the emotions to move an audience. Galba had been

---

[205]Cic. *Orat.* 37.128.

[206]Cic. *Orat.* 37.129-38.131.

asked to take over the defense of some slaves and free members of a corporation accused of the murders of several prominent citizens. He replaced another defense attorney by the name of Laelius who had pleaded the case with great thoroughness and precision but who had only succeeded in twice getting a continuance from the consuls. In preparation for the defense, Galba locked himself in a room with some of his educated slaves and practiced working up his emotions to such a fever pitch that when it was time to go to court, "he came out into the hall with flushed face and flashing eyes, like one, you would think, who had already conducted, and not merely prepared his case." Prepared with such vehement feelings, he went on to plead the case so forcefully with appeals to the mercy of the court that he won an acquittal for the accused. Cicero concludes from this:

> From this story . . . one may conclude, that of the two chief qualities which the orator must possess, accurate argument looking to proof and impressive appeals to the emotions of the listener, the orator who inflames the court accomplishes far more than the one who merely instructs it; that in short Laelius possessed precision, Galba power.[207]

Later in the same work, Cicero, through his mouthpiece in the discussion, used the evident lack of emotions in an opponent's speech as an argument against the very charges he brought! After describing the great pains his opponent went through to produce depositions, circumstantial evidence, and confessions under torture (which Aristotle called "preexistent proofs" in *Rh.*

---

[207]Cic. *Brut.* 28.89-90.

1.2.2), Cicero accused him of presenting "his case with perfect calmness, lackadaisically, and almost with a yawn." He goes on, as he says, to use "this great orator's manner of speaking, whether we call it wise restraint or a defect of eloquence, as an argument for breaking down his accusation." Cicero addresses him with these words:

'Come now, Marcus Calidius [!], would you present your case in that way if it were not all a figment of your imagination? And that eloquence of yours which you have always used so vigorously for the defense of others, is it credible that you should fail to invoke it for your own? What trace of anger, of that burning indignation, which stirs even men quite incapable of eloquence to loud outbursts of complaint against wrongs? But no hint of agitation in you, neither of mind nor of body! Did you smite your brow, slap your thigh, or at least stamp your foot? No. In fact, so far from touching my feelings, I could scarcely refrain from going to sleep then and there.'

Brutus, one of the interlocutors, responds to this with Cicero's conviction about the primacy of emotions in an argument:

"Can we hesitate whether to call it restraint or a defect? Why, every one must acknowledge that of all the resources of an orator far the greatest is his ability to inflame the minds of his hearers and to turn them in whatever direction the case demands. If the orator lacks that ability, he lacks the one thing most essential."[208]

Throughout other parts of the *Brutus*, Cicero hammers home his conviction of the importance of moving an audience through powerful words. At times the whole of oratory seems comprised of the expression of feeling, as when he argues through one of the characters in the dialogue that "the supreme orator is

---

[208]Cic. *Brut.* 80.277-78.

recognized by the people" and not necessarily by the trained critic through the incredible effects produced in them:

> When one hears a real orator he believes what is said, thinks it true, assents and approves; the orator's words win conviction. You, sir, critic and expert, what more do you ask? The listening throng is delighted, is carried along by his words, is in a sense bathed deep in delight. What have you here to cavil with? They feel now joy now sorrow, are moved now to laughter now to tears; they show approbation detestation, scorn aversion; they are drawn to pity to shame to regret; are stirred to anger wonder, hope fear; and all these come to pass just as the hearers' minds are played upon by word and thought and action.[209]

As a last piece of evidence of the great emphasis he placed on the arousing of emotions in his listeners, Cicero gives his picture of the ideal orator and says that the "one supreme characteristic of the orator" is "to inspire in the judge a feeling of angry indignation, or move him to tears or in short sway his feelings in whatever direction the situation demanded."[210] After evidence such as the above, there can be no doubt that for Cicero the use of emotional appeal throughout all parts of the speech was of primary importance.

"It was Cicero," writes Quintilian of his idol, "who shed the greatest light not only on the practice but on the theory of oratory; for he stands alone among Romans as combining the gift of actual eloquence with that of teaching the art."[211] It is no wonder then that Quintilian had the greatest respect for Cicero with whom he said he hardly liked to differ and whom he quoted on

---

[209]Cic. *Brut.* 49.186-188.

[210]Cic. *Brut.* 93.322.

[211]Quint. *Inst.* 3.1.20.

innumerable occasions.[212] One can expect then not to find anything new with regard to the use of emotions in Quintilian but only a rephrasing of Cicero's doctrines. Quintilian is in agreement with Cicero on the crucial quality of emotional appeals in a speech: "It is in its power over the emotions that the life and soul of oratory is to be found." He catches some of Cicero's addiction to the arousing of emotions when he says that "it is this emotional power that dominates the court, it is this form of eloquence that is the queen of all." He comments further:

> Proofs, it is true, may induce the judges to regard our case as superior to that of our opponent, but the appeal to the emotions will do more, for it will make them wish our case to be the better. And what they wish, they will also believe. For as soon as they begin to be angry, to feel favourably disposed, to hate or pity, they begin to take a personal interest in the case, and just as lovers are incapable of forming a reasoned judgement on the beauty of the object of their affections, because passion forestalls the sense of sight, so the judge, when overcome by the emotions, abandons all attempt to enquire into the truths of the arguments, is swept along by the tide of passion, and yields unquestioning to the torrent.[213]

Quintilian shares two of Cicero's central ideas. The first is that "there is scope for an appeal to the emotions . . . in every part of a speech." And the second is his statement that "the prime essential for stirring the emotions of others is, in my opinion, first to feel those emotions oneself."[214] Quintilian

---

[212]Quint. *Inst.* 7.3.8.

[213]Quint. *Inst.* 6.2.5-7.

[214]Quint. *Inst.* 6.2.26; also 6.2.2. Surprisingly, Quintilian (*Inst.* 6.2.26) seems to imply that the point of feeling the emotion oneself is something he discovered on his own and not something he read in Cicero: "But my design is to bring to light the secret

insists that a speech cannot be successful unless the orator genuinely feels the emotions being projected. He writes:

> Consequently, if we wish to give our words the appearance of sincerity, we must assimilate ourselves to the emotions of those who are genuinely so affected, and our eloquence must spring from the same feeling we desire to produce in the mind of the judge. Will he grieve who can find no trace of grief in the words with which I seek to move him to grief? Will he be angry, if the orator who seeks to kindle his anger shows no sign of labouring under the emotion which he demands from his audience? Will he shed tears if the pleader's eyes are dry? It is utterly impossible."[215]

In order to generate these emotions, he uniquely suggests the practice of vivid imagination resulting from "certain experiences which the Greeks call φαντασίαι, and the Romans *visions*, whereby things absent are presented to our imagination with such extreme vividness that they seem actually to be before our very eyes." Through this power of the mind, the orator can visualize the scene and circumstances of a murder, for example, and experience "the blood, the deathly pallor, the groan of agony, the death-rattle." In this way, the orator will stir up the appropriate emotions as if one were present at the actual occurrence.[216]

From all that has been derived from the various classical rhetorical

---

principles of this art, and to open up the inmost recesses of the subject, giving the result not of teaching received from others, but of my own experience and the guidance of nature." See also M. L. Clarke, *Rhetoric at Rome: A Historical Survey* (London: Cohen & West, 1953) 112.

[215]Quint. *Inst.* 6.2.27.

[216]Quint. *Inst.* 6.2.29-32.

theorists, it is quite clear that πάθος cannot be absent from any act of persuasion but, on the contrary, should assume precedence over even rational proofs. The latter may convince, but alone they will never persuade, that is secure the firm adherence of people's minds and hearts to the judgment proposed so that they will be mobilized into action. Emotional appeals, on the other hand, imbedded in the language of the speech and in the delivery of the orator, can so possess the souls of the listeners that they are conditioned, or as Aristotle would say, put into a certain frame of mind, to believe and act even in the face of slight reasons. All the great orators packed their speeches with emotions to intensify commitment to a stated choice and to reject its alternative, as the following classical examples demonstrate. The theory and practice of πάθος, as the third section of this chapter shows, operated as a very powerful proof in Paul's letter of persuasion to the Corinthians to secure their allegiance to his apostleship and his gospel.

B. The Use of Πάθος in Ancient Sources

For Cicero, Demosthenes was the ideal of the "vigorous style," by which he meant the eloquent use of πάθος, the ability to be on fire oneself and to set others on fire with emotions transmitted through the power of fiery words. Cicero was referring in particular to passages in Demosthenes' famous speech,

De Corona.[217] It is readily apparent that roiling emotions, particularly of anger and indignation, permeate Demosthenes' fiery speech against Aeschines. The reasons are evident in the accusation which Aeschines leveled against Demosthenes, causing him to be liable to capital punishment if the jury decided against him. At the least, such accusations impugned his good name, insulted his character, and minimized his outstanding achievements on behalf of the state. By the sheer eloquence of his words, as Aristotle would have it, Demosthenes had to put his jury into his own angry frame of mind and to convey what emotions of pain and righteous indignation caused by Aeschines' spitefulness and insult he was enduring. Moreover, he had to show the colors of the person who was the object of his anger, the one who was responsible for the dishonorable slight that questioned his integrity and implied the valuelessness of his noble deeds on behalf of his country. Last, Demosthenes had to refer to the occasion which gave rise to his anger and the desire for revenge for the pain it caused. At the same time, he had to concern himself with Ctesiphon, his friend, who was the object of Aeschines' indictment, an action primarily designed to take Demosthenes down.

In citing the following examples from Demosthenes and later from Cicero and Paul, it is difficult to convey the volcanic energy that would erupt from the words upon delivery. The person delivering the oration, the oration itself and

---

[217]Cicero (*Orat.* 38.133) says of the *De Corona*: "This speech certainly conforms so closely to the ideal [of arousing emotions] which is in our minds that no greater eloquence need be sought."

its delivery, the occasion and the audience are all unrepeatable factors in recapturing the power of the words as they are composed, uttered, and heard.[218] This point is illustrated in the interesting story of Aeschines, who was asked by the citizens of Rhodes (where he had moved after a humiliating lawsuit defeat in Athens) to read his splendid speech he had delivered against Ctesiphon and then was asked to read Demosthenes' defense. Cicero, who records this story, says in conclusion:

> This he did, in a very loud and attractive voice; and when everybody expressed admiration he said, 'How much more remarkable you would have thought it if you had heard Demosthenes himself!' thereby clearly indicating how much depends on delivery, as he thought that the same speech with a change of speaker would be a different thing.[219]

Cicero had said that whatever qualifications he had in the area of arousing emotions can be seen in his orations, "although books lack that breath of life which usually makes such passages seem more impressive when spoken than when read."[220] Seneca the Elder also reflects the dichotomy between the oratorical and the written word of the same person. He mentions the case of Cassius Severus who had an impressive talent as an orator with a delivery that

---

[218]Aristotle (*Rh.* 3.12.1-2) had something to say about the difference between spoken and written speeches. For a different opinion, see Quint. *Inst.* 12.10.52-55.

[219]Cic. *De Or.* 3.56.213. This experience can be repeated with any number of famous speeches throughout history. Lincoln's Gettysburg Address is an outstanding case in point. Although the full eloquent power of its sorrow-stricken grief and somber hope for remembrance can never be fully recaptured, yet it still pierces the heart on those occasions when there are war-dead men and women to be memorialized.

[220]Cic. *Orat.* 37.130.

"would have made any actor's reputation." The Elder Seneca quotes his friend Gallio as saying that "when [Cassius] spoke, he was king on the throne, so religiously did everyone do what they were told. When he required it, they were angry." However, "he was far greater heard than read. It happens to almost all people that they gain from being heard rather than read, but to a smaller degree: in him there was a vastly greater gulf."[221] In what follows, then, I cite speeches with clear evidence of strong emotions and attempt to isolate and name these various emotions to show how they function as a proof of the speaker's point and how they might plausibly affect the listeners in their judgments. This is undoubtedly subjective; but what should emerge is the feeling in the reader that some emotions, however one identifies and interprets them, are clearly at work for the text still to be read and enjoyed.

For a better appreciation of Demosthenes' response to Aeschines, it is

---

[221]Sen. *Controv.* 3.Pr.2-4. In this Preface and in his Preface to *Controv.* 9, Seneca Rhetor, as he was often called, talks of the distinction between gifted oratory and declamation, the latter referring to school exercises on themes based on particular law-court cases. Declamation was supposed to train students to take their places in the public arena, but it was highly criticized for its lack of contact with real life. In the Preface to *Controv.* 3, Seneca could say the following: "I know several cases of gifted speakers who did not match up to their reputation when they declaimed. In the forum they spoke to the admiration of all who heard them, but as soon as they retreated to our private exercises they were deserted by their talents. . . . And I remember that I once asked Cassius Severus why it was that *his* eloquence failed him in declamation." Cassius replies that a person can't do everything well and remarks: "Is there anything odd in a man not declaiming as well as he pleads? . . . When I speak in the forum, I am *doing* something. When I declaim I feel . . . that I am struggling in a dream. Again, the two things are quite different: it is one thing to fight, quite another to shadow-box." One may question whether Seneca's remarks are completely relevant to the statement in the text about the distinction between the delivered and the written word. While his comments may point in a slightly different direction, they do not alter radically the distinction we have made: the difference between *dicere* and *scribere*, the words Seneca uses.

helpful first to point out clearly the primary emotions which he is dealing with and which he hopes to arouse in his listeners and then to use Aristotle's analysis of these emotions to understand their nature. The main feelings in Demosthenes are anger and indignation sparked by the disdain, insult, spitefulness, and slander toward himself contained in Aeschines' indictment of Ctesiphon. Demosthenes must put the members of the jury in the right frame of mind by vehemently displaying these emotions and arousing within in them the same feelings, while concomitantly appealing to their sense of benevolence and gratitude toward him as a benefactor of the State for the honest discharge of his public office.

Anger, according to Aristotle, is "a longing, accompanied by pain, for a real or apparent revenge for a real or apparent slight, affecting a man himself or one of his friends, when such a slight is undeserved." The hope for revenge is the pleasurable side-effect of anger. A slight ($\dot{o}\lambda\iota\gamma\omega\rho\iota\alpha$) is "an actualization of opinion in regard to something which appears valueless." Things considered trifling or unimportant tend to be ignored. There are three kinds of spite: disdain, spitefulness, and insult. Disdain means looking down judgmentally on things. Spitefulness consists "in placing obstacles in the way of another's wishes" not for the advantage of the one who spites but to make sure no advantage accrues to the other. Insult consists "in causing injury or annoyance whereby the sufferer is disgraced" resulting in the pleasure of more fully showing one's own superiority. Dishonor is part of insult and slight. These are some of the dispositions and reasons for anger.[222]

As for the objects of anger, people are angry at those "who ridicule, mock, and scoff at them," all of which are gratuitous insults. People are angry "with those who speak ill of or despise things which they themselves consider of the greatest importance." Likewise "they are more angry with those who are their friends than with those who are not, for they think that they have a right to be treated well by them rather than ill." This is especially true "with those who have been in the habit of honouring and treating them with respect" but no longer do so. People are angry "with those who are of no account, if they slight them." People are angry "with those who are ungrateful, for the slight is contrary to all sense of obligation." People are angry "with those who do good to others, but not to them; for not to think them worthy of what they bestow upon all others also shows contempt."[223] The relevance of these psychological insights into the emotion of anger will become evident as the classical orations and Paul's response to the Corinthians are analyzed.

Indignation is a particular aspect of anger aroused through an unjust or mean and spiteful attack on one's dignity and honor. The rhetorical response to this attack is called βαρύτης, which, according to Liddell-Scott, is the

---

[222]Arist. *Rh.* 2.2.1-8.

[223]Arist. *Rh.* 2.2.12-27.

adoption of an injured tone.[224] Christopher Forbes describes it as "that quality

of speech which is appropriate to a strongly reproachful tone" and quotes a little

known but significant passage from Hermogenes' *On Rhetorical Forms* (2.8)

which is relevant to the discussion at hand.[225] Hermogenes writes:

> Indignation (βαρύτης) involves making use of all the
> reproachable figures of thought (ἔννοιαι). Whenever, speaking
> of one's own beneficial actions, one asserts reproachfully that
> they are being considered worthless, or are being depreciated; or
> even, contradictorily, that they should merit punishment rather
> than honour, this is 'indignation'.

In other words, as Forbes comments on this passage, indignation "was seen as

particularly appropriate to a speaker who had been badly treated." Hermogenes

goes on to talk about indignant speech when, according to Forbes' commentary,

one's "achievements were being credited to others, and whose good name had

been traduced. This was especially true if the value of his actual achievements

was being disputed." Irony, according to Hermogenes, was a popular way to

reflect indignation, as well as other forms of thought connected with irony such

as:

> . . . to raise a question as if it is doubtful . . . hesitating over
> matters on which everyone agrees before settling them . . . for
> example: 'And if you had actually done wrong rather than the

---

[224]Henry G. Liddell and Robert Scott, *A Greek-English Lexicon* (new [9th] ed.,
Henry S. Jones; Oxford: Clarendon Press, 1940) 808. The indignation discussed in the
text is completely different from the concept of τὸ νεμεσᾶν which is translated as
"indignation" in the LCL edition of Arist. *Rh.*

[225]Christopher Forbes, "Comparison, Self-Praise and Irony: Paul's Boasting and the
Conventions of Hellenistic Rhetoric," *NTS* 32 (1986) 1-30. The source for all the
quotations in the text are from 12-13. The quotation from Hermogenes is taken from
L. Spengel, *Rhetores Gracei* (BT; Leipzig: Teubner, 1853-56) 3.384ff.

things for which you are being honoured, how much more rightly
would you be hated, than spared?' Hesitation, followed by the
decision: 'I think much more so.'

This brief analysis of anger and indignation helps one to understand and

appreciate the effect of these two powerful emotions in the texts under

consideration, particularly Demosthenes' oration which is one sustained angry

rebuttal bristling with irony and invective.

In his exordium, after praising the benevolence of the people of Athens and

saying that the loss of goodwill, kindness, and fair-mindedness of the jury would

be the most painful of all losses, Demosthenes proceeds to respond not only to

the public charges but also to the "abusive aspersion of my private life." His

anger is evident in the words that immediately follow:

> Malicious as you are, Aeschines, you were strangely innocent
> when you imagined that I should turn aside from the discussion
> of public transactions to reply to your calumnies. I shall do
> nothing of the sort: I am not so infatuated. Your false and
> invidious charges against my political life I will examine; but
> later, if the jury wish to hear me, I will return to your outrageous
> ribaldry.[226]

Through the use of denunciatory verbs both for Aeschines' charges and his

person, Demosthenes not only conveys his own sense of outrage and indignation

but also attempts to neutralize the negative effects of Aeschines' previous

abusive speech in the minds of the jury. At one point, after detailing Aeschines'

traitorous association with Philip of Macedon and Alexander, Demosthenes turns

to the jury to ask them if they think Aeschines is Alexander's hireling or

---

[226]Dem. *De Cor.* 11.

Alexander's friend, a catch-22 situation since both are invidious. After a pregnant pause, during which there is an implied assent of voices and heads, Demosthenes says to Aeschines: "You hear what they say."[227] In such a short space of time, Demosthenes has managed to fill the audience with his own dispositions of anger and revulsion.

The invective against Aeschines becomes more and more blunt as Demosthenes advances into the oration. He touches upon the fact mentioned by Aristotle in discussing anger that a person who is inferior in birth, power, and virtue should highly esteem those superior to oneself. Demosthenes' indignation shows through as well:

> I must let you know who this man, who starts on vituperation so glibly . . . really is, and what is his parentage. . . . Hark to his melodramatic bombast: "Oh, Earth! Oh, Sun!, Oh, Virtue," and all that vapouring; his appeals to "intelligence and education, whereby we discriminate between things of good and evil report"—for that was the sort of rubbish you heard him spouting. Virtue! You runagate; what have you and your family to do with virtue? How do you distinguish between good and evil report? Where and how did you qualify as a moralist? Where did you get your right to talk about education? No really educated man would use such language about himself, but would rather blush to hear it from others; but people like you, who make stupid pretensions to the culture of which they are utterly destitute, succeed in disgusting everybody whenever they open their lips, but never in making the impression they desire.[228]

Demosthenes proceeds to talk about Aeschines' parents in a disparaging way. He piles one phrase upon another in various emotional outbursts of anger to

---

[227]Dem. *De Cor.* 52.

[228]Dem. *De Cor.* 126-128.

insult Aeschines. He calls Aeschines "this malignant mumbler of blank verse";
"a disreputable quill-driver"; "you third-rate tragedian"; "this monkey of
melodrama"; "our bombastic phrase-monger"; "this bumpkin tragedy-king";
"this pinchbeck orator"; "you incorrigible knave."[229] Demosthenes belabors
the jury with frequent assessments of Aeschines' lack of patriotism. Even more,
he accuses him of traitorous activity, one who found profit from his country's
foes.[230] Demosthenes lays before the jury his contention that it was not Philip
alone who brought disasters upon Athens:

> I solemnly aver that it was not one man, but a gang of traitors in
> every state. One of them was Aeschines; and, if I am to tell the
> whole truth without concealment, I will not flinch from declaring
> him the evil genius of all the men, all the districts, and all the
> cities that have perished. Let the man who sowed the seed bear
> the guilt of the harvest.[231]

Demosthenes' oath at this point shows the depth of his anger at the hypocritical
posture of Aeschines who can indict Ctesiphon on such a minor count when
Aeschines himself is guilty of betraying the entire nation.

Hermogenes himself points out a good example of Demosthenes' show of
indignation through the use of heavy sarcastic irony. He refers to the passage
in which Demosthenes reminds Aeschines of the loud applause the former had
received for the advice he had given in a speech to the council of Athens
concerning a grave crisis with Philip. He then says to Aeschines:

---

[229]Dem. *De Cor.* 139, 209, 243.

[230]Dem. *De Cor.* 198, 292, and *passim*.

[231]Dem. *De Cor.* 158-9.

> What part do you wish me to assign to you, Aeschines, and what to myself, in the drama of that great day? Am I to be cast for the part of Battalus [stammerer], as you dub me when you scold me so scornfully, and you for no vulgar role but to play some hero of legendary tragedy, Cresphontes, or Creon, or, shall we say, Oenomaus, whom you once murdered by your bad acting at Collytus? Anyhow, on that occasion Battalus of Paeania deserved better of his country than Oenomaus of Cathocidae. You were utterly useless; I did everything that became a good citizen.[232]

As Hermogenes comments:

> For in the use of the two names, 'Stammerer' and 'Oenomaus', the opposites of the names is signified. Thus in every way things are put forward as their opposites, which on the one hand is characteristically ironic, and on the other a means for achieving the effect of indignation.[233]

In this case the malicious epithet Aeschines used of Demosthenes ironically achieves the opposite effect. The 'Stammerer' convinces the Athenian council in their negotiations with Thebes while Aeschines "murders" the role of a tragedy-king!

Comparison is another way to display indignation and anger, especially when one's good name and achievements have been maligned. This Demosthenes does consistently throughout the oration in accounting for himself and his actions. In patriotism, in virtue, in integrity of life, in statesmanship, in oratory, in fortune, in decorations of honor, in honorable advice, Demosthenes outshines his accuser. One good example filled again with ironic indignation is the following:

---

[232]Dem. *De Cor.* 180.

[233]Quoted from Forbes, "Comparison, Self-Praise and Irony," 12.

Aeschines, . . . In respect of the business of which I am speaking
. . . I am a better citizen than you, in so far as I devoted myself
to a course of action that was unanimously approved, neither
shirking nor even counting any personal danger. . . . You are
proved after the event to have behaved throughout like a
worthless and most unpatriotic citizen; and now, by a strange
coincidence, those thorough-going enemies of Athens, Aristratus
at Naxos and Aristolaus at Thasos, are bringing the friends of
Athens to trial, while at Athens itself Aeschines is accusing
Demosthenes. And yet he who built his reputation on the
accumulated misfortunes of Greece deserves rather to perish
himself than to prosecute his neighbour; and the man who has
found his profit in the same emergencies as his country's foes
can make no claim to patriotism. You stand revealed in your life
and conduct, in your public performances and also in your public
abstinence. A project approved by the people is going forward.
Aeschines is speechless. A regrettable incident is reported.
Aeschines is in evidence. He reminds one of an old sprain or
fracture: the moment you are out of health it begins to be
active.[234]

There is one highly colorful passage in which Demosthenes minutely and vividly

describes the young Aeschines' occupation as his mother's assistant in her

performance of the initiation ritual of some Bacchic rites in which she was a

priestess. Mockingly, Demosthenes proceeds to relate:

At night it was your duty to mix the libations, to clothe the
catechumens in fawn-skins, to wash their bodies, to scour them.
. . and, when their lustration was duly performed, to set them on
their legs, and give out the hymn: "Here I leave my sins behind,
here the better way I find"; and it was your pride that no one
ever emitted that holy ululation so powerfully as yourself. I can
well believe it! When you hear the stentorian tones of the orator,
can you doubt that the ejaculations of the acolyte were simply
magnificent?. . . [You were] saluted by all the old women with
such proud titles as Master of the Ceremonies, Fugelman, Ivy-
bearer, Fan-carrier; and at last receiving your recompense of
tipsy-cakes, and cracknels, and currant-buns.

---

[234]Dem. *De Cor.* 197-98.

Demosthenes closes this derisive biography with the satirical comment: "With such rewards who would not rejoice greatly, and account himself the favourite of fortune?"[235] In one other example, heavy with sarcastic indignation at the arrogance of Aeschines to question his integrity as a statesman and a benefactor of the city, Demosthenes compares their respective careers. After some belittling differences, Demosthenes says: "And that is the good fortune enjoyed by you, who denounce the shabbiness of mine!" He follows this up immediately with another acrimonious jibe:

> Let me now read to you the testimony of the public services I have rendered, and you shall read for comparison some of the blank-verse you used to make such a hash of: "From gates of gloom and dwellings of the dead," or, "Tidings of woe with heavy heart I bear," or "Oh cruel, cruel fate!" Such a fate may the gods first, and the jury afterwards, allot to you—for your citizenship is as worthless as your mummery.[236]

Demosthenes never allows the jury to escape his high indignation as he barrages them with one trenchant passage after another against Aeschines whom he likewise pounds with ridicule.

While using this strategy against Aeschines and putting the jury in the same frame of angry and indignant mind that he has, Demosthenes creates a wholly different set of emotions to influence the jury. These emotions center on benevolence and gratitude. As has been shown in the previous chapter, Demosthenes portrays himself as the benefactor of the nation, a wise statesman,

---

[235]Dem. *De Cor.* 259-60.

[236]Dem. *De Cor.* 265-67.

a prophetic voice in the face of Philip's aggressive policies, an orator who speaks harsh truths. He does all this with proper modesty, yet it is calculated, since he was speaking after Aeschines, to leave the impression of an injured patriot and, worst of all, an insulted benefactor whose great deeds have been treated with spite and disdain by a contemptible person like Aeschines. Demosthenes meticulously details recent events in regard to Philip of Macedon's ambitious intentions to show the jury the contrast between his own sane and patriotic voice as well as his demanding but wise policies, which benefitted the men of the jury, and Aeschines' self-serving and callous disregard for the best interests of Athens. He reminds them that in the hour of most need, he came forward with counsel in a speech which he now asks them to devote careful attention to for two reasons, the first of which is

> . . . that you may understand that I, alone among your orators and politicians, did not desert the post of patriotism in the hour of peril, but approved myself as one who in the midst of panic could, both in speech and in suggestion, do what duty bade on your behalf.[237]

In closing his oration, Demosthenes remarks:

> There are two traits, men of Athens, that mark the disposition of the well-meaning citizen;—that is a description I may apply to myself without offense. When in power, the constant aim of his policy should be the honour and the ascendancy of his country; and on every occasion and in all business he should preserve his loyalty. That virtue depends on his natural disposition: ability and success depend on other considerations. Such, you will find, has been my disposition, abidingly and without alloy.[238]

---

[237]Dem. *De Cor.* 173.

[238]Dem. *De Cor.* 321.

His words are meant to fill the minds of his listeners with good feelings of gratitude toward him because of his benevolence to the nation in order to capture their votes that would exonerate him from the scurrilous attacks of Aeschines.

Demosthenes plays upon another emotion: fear and its opposite, confidence. Aristotle talks of fear "as a painful or troubled feeling caused by the impression of an imminent evil that causes destruction or pain." Whenever there are signs that misfortune is looming near, the approaching danger produces fear. Aristotle names one of these signs: "Injustice possessed of power is fearful, for the unjust man is unjust through deliberate inclination."[239] This is a significant observation in light of Demosthenes' insistent refrain in his defense to the jury: that Philip was out to enslave all Greece and particularly Athens and that Aeschines was his willing minion: "I saw a man enslaving all mankind, and I stood in his way. I never ceased warning you and admonishing you to surrender nothing."[240] Even though Philip had achieved his goals and Demosthenes' political efforts had come to nothing, yet Demosthenes highlights the fact that throughout the entire threat of danger his was the voice of sanity calling the men of the jury to confidence and belief in the Athenian principles of democracy and liberty and to a recognition that a commonwealth in subjection is "more dreadful than death itself." This ancient principle of

---

[239]Arist. *Rh*. 2.5.1-8.

[240]Dem. *De Cor*. 72.

freedom, inherent in the Athenian spirit, Aeschines was arraigning, according to Demosthenes, but he was vindicating. For pointing out the dangers of imminent war and for encouraging the people of Athens to stand firm, the men of the jury cannot listen to Aeschines' charges that Demosthenes was the author of terrors and dangers:

> For if you condemn Ctesiphon on the ground of my political delinquency, you yourselves will be adjudged as wrongdoers, not as men who owed the calamities they have suffered to the unkindness of fortune. But no; you cannot, men of Athens, you cannot have done wrongly when you accepted the risks of war for the redemption and the liberties of mankind.[241]

In defending himself, Demosthenes calls upon other emotions to dispose the jury toward his judgment of the case. These emotions which Aristotle treats as sources for arguments from πάθος Demosthenes exemplifies in his oration: his love and fidelity to the state (108-110, 258, 285, 299); shame and possible dishonor if the jury associates with Aeschines' actions and judgment (138, 206-07); pity for the sufferings of the state at the hands of Philip (45-48, 72, 298); praise for the bravery of the Athenians in battle and for their sense of righteousness (215-16). There is no question that Demosthenes' use of emotional appeals, particularly his anger and indignation at the outrage he suffered at the hands of one whom he branded a traitor, was instrumental in helping him win his case.

Cicero, who said in his *Brutus* that one of the two chief qualities of an

---

[241]Dem. *De Cor.* 206-08.

orator is "an impressive appeal to the emotions of the listener," one who "inflames the court," also makes πάθος a main ingredient of his persuasive speeches.[242] His ideal orator, a depiction of himself, was the speaker who could sway one's own feelings and those of the audience in whatever direction the situation demanded. All of his orations, in fact, seem to be one continuous play upon the emotions of the audience. Julius Severianus says: "Cicero per omnem orationem adfectum inserit."[243] And Cicero says through one of his protagonists: "There is no way in which the mind of the auditor may be aroused or soothed that I have not tried—I should say brought to perfection, if I really thought so, and if it were true I should fear to be called conceited."[244]

Cicero shows his art of πάθος with great mastery in the Cataline Orations which, as Solmsen says, are "one continuous effort to stir up *indignatio* or to arouse *odium.*"[245] The famous opening of the First Speech immediately begins with an impassioned tone of anger and alarm meant to arouse the Senate to fury at the treacherous plans of Cataline:

> In heaven's name, Cataline, how long will you take advantage of
> our forebearance? How much longer yet will that madness of
> yours make playthings of us? When will your unbridled
> effrontery stop vaunting itself? Are you impressed not at all that

---

[242]Cic. *Brut.* 22.89.

[243]From his *Praecepta artis rhet.* 18.365.19f (Halm) quoted from Solmsen, "The Orator's Playing Upon the Feelings," 401. The use of "adfectus" for emotion was coined by Quint. *Inst.* 6.2.8 as the Latin expression for πάθος.

[244]Cic. *Orat.* 28.132.

[245]Solmsen, "The Orator's Playing Upon the Feelings," 400-01.

the Palatine has a garrison at night, that the city is patrolled, that the populace is panic-stricken, that all loyal citizens have rallied to the standard, that the Senate is meeting here behind stout defenses, and that you can see the expression on the faces of the senators? Do you not appreciate that your plans are laid bare? Do you not see that your conspiracy is held fast by the knowledge of all these men? Do you think that there is a man among us who does not know what you did last night or the night before last, where you were, whom you summoned to your meeting, what decision you reached? What an age we live in! The Senate knows it all, the consul sees it, and yet—this man is still alive.[246]

Cicero goes on in these orations to appeal to the Senate's sense of honor as citizens of the greatest republic in the world, their fear of anything that would endanger the republic, their sense of security for themselves and their families. He arouses in them a loathing for Cataline's crimes which contravene the basic Roman virtues of reverence, law, and honor. He shows them his raging indignation that Cataline could flaunt his presence in public when everyone knew what his plans were. He calls upon the courage and wisdom of the senators to take a decisive stand against the man whom Cicero considers the worst enemy Roman has ever had. He even addresses himself to their respect for the guardian gods of Rome, whose omens seem to foretell Cataline's heinous intentions.

In the following passage, Cicero is facing the brazen Cataline and his co-conspirators in the audience. Seething with implacable hatred, Cicero erupts in tones and gestures of savage denunciation, as he lays bare before the Conscript

---

[246]Cic. *Cat.* 1.1-2.

Fathers Cataline's plot to destroy the republic:

> Go over with me, please, the events of the night before last.
> You will appreciate now that my concern for the safety of the
> Republic is much deeper than is yours for its destruction. I say
> that on the night before last you came to the street of the scythe-
> makers—I shall be precise—the house of Marcus Laeca. There
> you were joined by many of your accomplices in your criminal
> folly. You do not have the effrontery to deny it, do you? Why
> are you silent then? If you deny it, I shall prove it. In fact, I
> see some of those who were with you here in the Senate. In
> heaven's name! Where in the world are we? What State is ours?
> What city are we living in? Here, gentlemen, here in our very
> midst, in this, the most sacred and important council in the
> world, there are men whose plans extend beyond the death of us
> all and the destruction of this city to that of the whole world. .
> . . You cannot remain among us any longer; I cannot, I will not,
> I must not permit it.[247]

Cicero sustains this level of anger and outrage toward Cataline throughout the

first oration. Cicero seeks to paint Cataline's character in the bleakest of terms

to arouse the senators to shock over his deplorable personal scandals and public

crimes and to fear at Cataline's murderous intentions. He does this because

there are some in the Senate "who either cannot see what threatens us or

pretend that they cannot, who have fed Cataline's hopes by their feeble decisions

and put heart into the growing conspiracy by refusing to believe that it existed."

Cicero wants to arouse them to take action.

In his *Third Speech against Cataline* Cicero addresses the people and plays

upon their feelings of fear and reverence for the immortal gods who Cicero

claims helped to avert the dangers posed by Cataline. Cicero associates the

---

[247]Cic. *Cat*. 1.8-10.

exposure of Cataline's plots against the people and the Senate with the timing of the erection of a statue of Jupiter Optimus Maximus to convince the superstitious that Cataline's crimes were so heinous that the gods themselves had to intervene. He likewise arouses in them a sense of gratitude not only to the gods but also to himself for his vigilance in pursuing the traitors.

In the *Fourth Speech against Cataline* given before the Senate to decide the fate of Cataline and his conspirators, Cicero focuses on implanting in the senators feelings of grave concern for the preservation of their own lives and of the Roman people, while simultaneously instilling in them confidence in himself as their consul who will not shrink even to the peril of his own life from defending their decisions. Cicero asks them to keep faith with the common people and cast a vote for peace by putting the conspirators to death:

> Such being the case, gentlemen, the protection of the Roman people does not fail you; see to it then that you do not fail the Roman people. You have a consul kept from a multitude of dangers and plots, from the very jaws of death, not just to cling to life but to save you. All classes are united in purpose, will and voice to preserve the Republic. Beset by the brands and weapons of this vile conspiracy, the fatherland we all share extends to you the hands of a suppliant. To you she commends herself, the lives of all her citizens, the citadel and the Capitol, the altars of her household gods, the never dying fire of Vesta over there, the temples and shrines of all her gods, the walls and buildings of this city. Your lives, too, and the lives of your wives and children, the fortunes of you all, your houses and your hearths, depend upon the decision you have to make this day.[248]

His emotional tactics paid off. The conspirators were executed.

---

[248]Cic. *Cat.* 4.18.

In his *Pro Murena*, Cicero uses a completely different strategy to win his case, that of wit and laughter, a technique referred to in passing by Aristotle and analyzed more thoroughly by Cicero and Quintilian. The cause of laughter is uncertain, as Quintilian writes.[249] Laughter arises from a variety of things, not merely from the witty word or action but also "at those which reveal folly, anger or fear." And it is difficult to pinpoint the emotion on which a jest depends. Witticisms designed to raise laughter, Quintilian continues, "are generally untrue (and falsehood always involves a certain meanness), and are often deliberately distorted, and further, never complimentary. . . [and] never far removed from derision." He quotes Cicero, *De Or.* 2.58.236, as saying that "laughter has its basis in some kind or other of deformity or ugliness." When we point to some blemish in others, we call it wit (*urbanitas*), but when the same jest is turned on us we call it absurdity (*stultitia*). He says that laughter "frequently turns the scale in matters of great importance, . . . for instance, it often dispels hatred or anger." He proceeds to discuss the distinctions between wounding jests, gentle raillery, abusive wit against opponents, coarse jibes which rely on the ambiguity of words, and witty retorts that depend on many plays on persons, actions, words, and circumstances.

Cicero likewise goes into the nature of laughter, its source, its propriety for an orator, its limits in oratory, and the classification of things laughable. In

---

[249]Quint. *Inst.* 6.3.1-112. The remarks in the text are a brief digest of Quintilian's remarkable insights on wit and laughter.

asking whether laughter becomes an orator, Cicero responds through one of his

dialogue protagonists that it does on various grounds:

> For instance, merriment naturally wins goodwill for its author;
> and everyone admires acuteness, which is often concentrated in
> a single word, uttered generally in repelling, though sometimes
> in delivering an attack; and it shatters or obstructs or makes light
> of an opponent, or alarms or repulses him; and it shows the
> orator himself to be a man of finish, accomplishment and taste;
> and, best of all, it relieves dullness and tones down austerity,
> and, by a jest or a laugh, often dispels distasteful suggestions not
> easily weakened by reasonings.[250]

Cicero takes up the limits of laughter in a speech and cautions against ridiculing

outstanding wickedness or wretchedness, for the ridicule will backfire. He next

classifies witty sayings as having their point sometimes in facts and sometimes

in words, although the union of the two is particularly amusing. An orator can

express wit through ambiguity, the unexpected rejoinder, equivocation, play

upon words, the ironical inversion of verbal meanings, comparison, caricature,

understatement, assumed simplicity, hinted ridicule, personal retorts, and many

other methods which take words and facts and twist them to create or dispel

various emotions in the listeners.[251] The above discussion gives background

---

[250]Cic. *De Or.* 2.58.236. The other quotes and remarks in the text are taken from 2.54.216-71.289.

[251]Cicero, as always, is concerned with propriety in speech. He further suggests (*Orat.* 26.88-89) that the orator should use ridicule or witticisms that create laughter with care. It should "not be too frequent lest it become buffoonery; nor ridicule of a smutty nature, lest it be that of low farce; nor pert, lest it be impudent; nor aimed at misfortune, lest it be brutal, nor at crime, lest laughter take the place of loathing; nor should the wit be inappropriate to his own character, to that of the jury, or to the occasion; for all these points come under the head of impropriety. He will also avoid far-fetched jests, and those not made up at the moment but brought from home; for these are generally frigid. He will spare friends and dignitaries, will avoid rankling

for Cicero's strategy in his oration *Pro Murena*, but is also helpful background
to Paul's use of wit in 2 Corinthians 10-13 in the next section.

In *Pro Murena*, Cicero holds up Cato, the prosecutor, for ridicule for his
impracticality in prosecuting Murena, who was a consul-delegate, in a case of
ambitus or electoral malpractice in accepting bribes for votes at a time when the
state was in a serious crisis from Cataline's conspiracy. Cicero's wit in subtly
damning with faint praise Cato's dour Stoic virtues was calculated to dismiss
Cato as one straining at a gnat while Rome was burning. Cicero, with a hint
of ridicule, says in his opening lines that he will reply to Marcus Cato "who
organizes life according to the fixed pattern of a system and weighs with
scrupulous care the importance of all obligations."[252] When he does reply
later, Cicero raises the ploy of envy in the jurors at Cato's exceptional power
and prestige as a prosecutor. Cicero says he does not "like a prosecutor to
come into court with overweening power, an excessive force, overwhelming
influence or too much popularity." Cicero's reasoning is that Cato's acceptance
of the case might already seem a decision against Murena: "It will be creating
an unjust precedent, gentlemen, and a wretched state of affairs for men on trial
if the prosecutor's judgement is to count against the defendant as a presumption

---

insult; he will prod his opponents, nor will he do it constantly, nor to all of them nor
in every manner." Cicero considered wit and humor an outstanding mark of Attic style
and cites Demosthenes, though considered inferior in this by many, as more clever than
anyone. "Still he is not witty so much as humorous; the former requires a bolder
talent, the latter a greater art."

[252]Cic. *Mur.* 3.

of guilt."[253] Cicero's ploy forewarns the jury to judge the case on the strength of the evidence and not on the prestige of the prosecutor; in addition he already very subtly sets Cato up as a powerful figure about to be cut down to size by Cicero's incisive wit. His intent is to dismiss Cato as one filled with his own sense of self-importance and thus make him look laughable to the jury.

Cicero lays the groundwork for Cato's ultimate dismissal as a reasonable prosecutor by a mock-heroic description of Cato's stern morality based on Stoic precepts. Humorously, Cicero says he does not wish to censure his conduct but, perhaps, "reshape parts of it and improve them slightly." In extending Cato the left-handed compliment that "nature has framed you for integrity, serious-mindedness, self-control, strength of character and justice; in short a paragon of virtue," Cicero is really saying ironically that he has too much of a good thing for ordinary mortals. These virtues have made his set of beliefs "a little harsh and hard for reality or human nature to endure." Cicero suggests that virtue is in the middle. In essence Cicero is pleading with Cato for pity for his client, some evidence of the milk of human kindness, while addressing the same request to the jury. In one passage, after Cicero refers to Cato's great-grandfather's affableness and flexibility, he addresses Cato with these words:

> When you spoke with truth and conviction of his exceptional
> virtue, you said that you had an example to imitate in your own
> family. You certainly do have an example in front of you at
> home, but it has been easier for his character to be passed on to
> you who are a descendant than to each of us, and yet his example

---

[253]Cic. *Mur.* 60.

is there for me to copy as much as for you. If you sprinkle your sternness and severity with his courtesy and affability, your qualities will not become better—that is impossible— but they will at least be more agreeably seasoned.[254]

Through this witty observation, Cicero attempts to dispose the jury to accept the fact that Cato has been carried away by an overblown sense of duty unmixed with kindness and so to cause them to laugh Cato out of court.

At this point Cicero astutely turns from his focus on Cato to address the senators faced with the sedition of Cataline that could destroy Rome. He pleads with them to insure continuity with his consulship and its aims by exonerating and electing Murena to carry on the fight against the deadly perils posed by Cataline. He appeals to their well-being, patriotism, fear for the loss of Rome, pity for the expected death of Murena if Cataline got his way in the following words:

> Shall, then, a jury of such distinction and intelligence, selected from the most distinguished orders, give the same verdict as that ruthless cut-throat and enemy of the Republic? Believe me, gentlemen, you are going to give your verdict in this case not only on Lucius Murena's life but upon your own as well. We have come to the end of the road. . . . that monstrous plague that is Cataline will break out in all its violence where it threatens . . . it will suddenly swoop on the areas near the city; frenzy will be rampant in the city, terror in the Senate-house, conspiracy in the Forum, an army in the Campus Martius and desolation in the country-side. In every dwelling and every neighbourhood we shall fear fire and the sword. Yet, if only the Republic is furnished with its proper means of defense [the election of two consuls, Murena being one of them] these plans so long contrived, will easily be crushed by the measures taken by the magistrates and the watchful care of private citizens. . . . In this

---

[254]Cic. *Mur.* 66.

state of affairs, gentlemen, . . . I implore you, to assure tranquillity, peace, security, your own lives and those of the other citizens.[255]

Cicero ends the oration with an appeal to pity, mercy, and compassion for Murena from the senators: "Today, gentlemen, clad in sack-cloth and ashes, consumed by disease, worn out by his tears and his distress, he is your suppliant, gentlemen, he calls upon your protection, implores your pity, and looks to your power and resources."[256] Cicero draws forth all the emotional stops as he mentions the bust of Murena's father only yesterday wreathed in laurel in honor of his son, his mother who yesterday kissed a consul when she kissed her son but who today may have to see her son go off into exile, and the sorrowing crowds from Murena's town of Lanuvium where Juno Sospita, to whom all consuls must sacrifice, is worshipped. Needless to say, after a speech filled with such a variety of emotions so ably aroused, Murena was acquitted.

One more example of Cicero's art of emotional appeal should suffice to show the power of πάθος to persuade. It is his defense of his benefactor, Gnaeus Plancius, brought up before a special jury by Juventius Laterensis on the charge of *ambitus* in revenge for the latter having lost in the election to the aedileship. As background, it should be stated that it was Plancius who as quaestor in Macedonia and at the risk of his own position had shown great kindness to Cicero during his exile at a time when the great orator and former

---

[255]Cic. *Mur.* 85-6.

[256]Cic. *Mur.* 86.

consul was humiliated and in danger of reprisals from dead Cataline's associates. Now it was Cicero's turn to repay the favor by defending Plancius from the charge of buying votes. In his speech Cicero uses gratitude as the reason why he is defending his friend, a gratitude similar to what he feels toward the jury: "as I scan with careful eye each several member of the court, I see that there is no one of you who has not had my safety at heart, who has not laid me under the deepest obligations, and to whom I am not bound by the ineffaceable recollection of benefits received."[257] This *captatio benevolentiae* plays on the sacred obligation of gratitude which the members of the jury would understand and appreciate; for, as Aristotle had written, under the emotion of love, "men like those who are strongly attached to their friends and do not leave them in the lurch."[258] At the same time Cicero has nothing but feelings of admiration, benevolence, and esteem toward Laterensis whose friendship presents him with a dilemma: "the alternative of either damaging the reputation of a dear friend [Laterensis], if I pursue the line to which his speech has prompted me, or of betraying the cause of one [Plancius] to whom I am under a deep obligation."[259] Cicero argues that comparison between the two is out of the question. He goes on to show Laterensis that just because Plancius won the election, this does not mean Plancius is a better person than he is or that the

---

[257]Cic. *Planc.* 1.2.

[258]Arist. *Rh.* 2.4.27.

[259]Cic. *Planc.* 2.6.

people did Laterensis an injustice.

Cicero's strategy is to lift Laterensis up from debilitating envy and humiliation by pointing out that his [Cicero's] canvassing for votes for Plancius was done because he was "the only begetter and saviour of my life." Cicero says that Plancius' display of pity toward Cicero during his exile earned for Plancius the gratitude of everyone who was glad at his restoration. Cicero's appeal to the emotion of pity—pain that arises at the sight of someone else's undeserved bad fortune which one is fearful of suffering something similar—serves as a powerful proof toward the jury for his taking up Plancius' defense and for Plancius' uncontaminated success in the elections. Cicero also engages the emotions of neighborliness (9.22), the affection of the chieftains of the Macedonian states, who are in Rome on other business, for Plancius (9.28), filial love (9.29), the disinterested friendship of those who voted for him (19.46), in order to arouse in the jury a feeling of liking for the defendant because of those very qualities they admire in themselves. Cicero's peroration is an emotional *tour de force*. He relives the time of his exile and Plancius' vigilant, self-sacrificing care for him. Cicero draws tears from the gentlemen in the jury as he reminds them of their past tears for him in exile, "their yearning, their sorrow, their indignation." With emotion at its peak, Cicero says in conclusion to Plancius:

> What can I do save weep and lament, and link my fortunes with
> your own? Only those who gave life back to me can give life to
> you. Come what may,—stand up, I beg, that all may look on
> you,—my arms shall hold you to me, and I shall avow myself to

be not merely the interceder for your fortunes, but your partner
and your comrade; and none, I trust, will be so heartless or so
insensible, so forgetful, I will not say of my services to the
patriotic party, but of their services to me, as to tear from my
side the saviour of my person, and bid me live henceforth
without him. I cry your mercy for him, gentlemen, not as for
one whom my services have advanced, but as for one who has
watched over my welfare,[260]

The outcome of the trial is unknown, but the depth of the emotional pleas in this speech is enough to persuade anyone who reverences the same emotions in and toward themselves. This it seems was precisely Cicero's strategy.

Cicero's other speeches and his letters are replete with emotional arguments couched in language calculated to tug at the heart of the jurors or recipient rather than at their heads. Cicero's plea for the restitution of his house in *De Domo sua*, particularly 37.100-49.103, and his cries of affection and gratitude toward his brother in his *Epistulae ad Quintum Fratrem*, especially the third one with its threefold opening incantation of "*mi frater, mi frater, mi frater*," are further examples of his emotional style of writing to captivate an audience.

Though Demosthenes and Cicero remain the undoubted masters of emotional oratory, Isocrates and Aeschines are able to use πάθος to their advantage as well. In the case of Isocrates, however, although he called his written works "orations," the majority of them were never intended for delivery.[261] Nevertheless one can with a close reading hear the emotions

---

[260]Cic. *Planc.* 43.102.

[261]See A. Craig Baird, *Rhetoric: A Philosophical Inquiry* (New York: Ronald Press, 1965) 6, for the source of this remark.

embedded in the written composition. The reader can pick up Isocrates' outrage

and indignation at his youthful aggressor and his strong appeal for justice as he

arouses the democratic instincts of the jurors in his speech *Against Lochites*

(particularly 15-22); his anger and reproachful tone to the jurors in *Against*

Callimachus if they should violate the covenants, as well as his pleas for justice

and expediency in order to maintain civic concord (42-43; 55-57; 66-68); his

appeals to gentleness and mildness to end a useless war and his use of shame to

point out the imbecility of keeping mercenary troops in *On the Peace*; his

dismay at the slander against him and his teaching in the *Antidosis*, his sense of

dignity in the face of calumny by refusing to engage in the stock pathetic

devices of supplicating, imploring, bringing in children and friends before the

jurors (321), his deep passion for the power of persuasion as the index of all

that is human and social (254-55).

Aechines likewise utilizes the persuasive art of appeal to the emotions. He

employs a whole range of emotional appeals in *Against Timarchus* to discredit

him to such a degree that it would make it impossible for him ever to hold any

office or be a reliable advocate in anyone's case. Aeschines expresses an

unrelenting outrage and indignation at the lewd life Timarchus has led, outlining

in great detail his immorality to arouse the contempt of the jurors (40; the affair

with Misgolas, 44-49; the affairs with Pittalacus and Hegesandrus, 55-70); he

plays upon their emotions of honor and shame by recounting Timarchus' lack

of reverence in disowning his uncle and leaving him a pauper (103-04); he excites their sense of self-respect for justice and impartiality (190-95); he appeals to their pride and objectivity in not being swayed by the manipulation of words from his opponents (170-77); last, he recalls for the jurors the laughter from the crowd at the unconscious scatological wit involved in associating Timarchus with certain double-meaning words (82-85). Aeschines' skillful use of emotions had Timarchus disbarred from helping Demosthenes prosecute Aeschines in the matter of the embassy.

In his speech, *On the Embassy*, Aeschines is fighting for his life on charges of treason brought by Demosthenes. Aeschines seethes with anger and humiliation that his loyalty to Athens could be called into question and that the speech he made before Philip as part of delegation from Athens could be misconstrued by Demosthenes. He fills the jurors with great fear of defilement by unjust bloodshed and destruction on themselves and their households if they should listen to the lies of Demosthenes and send him to an unmerited death (87-88). He arouses the indignation of the jurors by pointing out Demosthenes' "deceit in a momentous matter, and his outrageous shamelessness" (58). He lets the jurors know that he feels keenly their lack of gratitude to him as their trustworthy ambassador because they set statues and give seats of honor and crowns "not to those who have brought you tidings of peace, but to those [their generals] who have been victorious in battle" (80). Last, he calls forth their pity and compassion by bringing his three children before the jurors and saying to them "whether you believe that I would have betrayed to Philip, not only my country, my personal friendships, and my rights to the shrines and tombs of my fathers, but also these children, the dearest of mankind, to me" (152). At the end of the speech he makes a great plea for mercy by bringing before the jurors his father, his brothers, his connections by marriage, again his three children to present them as objects of great pity if disaster should fall on him. His emotional arguments won the case.

Aeschines empties his arsenal of emotional appeals in his famous speech *Against Ctesiphon*, which is in reality one sustained exercise in anger and hatred for his arch-enemy Demosthenes. His total focus is to bring Demosthenes into such disrepute with the jurors that they will deem Ctesiphon's motion illegal and deny Demosthenes the crown. At the very beginning of the speech he attempts to fill the jurors with hatred toward those who in defiance of the laws outrage the constitution and circumvent democracy (3-8). He arouses great horror in the jurors by accusing Demosthenes of violating the sacred laws of friendship in putting to death "the man with whom at the same table you had eaten and drunken [sic] and poured libations, the man with whom you had clasped hands in token of friendship and hospitality," a charge that Demosthenes did not deny but answered in such a way that "called forth a cry of protest from the citizens and all the foreigners who were standing about the assembly" (224). He instills fear in the jurors by reminding them that no one is above the law, not even such a popular man as Demosthenes (230). He tells them they will be reproach to the future if they proclaim Demosthenes, for the character of the city will be likened to the cowardice of Demosthenes (247). As a last emotional ploy Aechines calls upon the reverence and honor the jurors owe to the sacred dead and to the memory of their heroic exploits by saying: "Think you not that Themistocles and those who died at Marathon and at Plataea, and the very sepulchres of your fathers, will groan aloud, if the man who admits that he has negotiated with the barbarians against the Greeks shall receive a crown" (259)? In a burst of dramatic anger Aeschines says: "Away with the fellow, the curse of all Hellas! Nay, rather, seize and punish him, the pirate of politics, who sails on his craft of words over the sea of state" (253). In spite of such skillful use of $\pi\acute{\alpha}\theta o\varsigma$, the jury was unmoved and gave the verdict in favor of Demosthenes.

From the above examples one can easily see how the power of emotional appeals sometimes overrides the logical and brings the audience to its knees in agreement. The authors cited above play upon the emotions embedded in the attitudes, motives, and values by which the people in the audience conducted their lives. Values like justice, loyalty, love, compassion and motives or ego-drives such as self-respect, honor, status, and avoidance of shame are all part of a particular audience's sources of behavior and as such are filled with emotional content. The orator, as we have seen in the above examples, in order to bring the audience to a pre-determined judgment identifies these emotions and through the instrumentality of language, especially connotative language, voice tones, and body movements produces effective results. If the particular orator is adept in understanding one's own emotions and intuitive in reading the character of the persons comprising the audience, the orator can speak persuasively. Paul, like the classical orators before him, uses emotional arguments to achieve his goal of influencing the Corinthians toward his way of thinking.

C. The Use of πάθος in 2 Corinthians 10-13

In defending his ministry to the Corinthians and calling them back to his interpretation of the gospel, Paul tries to set them on fire with passionate language that not only would express his own deeply felt emotions but also might influence the Corinthians to feel the situation as he experienced it. Paul sought to put the Corinthians into his own frame of mind and to arouse them to action on several counts: to pledge their sole allegiance to him as their legitimate apostle, to dislodge his opponents as pseudo-apostles, and to renew their commitment to Paul's authentic gospel. Paul's emotional arguments run the gamut of anger and indignation, hurt and insult, honor and shame, love and hate, fear and pity, gentleness and boldness, emulation and jealousy. He mediates these emotions in a variety of rhetorical techniques: through irony, exaggeration, *synkrisis*, wit, the *peristasis* catalogue, self-laudation, sarcasm, and generally through style and language that is filled with bold speech, violent protest, loving entreaties, harsh invectives, and warning curses. He frequently overlaps and intertwines these emotional appeals and their various configurations in speech to heighten the intensity of each feeling and thereby to create a doubly persuasive effect. Paul's emotional technique is evidence of what Cicero said of that "kind of eloquence which rushes along with the roar of a mighty stream," which "has the power to sway men's minds and move them in every possible way. Now it storms the feelings, now it creeps in; it implants new ideas and uproots the old."[262] Paul's impassioned style is such that it is difficult to capture the effect of the whole in the analysis of each emotion singly. And yet such a discursive examination is warranted to appreciate his vigorous use of $\pi\acute{\alpha}\theta o\varsigma$ as a proof of great persuasive power.

Before beginning the detailed analysis of the emotions Paul uses in his response to the Corinthians, I wish to discuss now the means he uses to express them so as not to interrupt later the flow of the discussion. I refer to those methods mentioned above which give verbal expression to the feeling he is experiencing. Facial expressions, voice inflection, gestures and other bodily movements are potent ways of conveying emotions; but it is in the choice and arrangement of words in patterned linguistic configurations which inflames the heart and sways the mind of the listener. The effective orator must not only feel the emotion personally but must arouse the same feeling in the audience. The orator does this through stylistic devices, since emotions are disembodied and indifferent, as it were, unless formulated into words that impinge on the

---

[262]Cic. *Orat.* 28.97.

desires, motives, and attitudes of one's listeners toward designated action.

Cicero forcefully underscores this when he says: "When, however, the speaker has discovered what to say and how to arrange his subject-matter, then comes the all-important question of the manner of presentation." By "manner of presentation" Cicero means delivery and use of language or style, this latter overshadowing all other qualities. Giving the substance of an argument may be sufficient for philosophy, where the style is "concentrated on the meaning, and words as such are not weighed"; but style is absolutely crucial "in suits at law which are wholly swayed by oratorical skill."[263] It is the style which constellates and materializes the emotions to act as a proof. In this regard, then, it is important for understanding the discussion on Paul's use of πάθος to consider what Cicero says about so-called "figures of thought" or what we have called above "configurations of the emotions." Cicero calls them "embellishments" (*ornamenta*), hardly an apt word for something so indispensable. These embellishments are certainly not adventitious but critical to the transmission of the emotional appeals. It is most illuminating for Paul's use of emotions to hear some of the figures Cicero enumerates, for Paul will engage the same stylistic techniques to express himself. The good orator will use the following figures:

> . . . he will treat the same subject in many ways, sticking to the same idea and lingering over the same thought: he will often speak slightingly of something or ridicule it: he will turn from

---

[263]See Cic. *Orat.* 26.51-55 for the quotes and thought.

the subject and divert the thought; he will announce what he is about to discuss and sum up when concluding a topic; he will bring himself back to the subject; he will repeat what he has said; he will use a syllogism; he will urge his point by asking questions and will reply to himself as if to questions; he will say something, but desire to have it understood in the opposite sense; he will express doubt whether or how to mention some point; . . . he will transfer to his opponent the blame for the very act with which he is charged; he will seem to consult the audience, and sometimes even with the opponent; . . . he will frequently provoke merriment and laughter; he will reply to some point which he sees is likely to be brought up; he will use similes and examples; . . . he will claim to be suppressing something; he will warn the audience to be on their guard; he will take the liberty to speak somewhat boldly; he will even fly into a passion and protest violently; he will plead and entreat and soothe the audience; he will digress briefly; he will pray and curse; he will put himself on terms of intimacy with his audience; . . . he will often exaggerate a statement above what could actually occur; his language will often have a significance deeper than his actual words.[264]

These are some of the ways emotions become crystallized into actual statements that affect the feelings of listeners to gain their allegiance to one's goals. In the following discussion we shall identify the emotions Paul experiences and the manner in which he projects them to the Corinthians to arouse in them a corresponding emotional state.

Anger, indignation and reproach are emotions which predominate in Paul's response in 2 Corinthians 10-13. They are the result of hurt and slight from his converts and insult and shame from outside agitators. Paul is angry because the Corinthians reject his apostleship and gospel and the false apostles slander his person and apostolic legitimacy. His angry reaction validates what his

---

[264]Cic. *Orat.* 40.138-39.

opponents say about him: "His letters are severe and powerful" (10:10). This particular letter bristles with strong, stinging emotions. His anger, however, is therapeutic both for himself and for the Corinthians because it is the healthy expression of profound love on Paul's part for the Corinthians and their salvation: God knows I love you (11:10) and I will spend myself for your sakes (11:15) and do anything to build you up (11:19) lest you be seduced into falling away from your sincere and complete devotion to Christ (11:3).

He is indignant that they so casually reject their marriage to Christ which he has gone through so much trouble to arrange (11:2). He reproaches them for enduring another gospel (by implication, a breach of relationship) so well (11:4). Paul teems with profound indignation that they could even think he or Titus took advantage of them (11:7-9; 12:17-18) after he had gone to so much trouble to bring the gospel of Christ to them free of charge (10:14; 11:23-28), and yet fail to see that the false apostles were the ones really taking advantage of them (11:20). Their failure to recognize the apostolic signs, wonders and deeds of power he had worked among them (12:12) through God's power (13:4), and yet their readiness to allow human distinctions of some pseudo-apostles (11:12,18) whose works were from the devil (11:13-15) to fascinate them hurts and insults Paul. Their slights anger Paul because he feels he has a right to be better treated by those on whom he has conferred so many spiritual gifts. Their ingratitude affronts him, for, as Aristotle said, this "slight is contrary to all sense of obligation" (12:11).[265] Their disdain for his person which they consider unimpressive and for his word which they say makes no great impact (10:10) outrages him. These are some of the major reasons why Paul is angry with the Corinthians. Their superficiality (10:7) and gullibility (11:4) threaten their very existence in Christ (11:3;13:5) and they remain complacent and naive in blithely putting up with ignorant fools (10:12; 11:19).

Paul's fullest anger is directed against his opponents. His rage is so intense that he is ready to go to war with them over their spiritual self-inflation which undermines the gospel (10:4-5). His anger escalates into outright hatred for them because they are threats to the pure virgin he has presented to Christ (11:1-3). He abominates them as false apostles (11:13) and exploitative ministers (11:20), whose practices of self-recommendation and *synkrisis* (10:12) exceed the bounds of proper self-laudation and border on blasphemy (10:18). He is highly indignant that they use him as a foil to show their alleged superiority (11:5-6; 12:11) and dishonor him by their belittling insults (10:10; 12:16). Paul literally fumes with outrage at the suggestion that they work on the same terms as he does (11:12) or that there is no proof of Christ working in him (10:7; 13:3). He is irate finally that they have alienated the Corinthians toward him by questioning his legitimacy as an apostle (10:2; 12:11) and shown disdain for a gospel that celebrates the meekness of Christ (10:1) by vaunting their own human accomplishments (11:12). For as Aristotle had written: "Men

---

[265]Arist. *Rh*. 2.24.

are angry with those who speak ill or despise things which they themselves consider of the greatest importance."[266] Clearly, Paul lets the Corinthians know that "his opponents are responsible for things which rouse men to anger and are people of the kind with whom men are angry."[267] How he puts them in his same frame of mind is a result of rhetorical techniques imbedded in his letter.

2 Cor 11:1-15 is a key passage for understanding Pauls' use of invective. Paul galvanizes in the Corinthians his anger toward the false apostles, first of all, by using a metaphor that exposes the latter's essential evil. They are nothing more than frauds ($\psi\epsilon\upsilon\delta\alpha\pi\acute{o}\sigma\tau o\lambda o\iota$, 11:13) who have hoodwinked the Corinthians by deceitful tricks into thinking they are real apostles of Christ. The are $\delta\acute{o}\lambda\iota o\iota$, crafty and treacherous, an echo of their criticism against his behavior (12:16). Paul pursues the image of disguise and masquerade by tracing it back to the ultimate trickster, namely Satan, who paraded himself as an angel of light (11:12-15). To follow the false apostles is, therefore, to follow an illusion (11:14). The false apostles will end up with the same destiny as the Evil One whose ministers they are (11:15). In creating this highly evocative image, Paul is essentially warning the Corinthians not to be taken in by the outward show of these pseudo-apostles. They are charlatans who are as far from being apostles of Christ as Satan is from being God. The gulf is

---

[266]Arist. *Rh.* 2.2.13.

[267]Arist. *Rh.* 2.2.27.

unbridgeable. Paul's shows his animosity and anger toward these infiltrators by a curt declaration of fact which is at the same time a slightly veiled criticism of the Corinthians' powers of discrimination: καὶ οὐ θαῦμα (11:14)! Paul is saying to the Corinthians: the fraudulence of these outside agitators should come as no surprise, if one knows anything about Satan's crafty camouflages. Paul is making an outright damnation of the false apostles. He is so incensed by their intrusion into his territory that he considers part of his ministry to be their unmasking: "What I am doing I shall continue to do, depriving at every turn those who look for a chance to say that in their much-vaunted ministry they work on the same terms as we do" (11:12). He is highly indignant that his apostleship could be compared to their alleged ministry and that the Corinthians could have the wool pulled over their eyes so easily.

The ironies in this comparison-theme abound in further expressions of anger and indignation. Earlier Paul had alluded to the self-recommendation and *synkrisis* of the false apostles (10:12) which implicitly were meant to spotlight in a negative way his own inadequacies and even legitimacy as an apostle. At the same time he refers to their scorn for his commonplace speaking ability and his unprepossessing physical appearance (10:10). Paul turns the tables at the point where he calls these self-recommended critics disguised ministers of Satan (11:11:15)! Outward appearances are negligible. What may seem externally flashy is in essence a sink-hole, while what is outwardly contemptible is a source of power. What counts is approval from God whose recommendation is accurate. Since the false apostles have been their own appraisers, they are blind

to their own disguise. Paul ridicules them before the Corinthians by finally

stating that their "much-vaunted ministry" is essentially a self-deception built

on the illusion of ministry in God's name (11:15). To follow them is to risk

damnation. Paul's trenchant critique issues not merely from extreme anger at

their intrusive methods but even more, from deep hatred for their very natures,

because ultimately they come unrecommended and therefore are unrecognizable

as ministers of God. All of Paul's intense dislike of these false apostles comes

out loud and clear with his castigation of them as minions of Satan. He trusts

that his emotions will put the Corinthians in the same frame of mind. It may

be argued that Paul indulges in hyperbole in imposing the imagery of satanic

disguise on the false apostles, but Paul's anger is such that he has to reach the

Corinthians at a deep emotional level to jar them into awareness.

Another method that Paul uses to express his anger and indignation is the

threefold reproachful use of the verb $\mu\epsilon\tau\alpha\sigma\chi\eta\mu\alpha\tau\iota\zeta\epsilon\iota\nu$ in 11:13-15. The verb

has clearly negative connotations with its overtones of duplicity and

spuriousness. This is evident from the way the verb is used in v. 13 and v. 15

as an *inclusio* for the its use in v. 14. In vv. 13 and 15 the verb refers to the

false apostles; in v. 14 it refers to Satan. In v. 13 the false apostles are noted

as disguising or transforming themselves into "apostles of Christ" and in v. 15

they are noted as transforming or disguising themselves as "ministers of

righteousness." The use of the verb in v. 14 of Satan as one who is disguised or transformed into "an angel of light" provokes a ready-made commentary on the nature and agency of the false apostles. Such a harsh indictment filled with hyperbole clearly conveys the depth of Paul's anger toward the false apostles. By a few deft strokes Paul has ironically dismissed the validity of their own self-assessment as well as the value of their appraisal of him.

The use of the verb also acts as a covert admonishment of the Corinthians for their ignorance and credulity in being taken in by the σχῆμα of a person. Paul's sarcastic reproach is especially fitting since it obliquely chides them for their arrogant insult to his dignity in treating his own σχῆμα as weak and contemptible, when it is actually filled with the power of God and Christ (12:9; 13:4). He is indignant that they could mistake the shadow image of the false apostles for the reality of his own authentic apostolic claims (10:7). Paul employs the rhetorical technique of emphasis through analogy, which "per.nits the hearer himself to guess what the speaker has not mentioned,"[268] by not openly drawing out the connections for the Corinthians but allowing them to draw their own embarrassing conclusions. Was Paul perhaps sparing their sensibilities by not overtly rubbing their noses in their lack of discernment and in their ill-fated allegiance? Was he indirectly correcting their notion of and preoccupation with σχῆμα as contrary to his preached gospel of a Christ who

---

[268]*Rhet. Her.* 4.54.67. Cicero (*Orat.* 40.139) writes that the orator's "language will often have a significance deeper than his actual words." See Quint. *Inst.* 9.2.44,65.

"was crucified out of weakness, but [who] lives by the power of God" (13:4)?[269]

Both the *peristasis* catalogue and the account of the rapture experience are basically the result of anger and indignation. There is no other provocation than these strong emotions which could have elicited Paul's self-revelations as a rebuttal to the slanders hurled at him from those whose true σχῆμα he exposed a few verses earlier. Though his own σχῆμα is weak, yet he is full of power. Paul displays his anger in the use of certain rhetorical techniques within his self-revelations, such as: "he will fly into a passion and protest violently"; and "he will urge his point by asking questions and will reply to himself as if to questions."[270] This last figure is known as *hypophora*, which occurs when we ask "our adversaries, or ask ourselves, what the adversaries can say in their favour, or what can be said against us; then we subjoin what ought or ought not to be said—that which will be favourable to us or, by the same token, be

---

[269]The remarks in the text are based on a standard rhetorical technique known as "covert allusion" or "veiled meaning" which is discussed by Demetr. *Eloc.* 5.289-94, Quint. *Inst.* 9.1.4,27 (compare also 9.1.14; 8.6.44; 9.2.46,65) and other ancient theorists and investigated by Fitzgerald (*Cracks*, 119-22) and Benjamin Fiore (*The Function of Personal Example in the Socratic and Pastoral Epistles*, 171-75). These writers recognize that sometimes through this indirect method "we shall, rather, blame some other persons who have acted in the same manner. . . .[Thus] the hearer is admonished without feeling himself censured" (Demetr. *Eloc.* 5.292). In effect, Paul is obliquely admonishing the Corinthians about their fascination with the σχῆμα of an apostle by pointing out to them the value of the σχῆμα of the false apostles; it is satanic! While Paul is extremely angry with the false apostles, yet he seems to spare the feelings of the Corinthians by not drawing out the inevitable comparison. Yet the irony is there and the Corinthians certainly get the point. Throughout the analogy, Paul's main focus is to fill the Corinthians with the same anger he has toward the false apostles so that they will reject them as credible ministers.

[270]Cic. *Orat.* 40.137-38.

prejudicial to the opposition."[271]

Paul protests vehemently through asking and answering his own questions that he is everything that the false apostles are and more. He intends his boasting, forced out of him under the power of his emotions, to answer the slanderous insult that he is not an apostle of Christ. After the revelations, two things happen which indicate that his anger has been spent. First, he interjects two examples of his weakness (11:32; 12:7-9) as if to repent having boasted under the pressure of his emotions; and secondly, he calls himself a fool, ostensibly for letting his anger compel him to blurt out: "I am more" (11:23) and then to reveal some very personal experiences. He blames the Corinthians for what he just did: "You have driven me to it" (12:11), seemingly to imply that his indignation at the hurt of their betrayal forced him to an uncalculated boast. His rationalization of his outburst is an effective emotional argument to explain what he had earlier disavowed, namely recommending himself.

At the same time his explanation is a bitter reproachful lesson to the Corinthians for their obtuseness in not accepting the Jesus he preached (11:4), namely one whose $\sigma\chi\hat{\eta}\mu\alpha$ was weak but who now "lives by the power of God" (13:4). Paul's anger at the false apostles and the Corinthians is directed more to this last point than to his own injured pride. He sees the gospel of these false apostles as radically defective and profoundly detrimental to the Corinthians. Their "preaching another Jesus" is what infuriates Paul, for as Aristotle said

---

[271]*Rhet. Her.* 4.23.33.

"men are angry with those who speak ill of or despise things which they themselves consider of the greatest importance."[272] Paul wants the Corinthians to feel the same emotions so they can reject the false apostles. If this anger causes him against his principles to boast to bring the Corinthians back to their senses, then he will use any means whatsoever to arouse them to action.

The war-like imagery of 10:3-5 embodies Paul's anger at the λογισμοί and πᾶν ὕψωμα which threaten his gospel. The polemical tone is not merely the outward show for some intellectual confrontation but the result of fierce emotions aroused because Paul sees his opponents engaged in a campaign of discreditation of him and by association his message. His opponents accuse him of walking κατὰ σάρκα, a broad category for a host of alleged apostolic deficiencies in his conduct, a criticism he will not meekly acknowledge because its underlying reasoning shows a superiority which is antithetical to "the knowledge of God" (10:5). His wrath at this kind of attitude surfaces in his language with its military metaphors, like τὰ ὅπλα τῆς στρατείας . . . πρὸς καθαίρεσιν ὀχυρωμάτων, . . . καὶ πᾶν ὕψωα ἐπαιρόμενον . . ., καὶ αἰχμαλωτίζοντες πᾶν νόημα (10:4-6). There is no ironic propriety here at the beginning of the passage to soften the blow but only straightforward frontal emotional assault on a clear and present danger. Paul is angry at the invasion of his community and he is out to do battle with enemy rivals. Interestingly

---

[272]Arist. *Rh.* 2.2.13.

enough, as another way of showing his hostility, Paul regularly damns his rivals with anonymity.[273] His usual references to them are: "some" (10:2; 10:12), "themselves" (10:12), "such people" (11:13), "many" (11:18), "anyone" (11:20), and other non-specific references contained in verbs. Paul's object in this non-naming of his rivals is to reduce them in stature and thus create animosity toward them in the minds of the Corinthians.

Honor and shame were pivotal values in the first-century Mediterranean world.[274] Paul uses these values as well as the emotions associated with them in 2 Corinthians 10-13 to dislodge his opponents in the minds of the Corinthians. He does this mainly through a reversal of these values which ironically gives new definition to who really belongs to Christ, one of the major slanders against Paul's legitimacy as an apostle. In doing this, he fills them with appropriate shame in order to bring them to repentance. Concomitantly, he faults them for their injury to his honor as their benefactor, using shame once again as a way of repairing the breach. Paul accomplishes this through the use of emotional appeals.

What is honor? Malina describes it as "the value of a person in his or her own eyes (that is, one's claim to worth) *plus* that person's value in the eyes of

---

[273]Edwin Judge ("Paul's Boasting in Relation to Contemporary Professional Practice," in *AusBR* 16 [1968] 41) suggests this unique observation.

[274]See Bruce Malina, *The New Testament World: Insights from Cultural Anthropology* (Louisville: John Knox Press, 1981); J. G. Peristiany, ed., *Honour and Shame: The Values of Mediterranean Society* (Nature of Human Society Series; Chicago: University of Chicago Press, 1966).

his or her social group."[275] Honor is entitlement to status and social repute

which carries with it a reciprocity of rights and obligations in the community.

In other words, honor is a claim to worth with obligation toward approved

behavior on the part of the one honored and at the same time it is a conferral

of worth by the honoring group with an obligation toward specific treatment of

the honored person in return. An affront is a disruption of this dialectic, a

physical or social challenge to one's honor. The result is shame which is taken

positively as "sensitivity about what others think, say, and do with regard to his

or her honor."[276] Aristotle defines shame as "a kind of pain or uneasiness in

respect of misdeeds, past, present or future, which seem to tend to bring

dishonour; and shamelessness as contempt and indifference in regards to these

same things."[277] Shame can be an emotion in the person with the claim to

honor because the person exceeds social boundaries or it can be an emotion in

the group conferring the honor because the group has withheld appropriate

social treatment.

Paul attempts to bring the Corinthians to an awareness of shame. They

have affronted his honor. They have denied him their obedience to his

leadership, their commendation of his benefactions, and their submission to his

gospel. On all three counts Paul has been dishonored. Instead of seeking

---

[275]Malina, *New Testament World*, 27. I am indebted to his discussion of honor and shame in the paragraphs above.

[276]Ibid., 48.

[277]Arist. *Rh.* 2.6.2.

satisfaction for these affronts or challenges to his honor at the level of the false apostles whose actions have deprived him of his reputation, Paul makes a radical reassessment of what constitutes honor and shame. This has to do with his interpretation of weakness and power, God-recommendation and self-recommendation, boasting in the Lord and boasting in oneself. Paul seeks honor in those things which characteristically bring dishonor: weakness and powerlessness (11:30-33; 12:7-10). His belonging to Christ is predicated on weakness, mistreatment, distress, persecutions and difficulties (12:10), all of which he considers badges of honor. He sees dishonor in what is normal practice, namely boasting and self-recommendation. There is great irony in the fact that Paul almost always associates himself with ἀφροσύνη (11:1,16 [2 times],17,19,21,23 [παραφρονῶν]; 12:11) when it is a question of boasting of his accomplishments but he never uses this word when it is a question of boasting of his weaknesses, an indication that he has reversed the traditional categories of honor and shame of his day.[278] He articulates this for the instruction of the Corinthians when he says: "I will do no boasting about myself unless it be about my weaknesses" (12:5) and "I willingly boast of my weaknesses instead" (12:10). Paul will not go beyond the μέτρον τοῦ κανόνος (10:13) allotted by God (see also 10:18); this is honor. To do otherwise (10:12-15) is shameless.

---

[278]The only possible exception to this would be 12:6, where the object of boasting is rather ambiguous. The closest antecedent is the experience of the rapture. It seems Paul is here saying that he is telling the truth about his experience and if he does talk about it, it is only to state it as a fact, not to boast of it, even though he could.

He arouses shame in the Corinthians by reminding them of his benefactions and goodwill toward them, free of every exploitation, unlike the false apostles whom he accuses of caring not for the Corinthians but for their own self-aggrandizement. With sarcastic irony he tells the Corinthians: "To my shame I must confess that we have been too weak to do such things" (11:21). The reality is, he has shown them great honor in not abusing them but by lavishing on them his total self (12:15). He reminds them several times that he is intent on their upbuilding, not their destruction (10:8; 12:19; 13:8). He protests to them that he came far to preach the gospel of Christ to them (10:14); he preached the gospel to them free of charge, even though he had a right to support (11:7); he used the support from other churches to minister to them (11:8); he was never a financial burden to them all the time he was with them (11:9; 12:13,14,16); nor did he or any of his associates ever take advantage of them (12:17). Paul uses these examples of his time, energy, and money, material things, to define the services he has rendered to them on behalf of the gospel. He has been their benefactor who has spent himself (12:15) to build them up. More than just these material things, Paul points out to them the spiritual signs of his apostleship he performed among them, namely, the signs and wonders and deeds of power (12:12). As if these were not enough to prove his apostolic credentials and benevolence, he is forced to augment his list with "a few further claims about the power the Lord has given us for your upbuilding" (10:8), namely his catalogue of hardships (11:23-28) and the abundance of his revelations (12:7), chief among which was the extraordinary journey to the throne of God (12:1-4).

All these actions suggest a man of honor who has upheld his obligations as a *bona fide* apostle and, even more, has excelled at them. He has an entitlement, therefore, to certain specific group treatment, namely a recognition of his worth and authority and ultimately the honorable response of their obedience. However, the obedience of the Corinthians is not yet perfect (10:6) and their acknowledgment of Paul's status is deficient (12:11). Paul experiences insult and scorn at their lack of honorable behavior to an apostle of his proven repute. He is dishonored by their capitulation to apostles whom they see as better recommended and whose program of disparagement to deprive Paul of his reputation they have so heedlessly swallowed. On a human level and even more on a spiritual level, Paul cannot let this challenge to his honor go unmet, for it would mean a loss of his status and the consequent detraction of his gospel. He must restore his honor among the Corinthians. He does this through his emotional appeal of putting them in his own frame of mind regarding his shame, so that they can be persuaded to render their obedience to him as their genuine benefactor. For the Corinthians not to experience appropriate shame for their behavior toward their benefactor would mean that they are shameless people who have transgressed the boundaries of dignified and acceptable human social interaction. The implication is that they would be considered social pariahs. Even more, they would be spiritual outcasts for having dishonored an authentic minister of God.

Paul's emotional argument from honor and shame is carefully worded so as not to lose the goodwill of the Corinthians. The emotion of shame which is associated with dishonor must be handled judiciously, since it is an emotion that is experienced by people who esteem and admire each other.[279] That is why Paul, as a counterpoint emotional argument, uses frequent expressions of his love for the Corinthians to attenuate any abrasiveness in his persuasion in order not to alienate them. Aristotle defined loving as "wishing for anyone the things which we believe to be good, for his sake but not for our own, and procuring them for him as far as lies in our power."[280] Aristotle associates this kind of loving with friendship. Paul attempts to show the Corinthians that he is their friend who loves them and wants to be loved in return. Aristotle says loving friends are

> . . . those who have done good either to us or to those whom we hold dear, if the services are important, or are cordially rendered, or under certain circumstances, and for our sake only; and all those whom we think desirous of doing us good. . . . who are liberal and courageous and just. . . . who do not live upon others; . . . who live by their exertions; . . . those who work with their own hands. . . . those who are strongly attached to their friends and do not leave them in the lurch. . . . those who do not dissemble with them; such are those who do not fear to

---

[279]As Aristotle (*Rh*. 2.6.14-15) writes: "And since no one heeds the opinion of others except on account of those who hold it, it follows that men feel shame before those whom they esteem. Now men esteem those who admire them and those whom they admire, those by whom they wish to be admired . . ."

[280]Arist. *Rh*. 2.4.1-2.

mention even their faults.[281]

Paul expresses many of these qualities of loving friendship to the Corinthians. He has brought them the gospel of Christ (10:14); he has exalted them at his own expense and that of other churches (11:7); he has loved them as God is his witness (11:11); he has been intent on their development (12:19; 13:10); he has sacrificed himself for their sakes (12:15); he has never taken advantage of them (12:17) but has been a selfless parent (12:14); he has not been afraid to point out their faults (12:20) or threaten them with punishment (13:2); he has challenged them to live the powerful life of Christ in them (13:3).

Paul articulates these feelings of deep love for the Corinthians to persuade them that he has only their best interests at heart, that he is their faithful friend who has always acted with unselfish love toward them. With characteristic ironic wit, he asks whether too much love on his part is a reason for less love on theirs (12:15). By way of contrast, he shows the Corinthians that the false apostles are not loving friends of theirs. They practice deceit toward them (11:13); they humiliate and take unfair advantage of them (11:20); they cast their superiority in their faces by their arrogant boasting (10:12; 11:12); they corrupt them with an adulterated gospel (11:3-4); they maltreat and slander Paul, their best benefactor (12:11-12). Through these negative emotions of love which he heaps on the false apostles, Paul intends to put the Corinthians in his own frame of mind toward them. At the same time, Paul is not afraid to tell

---

[281]Arist. *Rh.* 2.4.5-30.

the Corinthians that he is jealous of their love in the way God is jealous in a covenantal relationship (11:2), an aspect of Paul's love that will accept only unconditional allegiance to his person and gospel. Such great love, matched by deeds of power (his catalogue of hardships, his rapture experience and numerous other revelations), the false apostles would have a hard time emulating.

There is another major emotion which Paul utilizes to persuade the Corinthians and that is the emotion of fear. Aristotle defines fear as "a pained or troubled feeling caused by the impression of an imminent evil that causes destruction or pain." The evil must involve great pain and must be near at hand and threatening. Even "the signs of such misfortunes are fearful, for the fearful thing itself appears to be near at hand."[282] Paul expresses his fearful feelings for the Corinthians several times. His greatest fear is that they "may fall away from [their] sincere and complete devotion to Christ" (11:3) by listening to the false apostles. This would be the greatest of all possible evils; for it would nullify the reason why he came so far to preach to them (10:14) and why he endures all his hardships; it would also signify the failure of faith in the Corinthians to meet the challenge of the gospel of Jesus crucified in weakness but living now by the power of God (13:4). His other fears are of an ethical and a personal nature (12:20-21).

He projects fear in the Corinthians by severe warnings that when he comes to them this third time he will not spare them (13:2); he is ready to act boldly

---

[282]Arist. *Rh.* 22.5.1-15.

(10:2) and punish disobedience (10:6) with a militant use of God's spiritual weapons (10:4-5); and last, he is afraid he may not find them to his liking (12:20), so that he may have to confront them with the severity of the Lord's authority (13:10). He wants them to realize that his imminent coming will threaten some bold action on his part to redress the slanders against him and bring the Corinthians to obedience, something the Corinthians only feared from the remote words of his letters (10:11). One of the most cogent appeals to fear is the seed of doubt Paul instills in their minds, as he ends the letter, whether they have passed the test of faith or not. To fail this challenge of realizing that the weak, crucified Christ dwells in them is to face the wrath of God (13:5-7). Paul's strategy is to persuade the Corinthians by the emotional impetus of fear to beware of toying with his gospel and slighting his authority.

Paul's emotional appeals show up in his wit, the essence of which, as Quintilian writes, "lies in the distortion of the true and natural meaning of words."[283] Paul's wit is not primarily meant to create laughter but to be a conduit for his emotional commentary on the behavior of the false apostles and the Corinthians. There is, first of all, Paul's play on the word ἀνέχεσθαι. He compliments them mockingly on the fact that they are experts on putting up with things. Their main affinity, however, is for fools and foolishness! They endure the false apostles καλῶς (11:4) and ἡδέως (11:19), Paul says; certainly the Corinthians can endure his μικρόν (11:1; compare 11:16) as well. Paul's

---

[283]Quint. *Inst.* 6.3.90.

sarcastic observation operates on several emotional levels. He is angered that the Corinthians can so readily endure some other gospel when they can't pledge allegiance to the one he brought them (11:4). He expresses mock pity at the "sufferings" they are called upon to endure for this "gospel" (11:19). To show his indignation, Paul makes a pretense of weakness to deride their "wisdom" in enduring the claims of the false apostles (11:21). In this entire play on words and behavior, Paul burlesques the "boasts" of the false apostles which are no deeds of power at all and he pokes fun at the Corinthians for their misguided masochism.

As the foregoing analysis demonstrates, Paul has assembled a very powerful argument from πάθος. Through his letter he has managed to ignite in the Corinthians his own emotions of anger and ill will toward the false apostles, his feelings of hurt and insult resulting from slander and rejection, his sentiments of love for the Corinthians and fear for their spiritual health, and his passionate warnings about seeking the authentic criteria for approval, all with the object of persuading them to accept unconditionally his leadership and his gospel. Paul has used another critical proof urged by the rhetoricians for swaying an audience, namely that of putting his listeners into his own frame of mind. With this proof, delivery is all-important for documenting the effect on an audience, but it is impossible to recapture that rhetorical moment in which this letter was first spoken to the Corinthians. However, were this letter delivered by a competent actor today in front of an audience primed with the background of slander and rejection, one would be able to hear yet the emotional appeals of Paul to the Corinthians to accept him and his gospel. The effect on the Corinthians would be like a second conversion.

CHAPTER FOUR

ΛΟΓΟΣ : RHETORICAL REASONING

A. The Definition and Nature of Λόγος

"Lastly," as Aristotle writes, "persuasion is produced by the speech itself, in so far as it proves or seems to prove."[284] By this he means the last and most important of the three entechnic πίστεις, namely the λόγος of an argument, its rhetorical reasoning.[285] This type of reasoning is based on probable proofs and makes use of the two important instruments of all logical thinking, namely syllogism and induction. However, rhetorical reasoning is different from analytical reasoning which is based on scientific demonstration (ἀπόδειξις) containing evident and necessary propositions (or necessary signs which are called τεκμήρια) and leading to certain and inescapable conclusions.[286] Rhetorical reasoning is not a strict science. It is a δύναμις, a faculty or art of demonstrating the true or apparently true on any given

---

[284]Arist. *Rh.* 1.2.5.

[285]Apparently Spengel (Grimaldi, *Aristotle, Rhetoric II*, 5) saw λόγος as the only real entechnic proof and the other two as accidental or "as effective instruments of rhetorical argument not so much in themselves but as helpful means when faced with the stupidity of the auditors!"

[286] Arist. *Rh.* 1.2.17.

subject. As Cope writes, it "leads to no more certain result than $\pi\acute{\iota}\sigma\tau\iota\varsigma$, belief, a mode of conviction produced by the persuasion ($\tau\hat{\wp}$ $\pi\epsilon\acute{\iota}\theta\epsilon\iota\nu$) of the speaker."[287] It has propositions known as rhetorical syllogisms (or enthymemes) but very few of them are necessary; for, as Aristotle writes, "most of the things which we judge and examine can be other than they are." In other words, the material or subject of one's deliberation and examination in these propositions, namely human actions, will for the most part be only generally true or probable.[288] Even though the arguments and proofs used in rhetorical reasoning make it only a quasi-demonstration ($\grave{\alpha}\pi\acute{o}\delta\epsilon\iota\xi\acute{\iota}\varsigma$ $\tau\iota\varsigma$), yet the belief it produces may be more telling and powerful in the long run for judgment and action than a strict scientific demonstration which has intellectual appeal but may have little emotional power. The arrangement or disposition of the arguments in the rhetorical act is called the $\lambda\acute{o}\gamma o\varsigma$ by which the orator proves or seems to prove the issue at hand.

The understanding of rhetorical reasoning becomes clearer when the two fundamental ways in which all knowledge is acquired and conveyed are cited, namely the syllogism and induction. In their rhetorical form, Aristotle postulated the enthymeme as the syllogism and the example as induction. "Now," as Aristotle writes, "all orators produce belief by employing as proofs

---

[287]Cope, *Introduction to Aristotle's Rhetoric*, 142. See 67-99 for the relations and differences between scientific demonstration, dialectics, and rhetoric.

[288]Arist. *Rh.* 1.2.14.

either examples or enthymemes and nothing else."[289]   An example

(παράδειγμα) is proof from a single or limited number of particular cases from

which a universal rule is inferred.   An enthymeme is a proof from contingent

premises, one of which is unexpressed but understood, based on human actions

and motives resulting in probable conclusions.   Aristotle says that enthymemes

meet with greater approval, while arguments that depend on examples are less

likely to persuade.   Rhetorical speeches are characterized by the use of one or

the other or both, depending on what the orator sees as persuasive.   Again,

generally speaking, both the enthymeme and the example deal in probability,

drawing conclusions about what normally but not unreservedly happens.   Unlike

the irrefutable arguments of scientific logical demonstration, the enthymeme and

the example deal in matters that may be other than they are.   Both are

imperfect: the enthymeme because it omits one of its premises and the example

because it is satisfied with one or two instances, in contrast to true induction

which investigates all known examples, from which it makes a universal

statement.   There is then no absolute certainty to the conclusions drawn from

these two modes of the λόγος, only various degrees of probability.

Aristotle first treats of example which he says "resembles induction, and

induction is a beginning."[290]   It is the ἀρχή of syllogism, which basically

---

[289]Arist. *Rh.* 1.2.7-8 says: "Accordingly I call an enthymeme a rhetorical syllogism and an example rhetorical induction."

[290]Arist. *Rh.* 2.20.2.   See the following studies on example in ancient rhetorical theory: Bennett J. Price, *Paradeigma and Exemplum in Ancient Rhetorical Theory* (Ph.D diss., University of California at Berkeley, 1975); Benjamin Fiore, *The Function*

states a fundamental precept in any attainment of knowledge, namely, as Grimaldi succinctly puts it, "that while the mind cannot know the individual but only the universal the only way the intellect can reach the universal is through the particular."[291] This is to say that induction affords the evidence for the making of premises. Aristotle goes on to say that there are two kinds of examples: "namely, one which consists in relating things that have happened before, and another in inventing them oneself."[292] Another way of saying this is that the example is either real-historical based on past events ($\pi\rho\acute{\alpha}\gamma\mu\alpha\tau\alpha$ $\pi\rho o\gamma\epsilon\gamma\epsilon\nu\eta\mu\acute{\epsilon}\nu\alpha$) with real people or fictitious in which one invents a similar instance. The latter, a rather imaginative stretch of the meaning of induction, is subdivided into comparisons ($\pi\alpha\rho\alpha\beta o\lambda\acute{\eta}$) and fables ($\lambda\acute{o}\gamma o\iota$). In all three cases likeness is the key word; they are based on analogy.

Aristotle gives a case of an historical example which Grimaldi has lucidly symbolized:

> We have two statements of the same order . . . with one more familiar and accepted as true. The more familiar is used to establish the less familiar, or as [Aristotle] says, the major term

---

of Personal Example in the Socratic and Pastoral Epistles; K. Alewell, *Über das rhetorische PARADEIGMA: Verwendung in der römischen Literatur der Kaizerzeit* (Leipzig: A. Hoffman, 1913); H. Kornhardt, *Exemplum: eine bedeutungs-geschichtliche Studie* (Göttingen: Robert Noske, 1936); A. Lumpe, "Exemplum," *RAC* 6:1229-57; J. Martin, *Antike Rhetorik: Technik und Methodie* (Münich: C. H. Beck, 1974). Most of the above authors cite the thinking of the major Greco-Roman rhetorical theorists, historians, and orators regarding the nature and uses of example in education, oratory, and life.

[291]Grimaldi, *Aristotle, Rhetoric II*, 250.

[292]Arist. *Rh.* 2.20.2.

(A) is shown to be applicable to the middle term (B) by means of a term similar to the minor term (C). Thus if we wish to show that C is A, we can do so through the example D which is like C since both have the attribute B. But we also know that D has the attribute A. Therefore D is A, D is B, and so B is A (thus the major term belongs to the middle which is shown by way of D). Then: B is A; C (as we already know) is B; so C is A.[293]

This explanation will be helpful in exploring Paul's analogy regarding the false apostles in 2 Cor 11:13-15 Grimaldi goes on to say that arguments from example, whether historical or fictitious, "can move only from particular to particular in the same class and one particular must be better known and accepted." This is basically what Aristotle says about the induction-like aspect of example: "It is neither the relation of part to whole, nor of whole to part, nor of one whole to another whole, but of part to part, when both come under the same genus, but one of them is better known than the other."[294]

The first of the fabricated examples is comparison, a similitude or likeness borrowed from some other source to illustrate the point in question. The speaker sometimes invents an extended metaphor or simile from everyday real life as an analogy to the main point of the argument, expressing the comparison conjecturally, as Aristotle says in his expression ὅμοιον γάρ ὥσπερ ἂν εἰ τις ("for this would be the same as").[295] By way of contrast, the fable or tale is

---

[293]Grimaldi, *Aristotle, Rhetoric II*, 250.

[294]Arist. *Rh.* 1.2.19. Arguing from particular to particular results in a universal proposition, which, as has been repeatedly mentioned, is always open to objection since the process is built on probability. It is, in other words, an imperfect induction. Aristotle gives here a very good illustration of argumentation from example.

[295]Arist. *Rh.* 2.20.4.

not made up but taken from already existing literary works of poets, philosophers, and orators and used as proofs because of their common-sense sound of wisdom. This category would include the fables and tales of Aesop and Stesichorus mentioned by Aristotle.[296]

After this brief discussion on the invented examples, Aristotle goes on to say that if there are no enthymemes to employ for demonstrative proofs, then examples should be used, "for conviction is produced by these." However, if enthymemes are available, then they should be used first, since they meet with greater approval, and then examples can be used in corroboration: "For if they [examples] stand first, they resemble induction, and induction is not suitable to rhetorical speeches except in a very few cases; if they stand last they resemble evidence, and a witness is in every case likely to induce belief."[297]

---

[296]Grimaldi (*Aristotle, Rhetoric II*, 251-52) has an interesting brief historical overview of the fable, in which he quotes Theon (2nd century C.E.) as defining a fable as "a fictitious story picturing a truth." Cope (*Introduction to Aristotle's Rhetoric*, 254-56) gives further information. Aristotle (*Rh.* 2.20.5-6) gives a wonderful example of a fable from Stesichorus, who related the following fable to the people of Himera who had chosen Phalaris as dictator and were on the point also of giving him a bodyguard: "A horse was in sole occupation of a meadow. A stag having come and done much damage to the pasture, the horse, wishing to avenge himself on the stag, asked a man whether he could help him to punish the stag. The man consented, on condition that the horse submitted to the bit and allowed him to mount him javelins in hand. The horse agreed to the terms and the man mounted him, but instead of obtaining vengeance on the stag, the horse from that time became the man's slave." The moral of the story is: "Do you take care lest in your desire to avenge yourselves on the enemy, you be treated like the horse. You already have the bit, since you have chosen a dictator; if you give him a body-guard and allow him to mount you, you will at once be the slaves of Phalaris." Aristotle gives a further story from Aesop which serves as an excellent example of how a speaker can use a fable to argue a point.

[297]Arist. *Rh.* 2.20.9. Grimaldi (*Aristotle, Rhetoric II*, 257) quotes Spengel who illustrates this point by citing Arist. *[Pr.]* 916b 25ff: "Why are men more happy with examples and fables in speeches than with enthymemes? Is it because they rejoice both

The importance of παράδειγμα for Aristotle as an instrument in persuading others needs to be emphasized at this point, for its use is much more than an incidental ornament in an argument. In two places he says that examples, particularly the historical ones, are useful, especially in deliberative oratory, for it is by an "examination of the past that we divine and judge the future."[298] Example for Aristotle, therefore, functions demonstratively, on the basis of "the relative constancy of human behavior," to render "the repetition of the same behavior in analogous circumstances probable." In other words, as Carlo Natali continues, "the example serves to argue that a certain X is Y, inasmuch as it formulates, beginning from the example, a universal law of which X is a particular case."[299] A solidly probable deduction is made based on inferences from the past. In one sense, Aristotle is in agreement with the words of

---

in learning and in learning quickly? People in fact do learn more quickly through examples and fables. For those are things which they know and which are particular. But enthymemes are demonstrations from universals which we know less than the particular. Furthermore we place more trust in that for which there are several witnesses, and examples and fables are like witnesses; again, proofs by means of witnesses are more easy to come by. Further, too, men perceive likeness with pleasure and examples and fables show forth likeness."

[298]Arist. *Rh.* 1.9.40 and 2.20.8.

[299]Carlo Natali, "Paradeigma: The Problems of Human Acting and the Use of Examples in Some Greek Authors of the 4th Century B. C.," *RSQ* 19, 2 (Spring 1989) 141-152. Quotations are from 144. His article is somewhat opaque so that it is difficult to follow his thesis: to study the "origin of the *paradeigma* (in Latin: *exemplum*) from the problems of acting in practice, and its nature, not only as an instrument to be used in persuading others, but also as an instrument of use in finding a line of conduct" (142). In pursuit of his unique thesis, Natali investigates Aristotle's philosophical approach to example in which he "studies the reason for its validity, the mechanism of its functioning from a logical point of view, and the nature of the understanding to which it gives place" (143).

Isocrates who protreptically advises about the future in the following words taken from his *To Demonicus* 34: "When you are deliberating, regard things which have happened as examples of what will happen. For the unknown may be learned most quickly from the known."[300] In another sense, Aristotle goes beyond mere protreptics to the importance example has for argumentation and it is this philosophical analysis which makes his approach unique. As Natali writes:

> Aristotle . . . does not limit himself to advising us about the use of examples, but throws light onto what they are ('a sort of induction'), on how they function ('from particular to particular, passing through the universal'), and on what kind of knowledge is derived from them ('a particular and practical conclusion, that is an indication of concrete acting').[301]

More will be said below about the theory and use of example in other Greco-Roman writers. Here it is sufficient to point out in Aristotle's discussion of example the emphasis he places on its inductive quality and his recognition of the importance of the universal proposition.

Next Aristotle goes into a long discussion of maxims, about which a few words should be said since it has relevance to the rhetorical purposes of 2 Corinthians 10-13. Aristotle associates maxims, not with examples or another type of proverbial story which proceed inductively, but with enthymemes. His reasoning is quite simple. Since maxims do not concern particulars but "with

---

[300]This quotation is taken from George Kennedy, *The Art of Persuasion in Greece* (Princeton: Princeton University Press, 1963), 98.

[301]Natali, "Paradeigma," 147.

the objects of human actions, and with what should be chosen or avoided with reference to them" and since enthymemes deal with such things, maxims, therefore, "are the premises or conclusions of enthymemes without the syllogism."[302] Aristotle describes four kinds of maxims, depending on whether they have an epilogue or not. If the maxims are either clear as soon as they are uttered or else well-known and their content generally agreed on, they need no epilogue or additional demonstrative proof. On the other hand, as Aristotle writes, "in the case of matters of dispute or what is contrary to the general opinion, the epilogue is necessary," meaning that additional proofs are necessary. The latter needing an explanation are called either part of an enthymeme or enthymematic in character. Aristotle closes his discussion of maxims by saying that they add to the moral character of the speaker because if the maxims are good they show the speaker's moral preferences.

Following his discussion of example or rhetorical induction, Aristotle speaks of the other and more important half of rhetorical reasoning, namely enthymemes and their topics ($\tau \acute{o} \pi o \iota$), both the particular and the common topics. Enthymemes are truncated syllogisms, which means, first of all as stated above, that their premises and conclusions are never more than probable; and

---

[302]Arist. *Rh.* 2.21.1-2. See the entire discussion until 2.21.21. See also Grimaldi, *Aristotle, Rhetoric II*, 259-64, and Cope, *Introduction to Aristotle's Rhetoric*, 257-60 for commentary. Aristotle (*[Rh. Al.]* 11) writes: "A maxim may be summarily defined as the expression of an individual opinion about general matters of conduct."

secondly, that not all the premises are explicitly stated.[303] This latter point he

makes quite clear when he writes that the enthymeme, as a kind of syllogism,

is "deduced from few premises, often from fewer than the regular

syllogism."[304] The missing premise, and sometimes the conclusion, is

supplied by the listeners. A long series of arguments, Aristotle said, causes

obscurity and is simply a waste of words.[305] In fact, as he says in a later

context, those syllogisms are especially applauded where the hearer can

anticipate the conclusion as soon as the syllogism is begun, not because they are

superficial but because they are so understandable.[306] There are two kinds

of enthymemes: the demonstrative which "proves that a thing is or is not" and

"draws conclusions from admitted premises" [that is, admitted by the opponent];

---

[303]Aristotle (*Rh.* 1.2.9) defines the rhetorical syllogism in the following words: "When, certain things being posited, something different results by reason of them, alongside of them, from their being true, either universally or in most cases, such a conclusion in Dialectic is called a syllogism, in Rhetoric an enthymeme."

[304]Arist. *Rh.* 1.2.13.

[305]Arist. *Rh.* 2.21.3. An example of an enthymeme from the New Testament would be the Beatitudes from Matt 5:3-12. Jesus presupposes a missing premise which his listeners can supply. For instance, Jesus says: "Blessed are the poor in spirit: the reign of God is theirs." Here the missing but understood premise is: Blessed are those who possess the reign of God. Another good example is in John 9:33 where the blind man says: "If this man were not from God, he could never have done such a thing." His missing but implied first premise is: Only God can cure a person blind from birth (as implied in the man's previous sentence: "It is unheard of that anyone every gave sight to a person blind from birth"). The full argument following this first premise would be: This man cured me, a man blind from birth. Therefore, this man must be (from) God.

[306]Arist. *Rh.* 2.23.30.

and the refutative which "draws conclusions disputed by the adversary."[307]

At this point Aristotle launches into an examination of the τόποι of enthymemes. He is concerned here with what are known as the κοινοὶ τόποι, the common or general topics that have to do with the form of the inference, the so-called τόποι ἐνθυμημάτων or στοιχεῖα ἐνθυμημάτων.[308] Aristotle is not discussing here the special or particular τόποι which were earlier called εἴδη, which have to do with the content or material aspects of an enthymeme and which he had used as a methodology to develop statements for λόγος, ἦθος, πάθος.[309] Aristotle's interest here is in the common topics which are universally applicable to all arguments of all sciences.[310] The word *topic*, the

---

[307]Arist. *Rh.* 2.22.14-15.

[308]Aristotle (*Rh.* 2.22.13) writes: "Let us now speak of the elements of enthymemes (by element and topic of enthymeme I mean the same thing)."

[309]Aristotle's use of the particular topics had already been treated in 1.4-2.17. The study of the particular or special topics for ἦθος had been done in 2.12-17 and for πάθος in 2.2-11 and for λόγος in 1.4-15. The distinction between the special and the common τόποι is an important one but should not overly detain us here, since we are interested in the common topics and their formal (not material, as in the case of the special topics) disposition in the argument. The εἴδη or ἴδια, the specific topics, are those, as Aristotle said in 1.2.21, which are "peculiar to each species or genus of things"; or as he says in 1.2.22: "By specific topics I mean the propositions peculiar to each class of things." In other words, the special topics deal with the contents or material aspects confined specifically, for example, to physics or ethics or other sciences but not applicable across the board. For a revival of special topical theory in modern dress, see Carolyn Miller, "Aristotle's 'Special Topics' in Practice and Pedagogy," *RSQ* 17,1 (Winter 1987) 61-70.

[310]Friedrich Solmsen ("The Aristotelian Tradition in Ancient Rhetoric," in *Rhetorika: Schriften zur aristotelischen und hellenistischen Rhetorik* [ed. Rudolph Stark; Hildesheim, Georg Olms, 1968], 317-318) writes that the instructional system before Aristotle's taught the τόποι as nothing more than ready-made arguments on particular subjects, something after the fashion of models. Aristotle likened it to teaching an apprentice the art of shoe-making by giving the student a good number of ready-made

element of the enthymemes, is basically a source to go for arguments, a

storehouse of ready-to-use propositions as rhetorical arguments, a place of basic

rules for formulating self-evident and general principles applicable to all arts and

sciences. Aristotle describes τόπος as a head or class under which many

enthymemes are included.[311] There are 28 topics or types of argument which

Aristotle cites as useful for demonstrative or refutative enthymemes. As

Grimaldi puts it: "In brief the topics are seen by him [Aristotle] as varied, self-

evident, and general logical categories which enable one to refute or remonstrate

---

shoes but no blueprint on how to make them. Solmsen goes on to write: "[Aristotle] replaces this method by an altogether different system of τόποι, conceiving the τόπος as a 'type' or 'form' of argument of which you need grasp only the basic structural idea to apply it forthwith to discussions about any and every subject. Once you have grasped the τόπος of the 'More and Less' you will be able to argue: If not even the gods know everything, human beings will certainly not know everything; or, Whoever beats his father will certainly also beat his neighbors; or to form any other argument of the same kind, always proceeding from the less likely thing (which has nevertheless occurred) to the more likely. What matters in this system is the 'form' of the argument, this being perfectly independent of any particular subject-matter or content."

[311]Aris. *Rh.* 2.26.1. This is about the clearest definition Aristotle gives. Various other metaphors are used by Cicero and Quintilian to express this "source" quality of the κοινοὶ τόποι. Cicero (*De Or.* 2.34.146-47) has his interlocutor, Antonius, speak of "stock of cases and types . . . from which to dig out our proofs"; or "the ground over which you are to chase and track down your quarry"; or further on (162) "that source where no sequestered pool is land-locked, but from it bursts forth a general flood; to that teacher who will point out to him the very homes of all proofs. . ."; or (174) the commonplaces are imaged as veins of gold in the ground where the diligent digger can reveal the precious metal. Cicero (2.30.130) in the same work further explains the common topics as an alphabet; "For just as, whenever we have some word to write, we need not search out its component letters by hard thinking," so we should have "in readiness sundry commonplaces which will instantly present themselves for setting forth the case, as the letters do for writing the word." Cicero (*Part. Or.* 1.5) has one of his speakers call them "pigeonholes in which arguments are stored." Quint. *Inst.* 5.10.20-22 has some particularly apt metaphors: localities and haunts where one can find a particular bird or beast, or regions and shores where one can find various kinds of fish.

effectively and to do so with strong probability."[312] After he discusses each

of the 28 topics on real enthymemes, Aristotle devotes a chapter on the 9 τόποι

of apparent enthymemes or false inferences, which are divided into fallacies

based on language and those independent of language.[313]

It would be fruitless and redundant at this point to enumerate and discuss

each of the 28 τόποι for real enthymemes and the 9 for apparent enthymemes,

since we shall be selecting the major ones for explanation with appropriate

examples in the next two sections of this chapter. There various classical

speakers and Paul in his rebuttal to the Corinthians will illustrate the character

of the individual τόπος in the context of its oratorical usage.

Before leaving Aristotle's discussion of enthymemes, one should note the

importance he attaches to their use as proof in persuasive speech. Aristotle

considers enthymemes as the σῶμα τῆς πίστεως as well as the κυριώτατον τῶν

---

[312]Grimaldi, *Aristotle, Rhetoric II*, 293. Donald L. Clark (*Rhetoric in Greco-Roman Education*, 78) says that in his *Topics* Aristotle "treats hundreds of sources of arguments. Cicero in his own treatise on logic, the *Topica*, simplified the topics under seventeen main heads and many subdivisions."

[313]Thanks to Grimaldi (*Aristotle, Rhetoric II*, 338) for this distinction which is somewhat unclear in Aristotle, who uses παρὰ τὴν λέξιν for the verbal fallacies but has no comparable phrase for the fallacies not dependent on language. Grimaldi seems to coin the phrase ἔξω τῆς λέξεως for those false enthymemes "grounded on principles which result in false inference." Grimaldi (337) makes the thoughtful comment about Aristotle's apparent enthymemes: "This study of the sources of false enthymematic reasoning is not at all in aid of the technique of deception as a positive factor in rhetorical discourse. On the contrary it is an effort to unmask false reasoning on the part of others." He quotes Aristotle in his *Sophistici Elenchi* 165a 24-27: "It is the task of one who has knowledge about a thing to speak the truth about what he knows, and to be able to expose the individual who makes false statements."

πίστεων,[314] the most powerful of rhetorical arguments. As Georgiana Palmer has noted: "To be ἐνθυμηματικός (skilled in the handling of enthymemes) he [Aristotle] regards as the most important achievement for an orator and criticizes other writers on rhetoric for their neglecting this type of training."[315] However, there are certain precautions in the use of enthymemes. First, the speaker should not overuse them lest the speech become dry; and secondly, the speaker should never use an enthymeme to arouse emotion, because of a conflict of movements, nor to express one's ethical character, since this is not the function of demonstration.[316]

As for Aristotle's τόποι, Palmer states that "his classification as a whole did not meet with general acceptance." How else to explain Cicero's and Quintilian's acceptance of "his terminology and types only about a third of the time," considering "their strong understanding and knowledge of oratory together with their reverence for Aristotle." She reasons that they "would have kept more closely to this classification had it more closely corresponded to oratorical usage." What is more inexplicable, Cicero and Quintilian did not

---

[314]Arist. *Rh.* 1.1.3 and 11.

[315]Georgiana Paine Palmer, *The* τόποι *of Aristotle's Rhetoric as Exemplified in the Orators* (Ph.D. diss., University of Chicago; Chicago, IL, 1934) 3. See Arist. *Rh.* 1.1.3. Palmer's dissertation which discusses each of the 28 τόποι of Aristotle and gives numerous examples from ten Attic orators was of invaluable help in the next two sections of this chapter.

[316]Arist. *Rh.* 3.17.8.

retain some of the types most commonly used by orators.[317] Even though the classifications in various rhetoricians were different, the major τόποι were nonetheless widely used.[318]

Turning now to Cicero and Quintilian, we find a different terminology and typology for Aristotle's enthymeme. It is now called an epicheireme and its usual form has at least four or five premises as opposed to Aristotle's single premise and a conclusion.[319] We may pass over any more discussion of this difference as academic and not really germane to our subject and go on to say a few words about the τόποι in these two rhetorical theorists who give the name "loci communes" to Aristotle's term. According to Cope, "the communes loci of Cicero and Quintilian and the Latin Rhetoricians seem to be more comprehensive, and capable of a more extensive application" than those of Aristotle.[320] Even so, there seems to be a fluctuation in their thoughts

---

[317]Georgiana Palmer, *Aristotle's* τόποι, 2 and 82.

[318]Josef Martin (*Antike Rhetorik*, 110-119) gives the different classifications of the topics from Neocles (by way of Anonymous Seguerianus), Cicero, Quintilian, Apsines, Minucianus (with 33 τόποι). Grimaldi (*Aristotle, Rhetoric II*, 292) cites in addition Themistius' (ca. 320-380 C.E.) analysis and classification from Book 2 of Boethius' *De topicis differentiis* and that of Maximus Planudus (see Spengel, *Rhetores Graeci*, 5.404ff.).

[319]See Cic. *Inv. Rhet.* 1.34.57-41.77 and Quint. *Inst.* 5.14.5-23. Cicero does discuss Aristotle's tripartite system but finds the five-parts division more suitable, mainly because he feels each premise needs to be proved. Solmsen ("Aristotelian Tradition in Rhetoric," 329, n.66) has references on the discussion of enthymeme and epicheireme in various classical theorists.

[320]See Cope, *Introduction to Aristotle's Rhetoric*, 130. George Kennedy (*The Art of Persuasion in Greece* [Princeton: Princeton University Press, 1963], 102) writes: "None of Aristotle's topics should be confused with *loci communes*, those commonplaces or expanded formulae which were a leading aspect of the knack of

between the *loci communes* as synonymous at times with Aristotle's conception

of τόποι and at other times with the pre-Aristotelian type of ready-made

arguments on the most common and general subjects.[321]   This intricate

discussion need not detain us here since we will be interested only in certain

individual τόποι with examples in the following two sections.

The use of example in Cicero, Quintilian, and other Greco-Roman

rhetoricians offers some interesting additions to Aristotle's treatment.   One is

the notion of negative examples first introduced in the *Rhetorica ad Alexandrum*,

where the author states that the speaker should point out actions occurring

against reasonable expectations which cause incredulity and can discredit advice

---

oratory as taught by the sophists. The conclusion of the *Sophistical refutations* shows
that Aristotle was well aware of the existence of these, but they were unscientific and,
thus, play no part in his theory.   Conversely, the topics of Aristotle were not,
apparently, recognized as such by any of the orators; although they use many of the
arguments he classifies, they do not apply any collective term to them."   This last
thought seems to agree with Georgiana Palmer's statement above.

[321]Cope (*Introduction to Aristotle's Rhetoric*, 130-31) and Solmsen ("Aristotelian
Tradition in Ancient Rhetoric," 330-35) have good discussions of the meaning of *loci
communes* and their contrast with the τόποι of Aristotle.   Cope (130) writes that "it
seems that any subject or topic of a general character, that is capable of bring variously
applied and constantly introduced on any appropriate occasion, is a locus communis."
Quoting Bacon (*de Augm. Scient.* Lib. v. c.3), Cope (131) equates Cicero *loci
communes* with the *Promptuaria* or "stock of ready-made arguments and speeches upon
the most common subjects of controversy."   Cope uses Cicero (*Brut.* 12.46-47) as
evidence for this, where Cicero states that this meaning of commonplaces goes back to
Protagoras and Gorgias. See the following for sorting out this distinction as well as the
meaning of *loci communes* and examples: Cic. *Orat.* 36.126; Cic. *De Or.* 3.27.106-7;
Cic. *Inv. Rhet.* 2.16.50; *Rhet. Her.* 2.3.5; 9.13; 10.14; 15.22; 16.24; 17.26; 30.48-9;
Quint. *Inst.* 5.10.23-52; 5.10.53. Solmsen (332, n.74) makes the interesting comment:
"It is generally and probably rightly assumed that Cicero borrows the *loci* of the *De
orat.* (and similarly those included in the *Topica* and the *Part. orat.*) from a
contemporary Academic system which in turn shows Stoic influence. . . . From our
point of view, however, the immediate source of Cicero's *loci* is less important than the
fact that he reverts to Aristotle's method."

that is based on probability. Likewise the speaker should employ example in general to illustrate one's case, "in order that your audience may be more ready to believe your statements when they realize that another action resembling the one you allege has been committed in the way in which you say that it has occurred."[322] Both of these statements will be useful in interpreting Paul's negative example of the false apostles as ministers of Satan.

In the *Rhetorica ad Herennium* the author talks of *similitudo* (comparison) which is defined as "a manner of speech that carries over an element of likeness from one thing to a different thing," used, among others, in the form of contrast and negation. The author also speaks of *exemplum* which is "the citing of something done or said in the past, along with the definite naming of the doer or author," for the same motives as comparison above. The author also makes note of simile (*imago*) which is "the comparison of one figure with another, implying a certain resemblance between them."[323]

Cicero defines an *exemplum* as that which "supports or weakens a case by appeal to precedent or experience, citing some person or historical event."[324]

---

[322]Arist. *[Rh. Al.]* 8. See also 14.

[323]*Rhet. Her.* 4.49.59-62. The notion of *exemplum* corresponds to Aristotle's παράδειγμα; that of *similitudo* to παραβολή; that of simile to his εἰκών in *Rh.* 3.4 where he discusses it as a point of style. Quintilian (*Inst.* 5.24) advises that this kind of comparison "should be more sparingly used in oratory than those comparisons which help to prove our point, although a few lines before he remarked that "*simile* has a force not unlike that of *example*." His caution is probably based on the fact, as he says, that it is "always possible to be misled by appearances in the use of similes."

[324]Cic. *Inv. Rhet.* 1.30.49.

Cicero here goes beyond Aristotle in not insisting only on a past event. In his other later works he goes beyond the mere function of *exemplum* within a proof and talks about its effectiveness, along with comparison, in the area of πάθος as extremely moving.[325] He writes in another work about the importance of the study of history as one of the many subjects the orator must be educated in and concludes: "Moreover, the mention of antiquity and the citation of examples give the speech authority and credibility as well as affording the highest pleasure to the audience."[326]

Quintilian adds a new note to the meaning of historical example. He writes: "The most important proofs of this class [use of similitude in proof] is that which is most properly styled example, that is to say the adducing of some past action real *or assumed* (*ut gestae*) which may serve to persuade the audience of the truth of the point which we are trying to make."[327]

Alongside the notion of example as the citation of a past event as inductive proof, there is another aspect of example which is normally not included in the term παράδειγμα in the rhetorical treatises, although it is used in this latter sense by Isocrates in his orations.[328] This is the case of personal example.

---

[325]Cic. *De Or.* 3.53.205: "tum duo illa quae maxime movent, similitudo et exemplum."

[326]Cic. *Orat.* 34.120. See also his *Part. Or.* 11.40 where it is said that an example "maximam . . . facit fidem."

[327]Quint. *Inst.* 5.11.6.

[328]See Isoc. *Adv. Soph.* 17.

Natali puts it well when he writes: "This is the case in which one person is himself an example, that is to say, when no preceding case analogous to the present is indicated as a model to be followed, but rather the whole life of one person assumes an emblematic character."[329] Quintilian would certainly resonate with this notion of personal example as instrumental for the effectiveness of a rhetor as well as of a teacher of rhetoric who must model for students by "the living voice" of a good life, as was shown quite early on in this paper.[330] This meaning of example as a personal demonstration of the truth of one's words to move people to action seems more oriented toward ἦθος than it does toward λόγος which sees example as a proof in rhetorical reasoning to persuade people into belief and action. There is a fine line here, since the objects are the same, namely to persuade, even though the methods (including the use of πάθος by way of moving examples) are the same. Whatever the method, the example in its full meaning, to adopt the words of Fiore, "cogently attests the desirability or advantage of a recommended action, attitude, or association, or the harm in those disapproved of. Similarly, it might bolster the authority of the exhorter-admonitor or even offer vindication from undeserved

---

[329]Natali, "Paradeigma," 147. He goes on to discuss how historiography in the second half of the 4th century B.C.E., under the influence of Isocrates and his school which assigned a different meaning to παράδειγμα, developed a moralizing and evaluative tendency toward the presentation of ethical models rather than an objective narration of facts.

[330]See Quint. *Inst.* 2.2.5-8 where the great rhetorician gives a magnificent description of a good teacher of rhetoric.

criticism."[331]

These words of Fiore already adumbrate some of the uses Paul makes of example together with enthymemes in his letter of persuasion to the Corinthians. Paul's use of λόγος, at the heart of which, as has been demonstrated, are the enthymeme and example, is meant to offer rational proof through his written word to convince the Corinthians to adopt his gospel and recognize his apostolic authority. He uses both enthymeme and example to promote himself, to denigrate his opponents, and to capture, through appeal to their intellects, the allegiance of the Corinthians. Before showing how Paul does this, we need to see how λόγος plays out practically in the writings of the classical orators.

From the above analysis there is no doubt that the λόγος of the speech is a crucial method of proof. The arguments of the speech and their arrangement act as a "warrant of credibility," as Quintilian says, to what needs to be proven or defended against accusations, so that a favorable judgment is rendered.[332] However, as Aristotle and Quintilian warn, the λόγος of the speech must not resemble the prolonged and minute process of a dialectical inquiry. Although brilliant, the speech would be counterproductive. The λόγος must be seasoned with appeals to the emotions of the judges and with

---

[331]Fiore, *Function of Personal Example*, 36.

[332]Quint. *Inst.* 5.10.9: "To all these forms of argument the Greek give the name πίστεις, a term which, though the literal translation is *fides* 'a warrant of credibility,' is best translated by *probatio* 'proof'."

other oratorical ornaments to breathe life into the logical arguments.[333] And

yet without the structure of proofs to give form to the persuasion, the other

elements of ἦθος and πάθος would dissolve into mere emotional harangue.

B. The Use of Λόγος in Ancient Sources

Enthymemes and examples, the key constituents of rhetorical reasoning,

abound in the classical orators. These writers exemplify the actual practice

behind the theory of λόγος to persuade through rational proofs. In the majority

of cases they use the rhetorical syllogism, the enthymeme, to argue their point.

In doing so they rely upon a collection of ready-made and popular types of

arguments known as τόποι which they use as the formal basis for their

enthymemes. The individual τόπος may be an argument from probability, from

authority, from consequences, from the more or less, and from other

acknowledged sources which, using Aristotle's classification in his *Rhetoric*,

amount to 28 topics. These serve as the elements in a rhetorical syllogism.

In this particular section on how the classical authors use enthymemes and

---

[333]See Quint. *Inst.* 5.14.28-35: "We . . . have to compose our speeches for others
to judge, and have frequently to speak before an audience of men who, if not
thoroughly ill-educated, are certainly ignorant of such arts as dialectic: and unless we
attract them by the charm of our discourse or drag them by its force, and occasionally
throw them off their balance by an appeal to their emotions, we shall be unable to
vindicate the claims of truth and justice. Eloquence aims at being rich, beautiful and
commanding, and will attain to none of these qualities if it be broken up into conclusive
inferences which are generally expressed in the same monotonous forms: on the
contrary its meanness will excite contempt, its severity dislike, its elaboration satiety,
and its sameness boredom" (29-30).

examples and in the next one on Paul's practice, it is impossible to define and exemplify each τόπος, for the project would be lengthy, daunting, and undoubtedly confusing. The reasons for this are in Aristotle and in the present writer. Oftentimes, as Palmer suggests, it is difficult, from the sometimes short definition and few examples Aristotle gives of each topic, to determine the meaning of a topic, how far each one extends, when one overlaps or coincides with another, and whether the examples he gives are meant to be limiting or representative. The complexity is compounded by the varied uses the Latin writers, particularly Cicero and Quintilian, make of the topics in their systems and by the freedom in citing parallel examples never intended for a particular topic by Greek and Latin orators and even modern commentators.[334]

Since it would be too far-ranging to explicate and illustrate each of the 28 topics in the classical authors, not to mention the advisability or relevance of this for 2 Corinthians 10-13, I will discuss about six or seven τόποι together with maxims and examples which seem to be helpful in understanding Paul's use of rational argumentation, the last in our discussion of the three methods of

---

[334]Palmer, *Aristotle's τόποι*, 1-3, whose reservations I share. Her study and the numerous references she gives in the classical authors of examples of the various topics has been invaluable in understanding Aristotle's discussion. She refers frequently to Aristotle's *Top.* for further explanation of an individual τόπος and makes liberal use of Leonard Spengel's monumental work on Aristotle's *Ars Rhetorica* to cite his numerous illustrations of Aristotle's topics in the classical orators. In this regard, Palmer makes the interesting observation that it is "ridiculous to search for the effect of Aristotle's Rhetoric on the speeches" in the ten Attic orators she discusses, "most of which must have been delivered before its publication." She says that whatever influence there was, it was the other way. I take this to mean that Aristotle systematized the theory of these τόποι from his careful observations of the actual practice of the orators of his day.

proof in persuasion.[335] My applications and conclusions will be tentative, since the use of this methodology is relatively new. I will provide in this section first the meaning of the individual topic and its illustration in several classical orators and then in the next section give Paul's own use of enthymeme and example to persuade through λόγος instead of doing an immediate application to Paul after each one. This separate treatment, consistent with the divisions of the previous two chapters of this paper, will preserve the fluency and impact of Paul's arguments when they are seen as a whole, although the other approach, at least in this chapter, has the merit of easy recall of the individual topic.

Aristotle's eleventh topic, designated as an argument ἐκ κρίσεως, is one of the clearest and easiest with which to begin.[336] It is an argument based on the appeal to authority. As Aristotle writes:

> Another topic is that from a previous judgement in regard to the same or a similar or contrary matter, if possible when the judgement was unanimous or the same at all times; if not, when it was at least that of the majority, or of the wise, either all or most, or of the good; or of the judges themselves or of those whose judgement they accept, or of those whose judgement it is not possible to contradict, for instance, those in authority, or of those whose judgement it is unseemly to contradict, for instance,

---

[335]The individual topic under discussion will be numerically referred to by its sequence in Aristotle's *Rhetoric* and given its name based on Palmer's nomenclature.

[336]Palmer (*Aristotle's* τόποι, 41-42) says that this topic "vies with the thirteenth for second place in frequency among orators." She has noted over a hundred cases of each.

the gods, a father, or instructors.[337]

It is evident that this is a topic that is extrinsic to the argumentation since it does not relate precisely to the internal veracity of the propositions but refers their truth or denial to some outside witness who is considered to be knowledgeable and truthful. That is why, as Aristotle remarks a few chapters later, an argument may also be refuted based on an objection "derived from the former decisions of well-known men."[338]

It is the presence of a witness, the witness' authority, and the witness' immediate or mediated knowledge, as Grimaldi writes, that is "our motive for giving consent." The witness' statements can range over any aspect of reality and "our certitude can vary in accord with the capability and quality of the authority."[339] This authority, as Aristotle indicates, can comprise anyone whom the audience sees as credible. The argument from authority can be used for amplification purposes in the case of promoting oneself or another, showing one's superiority, supporting a mode of behavior, establishing a fact, demanding allegiance, refuting adversaries, and for many other reasons.[340]

As for examples of the use of the argument from authority, Aristotle gives

---

[337]Arist. *Rh.* 2.23.12. This topic can be found in Cic. *Inv. Rhet.* 1.30.48; 2.22.68; *Rhet. Her.* 2.13.19; 2.30.48; Quint. *Inst.* 5.11.17-18, 36-44 where he discusses all kinds of *testimonia*.

[338]Arist. *Rh.* 2.25.7.

[339]Grimaldi, *Aristotle, Rhetoric II*, 312. See Arist. *Rh.* 1.15.1-26 for his discussion on witnesses.

[340]See Palmer, *Aristotle's τόποι*, 42.

some himself after his definition. He writes: "If the awful goddesses [the Eumenides] were content to stand their trial before the Areopagus, should not Mixidemides?" Or: "Helen was a virtuous woman, wrote Isocrates, because Theseus so judged." Lysias uses this argument to amplify the character of his clients in his speech *Against Agoratus*: "Some had served you several times as generals, and then had handed on the city with added greatness to their successors in authority; some had held other high offices, and had borne the expense of many naval equipments: never before had they met with any disgraceful censure from you."[341] Isocrates, in his speech *Aegineticus* which he wrote for a litigant, has the person promoting his own character with the following conclusion:

> . . . pray consider how strong and how just are the claims with which I have come before you; there is, first, my friendship with those who have left the inheritance, a friendship of ancient origin, handed down from our fathers, and in all that time never broken; second, my many great acts of kindness done for them in their adversity; third, there is a will which my opponents themselves acknowledge; and lastly, the law, which supports the will, a law that in the opinion of all Greeks is regarded as wisely made. Of my statement the best proof is this — although the Greek states differ in opinion about many other enactments, they are of one accord concerning this one.[342]

Demosthenes uses the argument from authority on behalf of himself:

> Therefore, up to the date of those transactions it is shown by common consent that my conduct was entirely beneficial to the commonwealth. The proofs are, that my speeches and notions were successful at your deliberations; that my resolutions were

---

[341]Lys. 13 (*Against Agoratus*) 13.63.

[342]Isoc. 19 (*Aegineticus*) 19.50.

carried into effect; that thereby decorations came to the city and to all of you as well as to me; and that for these successes you thanked the gods with sacrifices and processions.[343]

Demosthenes in another passage argues that Ctesiphon's petition for a crown was warranted because Demosthenes had given a benefaction out of his own pocket that deserved gratitude and formal thanks rather than be subjected to an audit: "That this distinction is recognized both in the statutes and in your moral feelings I can prove by many instances." He proceeds to enumerate several cases and then concludes: "To prove the truth of my statement, please take and read the actual words of the decrees made in the cases I have cited." Demosthenes even calls Aeschines as an authority who "himself testifies that I have been crowned for matters in which I was audit-free" because he did not object at the time the decree was drawn in Demosthenes' favor.[344]

In his defense of Milo at the murder of Clodius, Cicero uses the argument from divine authority by citing an example from Aeschylus' *Eumenides* where Orestes is acquitted by Athena's casting-vote: "And so, gentlemen, it is not without reason that even in their fictions accomplished poets have narrated how one, who, to avenge a father, had slain a mother, was, though the human vote was divided, acquitted by a sentence that proceeded not merely from a divine being, but from the wisest of the goddesses."[345] In his third oration against

---

[343]Dem. *De Cor.* 86.

[344]Dem. *De Cor.* 114-118.

[345]Cic. *Mil.* 3.8.

Cataline, Cicero uses the erection of the statue of Jupiter Optimus as "clear proof of the intervention" of the god and says: "When the statue had been placed in position and turned towards yourselves and the Senate, both Senate and people saw the plots against the safety of you all brought into the light of day and laid bare."[346] And Quintilian cites Cicero's *Pro Ligario* "where he admits the cause of Caesar to be the better because the gods have decided in his favour."[347] There are other numerous examples but these suffice to show how the argument from authority works to prove a point.[348]

Another topic that is most common is topic four, the argument $\dot{\epsilon}\kappa\ \tau o\hat{v}$ $\mu\hat{\alpha}\lambda\lambda o\nu\ \kappa\alpha\dot{\iota}\ \hat{\eta}\tau\tau o\nu$, one that is derived from the more and less (*a maiori, a minore*). Aristotle describes it in this fashion:

> For instance, if not even the gods know everything, hardly can men; for this amounts to saying that if a predicate, which is more probably affirmable of one thing, does not belong to it, it is clear that it does not belong to another of which it is less probably affirmable. And to say that a man who beats his father also beats his neighbours, is an instance of the rule, that, if the less exists, the more also exists. Either of these arguments may be used, according as it is necessary to prove either that a predicate is

---

[346]Cic. *Cat.* 3.9.21.

[347]Quint. *Inst.* 5.11.42. Quintilian cites another example of the authority of the gods from Cic. *Har. Resp. passim*, where Clodius had asked the soothsayers about certain unusual manifestations at the time and the reply was that they were due to the profanation of sacred rites. Clodius used this to argue against Cicero rebuilding his house on the spot which Clodius had consecrated after tearing down Cicero's first house while he was in exile.

[348]Palmer (*Aristotle's* τόποι, 42) cites numerous other citations from Greek orators.

affirmable or that it is not.[349]

There are three parts to this argument, as Spengel notes: from the more, from the less, and if neither more nor less.[350] Aristotle gives several examples, of which the following two are readily intelligible: "If generals are not despised because they are frequently defeated [or perhaps: "are put to death"], neither are the sophists; or, if it behooves a private citizen to take care of your reputation, it is your duty to take care of that of Greece." This is a kind of *a fortiori* argument working from the principle that every greater contains a lesser. Aristotle gives the logical ground for this argument in the quotation above which is paraphrased by Grimaldi: "if something is not present where . . . it should more likely be present, then obviously it is not present where it should less likely be."[351] There are numerous examples. One is from Demosthenes who says against Conon's assault and battery of Ariston:

> For if he has trained up his sons in such fashion that they feel no fear or shame while committing in his presence crimes for some of which the punishment of death is ordained, what punishment do you think too severe for him? I think these actions are a proof that he has no reverence for his own father; for if he had honoured and feared him, he would have exacted honour and fear from his own children.[352]

---

[349]Arist. *Rh.* 2.23.4. See also Cic. *Top.* 4.23; Cic. *De Or.*, 2.40.172; Quint. *Inst.* 5.10.86-93. Palmer (*Aristotle's τόποι* 18 n.3) has a brief discussion of where she perceives Quintilian to diverge from Aristotle's strict definition.

[350]Cited by Palmer, *Aristotle's τόποι*, 18.

[351]Grimaldi, *Aristotle, Rhetoric II*, 299.

[352]Dem. *Con.* 23.

Isaeus, the 4th century B.C.E. orator, uses this same argument in a speech he
wrote for a man who was involved in an inheritance. The kinship claims are
too difficult to go into here but one can get the flavor of the argument in the
following words:

> Is Ciron's daughter or his brother the nearer kin to him? Clearly
> his daughter; for she is his issue, while the brother is only born
> of the same stock. Next, is the brother nearer kin or the
> daughter's children? Certainly the daughter's children; for they
> are lineal descendants and not mere collaterals. If then our rights
> are so far superior to those of a brother, *a fortiori* we are still
> more to be preferred to our opponent, who is only a nephew.[353]

A very good example is from Isocrates in his famous self-defense oration:

> But, though there are many anomalies in my situation, it would
> be the crowning absurdity of all if, when the men who have paid
> me money are so grateful to me that they are still even now
> devoted to me, you on whom I have spent my means should
> desire to penalize me. It would be even more absurd, if,
> whereas Pindar, the poet, was so highly honoured by our
> forefathers because of a single line of his in which he praises
> Athens as "the bulwark of Hellas" that he was made "proxenos"
> and given a present of ten thousand drachmas, I, on the other
> hand, who have glorified Athens and our ancestors with much
> ampler and nobler encomiums, should not even be privileged to
> end my days in peace.[354]

Lysias also affords a strong example in a speech he wrote for an Athenian
accused of removing a sacred olive stump which was formerly punishable by
death but at this time only by exile and confiscation of property:

> But the fact is that I have as great a regard for them [the sacred
> olive stumps which he had on his other property which he could
> have cleared away, if he wanted to, with less notice] as for my

---

[353]Isae. 8 (*On the Estate of Ciron*) 33.

[354]Isoc. *Antid.* 166.

native land and my whole property, realizing that it is the loss of both of these that I have at stake. And you yourselves I shall produce as witnesses [argument from authority] to that fact; for you supervise the matter every month, and also send assessors every year, none of whom has ever penalized me for working the ground abut the sacred olives. Now surely, when I pay so much regard to those small penalties, I cannot so utterly disregard the perils involved for my person. You find me taking all this care of the many olive-trees upon which I could more freely commit the offence, and I am on my trial to-day for clearing away the sacred olive which it was impossible to dig up unobserved![355]

In his famous speech against Timarchus, Aeschines expresses this argument in the form of a rhetorical question after he detailed Timarchus' many crimes of bribery, blackmailing, and adultery:

But what do you expect? If a man at Athens not only abuses other people, but even his own body, here where there are laws, where you are looking on, where his personal enemies are on the watch, who would expect that same man, when he had received impunity and authority and office, to have placed any limit on his license?

Aeschines barrages Timarchus with a series of *a fortiori* arguments at the beginning of his speech as he recites the laws of the great Athenian lawgiver, Solon, and shows how Timarchus' way of life precludes his ever occupying political office. One can get the background of the arguments with which Aeschines hammers Timarchus:

Because if a man is mean toward those [one's parents] whom he ought to honour as the gods, how, pray, he [Solon] asks, will such a man treat the members of another household, and how will he treat the whole city? . . . Man, if you fail to take up arms in behalf of the state, or if you are such a coward that you are unable to defend her, you must not claim the right to advise her,

---

[355]Lys. 7 (*On the Olive Stump*) 25-26.

either. . . . For the man who has made traffic of the shame of his own body, he [Solon] thought would be ready to sell the common interests of the city also. . . . For he [Solon] believed that the man who has mismanaged his own household will handle the affairs of the city in like manner; and to the lawgiver it did not seem possible that the same man could be a rascal in private life, and in public life a good and useful citizen.[356]

Palmer indicates several ways this line of argument is most frequently applied. She writes that this topic may be used in a character argument: "A man who has done this would certainly not hesitate to do that." Sometimes it is used to bring out an εἰκός argument which is based on likelihood. She quotes Demosthenes in his famous *On the Crown* oration: "If my acts provided a case against Ctesiphon, Aeschines would be even more ready to use them to attack me instead "(13). She says that "Demosthenes and Isocrates both appeal to αἰδώς in using this τόπος," which would be expressed in words like: "Can you permit such people to do well and not strive to do better than they?" The topic is used in cases of appeal to authority or previous judgment as when a person might say: "Your ancestors (or you yourselves on former occasions) punished much slighter wrongs than this. Will you then hesitate to pronounce judgment on so great a criminal?"[357] Lysias writes a speech for a client brought up on charge of taking bribes. He argues: "For I should be a madman, gentlemen, if, after spending my patrimony upon you in pursuit of distinction,

---

[356]Aeschin. *In Tim.* 108 and 28-30 for both quotations.

[357]Palmer, *Aristotle's τόποι*, 20-21.

I accepted bribes from others with the aim of injuring the State."[358]

Quintilian cites some of Cicero's uses of this argument, many of which are put into the form of a rhetorical question. As an example of something from the greater to the lesser, Cicero says: "Shall we suppose that which alarms whole armies caused no alarm to a peaceful company of lawyers?"[359] As an argument from something more difficult to something less difficult, there is Cicero's ironical statement: "Mark, Tubero, I pray, how I, who flinch not from confessing my own fault, dare not to acknowledge that of Ligarius!"[360] As an example of arguing from something less, Cicero writes: "Really! Is the knowledge that the men were armed sufficient to prove that violence was offered, and the fact that he fell into their hands insufficient?"[361]

Topic seven is a fairly straightforward one. It is called argument ἐκ ὁρισμοῦ or one derived from definition. Aristotle says of it after a number of examples: "It is by definition and the knowledge of what the thing is in itself that conclusions are drawn upon the subject in question."[362] Palmer gives a fuller explication:

The method is so to state some particular aspect of the thing

---

[358]Lys. 21 (*On a Charge of Taking Bribes*) 22.

[359]Cic. *Caecin.* 15.43.

[360]Cic. *Lig.* 3.8. Cicero is saying that if he is willing to confess his own fault, surely he will not hesitate to admit Ligarius' smaller offence.

[361]Cic. *Caecin.* 16.45.

[362]Arist. *Rh.* 2.23.8.

under discussion as to make it correspond to something else, and usually to something about which the audience has a settled opinion; or else to give a definition of the other thing which brings it to coincide with that under discussion.[363]

Cicero adds further clarification. After saying that one must give a brief, clear definition of the word whose meaning is being sought and the reasons for it, he writes: "Then it will be necessary to show the connexion between the act of the accused and your definition . . . and then support the whole argument by a common topic in which you magnify or inveigh against the enormity of the deed itself, its heinousness or at least its guilt."[364]

Cicero gives an example which clarifies what has been said so far: "If sovereignty be the grandeur and glory of the State, it was violated by the man who delivered up to the enemy an army of the Roman people, not by him who delivered the man that did it into the power of the Roman People."[365] Aristotle exemplifies this argument also when he says:

When Iphicrates desired to prove that the best man is the noblest, he declared that there was nothing noble attaching to Harmodius and Aristogiton, before they did something noble; and, "I myself am more akin to them than you; at any rate, my deeds are more akin to theirs than yours."[366]

Isocrates in his self-defense speech says that he will tell the jury about wisdom

---

[363]Palmer, *Aristotle's* τόποι, 29.

[364]Cic. *Inv. Rhet.* 2.17.53-56. See also Cic. *Part. Or.* 12.41; Quint. *Inst.* 5.10.54-64.

[365]Cic. *De Or.* 2.39.164.

[366]Arist. *Rh.* 2.23.8. See Isae. 5 (*On the Estate of Dicaeogenes*) 47 for a similar one in content.

and philosophy and then concludes:

> It is true that if one were pleading a case on any other issue it would be out of place to discuss these words (for they are foreign to all litigation), but it is appropriate for me, since I am being tried on such an issue, and since I hold that what some people call philosophy is not entitled to that name, to define and explain to you what philosophy, properly conceived, really is.[367]

Isocrates gives another argument from definition from the same speech which

is paradoxical:

> I come now to the question of "advantage"—the most difficult of the points I have raised. If anyone is under the impression that people who rob others or falsify accounts or do any evil thing get the advantage, he is wrong in his thinking; for none are at a greater disadvantage throughout their lives than such men; none are found in more difficult straits, none live in greater ignominy; and, in a word, none are more miserable than they.[368]

Demosthenes uses this argument from definition when he challenges Aeschines

to tell him what are the duties of an orator, when Aeschines accuses him of

cowardice. Demosthenes then claims to be such a responsible orator:

> Make as strict an inquiry as you will into everything for which an orator is responsible; I ask no indulgence. But for what is he responsible? For discerning the trend of events at the outset, for forecasting results, for warning others. That I have always done. Further, he ought to reduce to a minimum those delays and hesitations, those fits of ignorance and quarrelsomeness, which are the natural and inevitable failings of all free states, and on the other hand to promote unanimity and friendliness, and whatever impels a man to do his duty. All that also I have made my business: and herein no man can find any delinquency on my part.[369]

---

[367]Isoc. *Antid*. 270.

[368]Isoc. *Antid*. 281.

[369]Dem. *De Cor*. 246.

These words are in reply to Aeschines, who used a similar argument from definition to defame Demosthenes, who reproached Aeschines for inconsistency in serving Philip when he had previously asked the Greeks to oppose him. Aeschines says that this charge can be brought against any of the Athenians who help the people they formerly oppose:

> For in order to attain the highest good the individual, and the state as well, is obliged to change front with changing circumstances. But what is the good counsellor to do? Is he not to give the state the counsel that is best in view of each present situation? And what shall the rascally accuser say? Is he not to conceal the occasion and condemn the act? And the born traitor—how shall we recognize him? Will he not imitate you, Demosthenes, in his treatment of those whom chance throws in his way and who have trusted him? Will he not take pay for writing speeches for them to deliver in the courts, and then reveal the contents of these speeches to their opponents? [After some examples of the latter]: That conduct, and conduct like that, defines the traitor.[370]

The examples show how one can exonerate or accuse by defining the subject and then drawing conclusions from one's definition which in the majority of cases is a definition generally accepted by most sensible people.

Another topic which Paul seems to use is topic twenty-two, known as τὸ τὰ ἀνομολογούμενα σκοπεῖν or an argument consisting "in examining contradictories." Aristotle goes on to say that this topic, which is appropriate to refutation, consists in looking for inconsistencies

whether in dates, actions, or words, first, separately in the case

---

[370]Aeschin. *Embassy* 165. See Lys. 3 (*Against Simon*) 41-43 on the definition of unpremeditated assault and the injustice of excessive punishment; and 27 (*Against Epicrates and His Fellow-Envoys*) 8 for an intricate argument on punishing the guilty.

of the adversary, for instance, "he says that he loves you, and yet he conspired with the Thirty;" next, separately in your own case, "he says that I am litigious, but he cannot prove that I have ever brought an action against anyone"; lastly, separately in the case of your adversary and yourself together: "he has never yet lent anything but I have ransomed many of you."[371]

Palmer comments: "The first two examples . . . cite instances to point out the falsity of statements of the other side, in one case to bring him into disrepute, in the other to discredit the aspersions he has cast upon one's character. The third shows . . . any sort of contrast."[372] Aristotle's topic seems to coincide with the type of oratory mentioned in the *Rhetoric to Alexander* called investigation, which is the "exhibition of certain intentions or actions or words as inconsistent with one another or with the rest of someone's conduct." In this situation, the investigator "must try to find some point in which either the speech that he is investigating is self-contradictory or the actions or the intentions of the persons under investigation run counter to one another."[373] Some examples will show the point of this topic.

Isaeus has an example of the first type of contradiction Aristotle mentions, namely the inconsistency between one's actions and one's words. In the case of an inheritance dispute over a deceased Astyphilus, the speaker, the dead man's half-brother and first cousin to his opponent who claims his own son should get the legacy, says:

---

[371]Arist. *Rh.* 2.23.23.

[372]Palmer, *Aristotle's τόποι*, 68-9.

[373]Arist. *[Rh. Al.]* 5.

When, however, my brother's remains were brought home, the person who claims to have been long ago adopted as his son did not lay them out or bury them, but Astyphilus's friends and companions-in-arms, seeing that my father was ill and I was abroad, themselves laid out the remains and carried out all the other customary rites, and conducted my father, ill though he was, to the tomb, well knowing the affection in which Astyphilus held him.[374]

Demosthenes has many examples of the second instance Aristotle cites of this topic, namely the contradiction between the accusations of the other side and the acts of the speaker. Demosthenes, incensed that Aeschines is blaming him for the dishonorable peace with Philip, says:

Why, you, you—but I can find no epithet bad enough for you—was there any single occasion when you, having observed me in your presence trying to rob the state of a negotiation and of an alliance which you have just described as of the greatest importance, either made any protest, or rose to give the people any information whatsoever about the proceeding which you now denounce? Yet if I had really intrigued with Philip to stop a Panhellenic coalition, it was your business not to hold your peace, but to cry aloud, to protest, to inform the people. You did nothing of the sort. No one ever heard that fine voice of yours.

Then Demosthenes goes on to show the contradiction in Aeschines' behavior:

If at one and the same time you were inviting the Greeks to make war and sending envoys to Philip to negotiate peace, you were playing a part worthy of Eurybatus the imposter, not of a great city or of honest men. But it is false; it is false! For what purpose could you have summoned them at that crisis? For peace? They were all enjoying peace. For war? You were already discussing terms of peace. Therefore it is clear that I did not promote, and was in no way responsible for, the original

---

[374]Isae. 9 (*On the Estate of Astyphilus*) 4. Other examples of this topic are Isoc. 18 (*Against Callimachus*) 47-48; Lys. 12 (*On the Murder of Eratosthenes: Defense*) 25-29, 39-40; Lys. 10 (*Against Themnestus I*) 2-3.

peace, and that all his other calumnies are equally false.[375]

There is another dramatic passage in which Demosthenes backs Aeschines into a corner by showing the inconsistency of his behavior:

> I should like to ask Aeschines a question: when all that was going on, when the whole city was a scene of enthusiasm and rejoicing and thanksgiving, did he take part in the worship and festivity of the populace, or did he sit still at home, grieving and groaning and sulking over the public successes? If he was present as one of the throng, surely his behaviour is scandalous and even sacrilegious, for after calling the gods to witness that certain measures were very good, he now asks a jury to vote that they were very bad—a jury that has sworn by the gods! If he was not present, he deserves many deaths for shrinking from a sight in which every one else rejoiced.[376]

Cicero in his orations shows developed skills in using this topic. The examples are legion. Cicero employs a clever tactic in response to Clodius who has razed Cicero's house and consecrated the ground so that Cicero had to argue for its repossession:

> But what did the expert and astute formulator of laws enact? "That it may please you, that you may command, that Marcus Tullius be interdicted from fire and water?" A cruel, a shocking measure this, and one not to be tolerated, be the citizen who is its victim never so far gone in crime! But the actual phrase was not "that he be interdicted." How then did it run? "That an interdict *have* been passed upon him." O abominable and

---

[375]Dem. *De Cor.* 22-24.

[376]Dem. *De Cor.* 217. See also 17 and 316-17; *De Falsa Leg.* 166, 229-231 for a contrast between the actions and character of Demosthenes and Aeschines. Likewise see Aeschin. *In Ctes.*141-154 who accuses Demosthenes of three great crimes, ending with great pathos: "O man of all mankind most useless for great and serious deeds, but for boldness of words most wonderful, will you presently undertake to look this jury in the face and say that over the disasters of the city you must be crowned?" Literally, there are dozens of passages in both *De Cor.* and *In Ctes.* which exemplify topic twenty-two.

> monstrous wickedness! Behold! Clodius has formulated a law
> for you in phrases more vile than his own vile tongue, for he
> enacts that an interdict *have* been passed upon one upon whom
> an interdict has not been passed! I ask your kind pardon, my
> good Sextus, since you have lately turned logician, and are
> smacking your lips over your performances in this direction as
> well as in others, but is it possible to propose to the assembly, or
> to ratify in any form of words, or to corroborate by vote, an
> enactment enjoining the existence of a state of affairs which does
> not exist?[377]

This is a good example of a refutative syllogism which Aristotle says, as

mentioned earlier, is always more striking since the opposite propositions are

closely juxtaposed.[378] In another passage Cicero uses this topical argument

to refute the charges against him, citing minutely his actions in his visit to Sicily

to investigate the accusations of extortion against Verres. He says the

promptness of his return to Rome, his carefulness in collecting witnesses and

documents, and his conscientious regard for propriety at not imposing himself

on the citizens there caused no trouble or expense, official or unofficial, to

anyone. He responds in typical ironic fashion to the slanders against him:

> Upon my return from Sicily to Rome, Verres and his friends,
> with characteristic good taste and delicacy, tried to discourage
> my witnesses by circulating stories of my having accepted a
> heavy bribe to make my prosecution a sham: and although none
> of the witnesses believed this—those from Sicily being men who
> had learnt my character when I was quaestor in the province, and
> those from Rome men of shining reputation, to whom my
> character, and that of each of my supporters, is as familiar as

---

[377]Cic. *Dom.* 18.47.

[378]The passage referred to is *Rh.* 2.23.30: "Refutative enthymemes are more
popular than those that serve to demonstrate, because the former is a conclusion of
opposites in a small compass, and things in juxtaposition are always clearer to the
audience." See also 3.17.14.

their own is familiar to the world—none the less I did feel misgivings lest my honour and integrity should be distrusted, until we came to the challenging of the judges.[379]

There are many more variations to this topic than we have suggested, for instance, the contrast with one's opponents to people of former times and the topic's use in comparison arguments, as in "no one who did this would have done that"; but the above gives the flavor of the topic, which Aristotle suggests using for amplification but which Palmer notes is more used in cases where there is depreciation.[380]

The very next topic, number twenty-three, needs mentioning because it is closely related to the preceding one. This is one used in cases of slander, where the speaker states the reason for the calumny in order to dispel it. Aristotle writes: "Another topic, when men or things have been attacked by slander, in reality or in appearance, consists in stating the reason for the false opinion; for there must be a reason for the supposition of guilt."[381] As Palmer rewords it: "This type denies the charge, shows why the charge was apparently true and by this explanation refutes it."[382] A good example is from Demosthenes who explains to the Athenians that the reason why they fell into Philip's trap was the "baseness and stupidity . . . of the other Greek states" who helped them

---

[379]Cic. *Verr.* 2.1.6.17.

[380]Palmer, *Aristotle's τόποι*, 71-2.

[381]Arist. *Rh.* 2.23.24.

[382]Palmer, *Aristotle's τόποι*, 72.

"neither with money, nor with men, nor with anything else." This is the reason why the Athenians accepted Philip's suggestion. Demosthenes concludes with the words which illustrate the present topic: "The peace conceded to him at that time was due to the causes I have named, and not, as Aeschines maliciously insists, to me; and the misdeed and the corruption of Aeschines . . . will be found to be the true cause of our present troubles."[383] Isocrates offers another good example. He laments the slander of a certain sophist against him who said that he held poetry in contempt and would do away with "all the learning and teaching of others, and that I assert that all men talk mere drivel except those who partake of my instruction." These aspersions force Isocrates to respond to clear up the misapprehension:

> Now I could not possibly convey to you how troubled and disturbed I was on hearing that some accepted these statements as true. For I thought that it was so well known that I was waging war against the false pretenders to wisdom and that I had spoken so moderately, nay so modestly, about my own powers that no one could be credited for a moment who asserted that I myself resorted to such pretensions. But in truth it was with good reason that I deplored at the beginning of my speech the misfortune which has attended me all my life in this respect. For this is the cause of the false reports which are spread about me, of the calumny and prejudice which I suffer, and of my failure to attain the reputation which I deserve—either that which should be mine by common consent or that in which I am held by certain of my disciples who have known me through and through. However, this cannot now be changed and I must needs put up with what has already come to pass.[384]

---

[383]Dem. *De Cor.* 20. See also his 57 (*Against Eubulides*) 8-19.

[384]Isoc. *Panthaen.* 20-21. His *Antidosis* is really a sustained defense of his life and teachings. See especially 150ff. See also Isae. 5 (*On the Estate of Dicaeogenes*) 5-12; Lys. 9 (*For the Soldier*) 13ff; Isoc. 16 (*On the Team of Horses*) 38. These passages,

These examples above should suffice to illustrate the theory and practice of enthymemes and their τόποι as a background to our investigation of Paul's usage in 2 Corinthians 10-13. However, there is one aspect of enthymemes that needs to be further illustrated: the maxim.

Aristotle classifies the maxim under his discussion of the enthymemes and devotes several pages to its explanation.[385] It will be earlier remembered that maxims are enthymemes because like them they are also concerned with the "objects of human actions, and with what should be chosen or avoided with reference to them." Maxims are abbreviated syllogisms and consequently function as proof. They are "the premises or conclusions of enthymemes without the syllogism", as Aristotle says giving a few samples: "He is no lover who does not love always"; and "There is no man who is really free"; and "Being a mortal, do not nourish immortal wrath."[386] The *Rhetorica ad*

---

a mere sampling of the hundreds of citations, offer explanations of what appears to be the accusations or evidence against the speaker. They are defense speeches.

[385]Arist. *Rh.* 2.21.1-21. See also Arist. [*Rh. Al.*] 11; *Rhet. Her.* 4.17.24; also Quint. *Inst.* 5.10.1; 8.5.3. See also Grimaldi, *Aristotle, Rhetoric II*, 260-61, and Cope, *Introduction to Aristotle's Rhetoric*, 257-60.

[386]Arist. *Rh.* 2.21.2-6. When in this section Aristotle says that a maxim becomes an enthymeme "when the why and the wherefore are added" (2.20.2), he adds a bit of confusion to the notion of enthymeme which earlier had been described as itself an abbreviated syllogism. Cope (*Introduction to Aristotle's Rhetoric*, 102-3) contends that incompletion as to form is the mark of the enthymeme. Grimaldi (*Aristotle, Rhetoric II*, 262) disagrees with Cope and says that an enthymeme is an ordinary syllogism with two premises and a conclusion. However, 257 Cope (257) writes, paraphrasing Aristotle, that "if we add the reason of this general maxim in the shape of a premise we have a regular enthymeme." Aristotle supports this statement further in a later remark (*Rh.* 3.17.17) which should be quoted: "One should also sometimes change enthymemes into moral maxims; for instance, 'Sensible men should become reconciled when they are prosperous; for in this manner they will obtain the greatest advantages,'

Alexandrum reflects the general thinking on a maxim at the time of Aristotle:

> A maxim may be summarily defined as the expression of an individual opinion about general matters of conduct. Maxims have two modes, one agreeing with accepted opinion, and the other running counter to it. When you say something that is usually accepted, there is no need to produce reasons because what you say is not unfamiliar and does not meet with incredulity; but when what you say is paradoxical, you must specify the reasons briefly, so as to avoid prolixity and not arouse incredulity.[387]

The author goes on to say that one develops maxims from the particular nature of the case, as in the following example: "I do not think it possible for a man to become an able general if he is without experience of affairs"; or by using hyperbole, as in the following sardonic maxim: "I think that thieves commit worse outrages than highwaymen, because the former rob us of our property by stealth, the latter openly"; or by drawing a parallel, as in "I think that those who cheat people out of money act exactly like those who betray their country, because both of them after being trusted rob those who have trusted them."[388]

Other examples of maxims are: "Every beginning is difficult"; "Least in the habit of giving reverence to the virtues is he who has always enjoyed the

---

which is equivalent to the enthymeme: 'If men should become reconciled whenever it is most useful and advantageous, they should be reconciled in a time of prosperity'." My contention is that both are normally abbreviated syllogisms where one of the premises is missing but assumed, as in "Blessed are the poor in spirit, for the reign of God is theirs." One of the qualities in a maxim is its brevity and pithy encapsulation of a general truth reflective of a moral stance in human activity. If it were too long, it would not be easily memorizable.

[387]Arist. [*Rh. Al.*] 11.

[388]Ibid.

favours of fortune"; "A free man is that man to be judged who is a slave to no base habit"; "As poor as the man who has not enough is the man who cannot have enough"; "Choose the noblest way of living; habit will make it enjoyable." These are examples where no reason is needed, where brevity is the soul of wit. Other maxims which are not so readily intelligible are supported by some reason, as for example: "Those who have cultivated a man's friendship for his wealth one and all fly from him as soon as his wealth has slipped away. For when the motive of their intercourse has disappeared, there is nothing left which can maintain that friendship."[389]

Quintilian has an interesting discussion and several apt examples of the maxim, called *sententia* in Latin and γνώμη in Greek. Both names, he says aptly, are "derived from the fact that such utterances resemble the decrees or resolutions of public bodies." Sometimes the maxim refers to things in general as in his quotation from Cicero: "There is nothing that wins the affection of the people more than goodness of heart."[390] At other times it makes a personal reference: "The prince who would know all, must needs ignore much."[391] At still other times a reason may be added to the statement: "For in every struggle,

---

[389]All the examples in this paragraph are taken from *Rhet. Her.* 4.27.24-25. The anonymous author, after citing other examples, ends with this advice for those drawing up an argument: "We should insert maxims only rarely, that we may be looked upon as pleading the case, not preaching morals. When so interspersed, they will add much distinction. Furthermore, the hearer, when he perceives that an indisputable principle drawn from practical life is being applied to a cause, must give it his tacit approval."

[390]Cic. *Lig.* 12.37.

[391]Quintilian quotes from Domitius Afer; no citation.

the stronger seems not to suffer wrong, even when this is actually the case, but

to inflict it simply in virtue of his superior power."[392] Sometimes, the maxim

may be double, as in: "Complaisance wins us friends, truth enmity."[393]

Quintilian gives a striking maxim that is produced by opposition of words, the

effect of which is evident in the Latin: "Mors misera non est, aditus ad mortem

est miser" (Death is not bitter, but the approach to death). He offers the

following thought-provoking maxim cast in the form of a direct statement: "The

miser lacks/That which he has no less than what he has not."[394] He ends his

discussion with the monitum:

> . . . we must be careful as always, not to employ them too
> frequently, nor at random, nor place them in the mouth of every
> kind of person, while we must make certain that they are not
> untrue. . . . Such reflexions are best suited to those speakers
> whose authority is such that their character itself will lend weight
> to their words. For who would tolerate a boy, or a youth, or
> even a man of low birth who presumed to speak with all the
> authority of a judge and to thrust his precepts down our
> throat?[395]

Demosthenes is fond of making moral reflections in the form of maxims

in his orations. He chides Aeschines for his preoccupation with fortune and

says: "Seeing that a man who thinks he is doing well and regards himself as

highly fortunate, is never certain that his good fortune will last till evening, how

---

[392]Quoted from Sall. *Jug.* 10.

[393]Quoted from Ter. *An.* 1.1.41. Cicero (*Amic.* 24.89) quotes this same maxim.
Quintilian may have read it directly in Terence or else lifted it from Cicero.

[394]Quoted from Publil. *Syr. Sent.* 486.

[395]These words and all the previous examples are taken from Quint. *Inst.* 8.5.1-8.

can it be right to boast about it, or use it to insult other people?"[396] Another

would be Demosthenes' remarks on treason: "Men of Athens, it is not because

he wants to do a traitor a good turn that a man spends his money; nor, when he

had once got what he paid for, has he any further use for the traitor's counsels.

Otherwise, treason would be the most profitable of all trades." He then

cautions the jury to look at the present issue and even though the right time for

action in this instance has passed, he says "for wise men it is always the right

time to understand history."[397]

Aeschines quotes Euripides to prove his point against Timarchus: "I know

too well the man is such/As is the company he loves to keep."[398] Isocrates

defends his students who choose an education in oratory by saying: ". . . he

must not hasten to seek to rule over others before he has found a master to

direct his own thoughts, and he must not take as great pleasure or pride in other

advantages as in the good things which spring up in the soul under a liberal

education."[399] Isocrates in another oration echoes these thoughts when he

writes about those who have no care for the education of the mind: "They fail

to see that nothing in the world can contribute so powerfully to material gain,

to good repute, to right action, in a word to happiness, as virtue and the

---

[396]Dem. *De Cor.* 252.

[397]Dem. *De Cor.* 47-48.

[398]Aeschin. *In Tim.* 152.

[399]Isoc. *Antid.* 290.

qualities of virtue." He then appends the reason: "For it is by the good qualities which we have in our souls that we acquire also the other advantages of which we stand in need."[400] Through the young king, Isocrates lectures the king's subjects: ""Do not do to others that which angers you when they do it to you. . . . Practice nothing in your deeds for which you condemn others in your words." He goes on to give another maxim: "Do not think that getting is gain or spending is loss; for neither that one nor the other has the same significance at all times, but either, when done in season and with honour, benefits the doer."[401]

Cicero gives several examples of maxims in his writings. In his speech delivered before the people upon his return from exile, he writes of his joy in Rome and how much he has always appreciated her but seeing her now, after his return, he is even more ecstatic: "But as good health is sweeter to those who have recovered from grievous sickness than to those who have never known physical infirmity, so these are all the more keenly appreciated in their loss than in their continued enjoyment."[402] Cicero quotes a well-known saying of Cato which amounts to a maxim: "Some men are better served by their bitter-tongued

---

[400]Isoc. 1 (*On the Peace*) 32. This is an echo of Socrates (Pl. *Ap*. 30B): ". . . not from your possession does virtue spring, but from virtue spring possessions and all other good things to mankind in private and in public life." Thanks to George Norlin, *Isocrates II* (LCL), 32, n.b, for this connection.

[401]Isoc. *Nic*. 61; 50 for both quotations. The entire last part of the treatise seems to be a concatenation of one maxim after another on justice, temperance, fidelity in marriage, performance of duty, virtue.

[402]Cic. *Red. Pop*. 1.4.

enemies than by their sweet-smelling friends." And he gives the reason: "Because the former often tell the truth, the latter, never."[403] He also quotes Aristotle in the same work in which he quotes Cato when the question is raised about old friendships: "Men must eat many a peck of salt together before the claims of friendship are fulfilled."[404] Another example of a maxim made to order by Cicero for a client is the following on behalf of Marcellus, an antagonist of Julius Caesar: "That citizen knows neither gratitude nor justice who, when released from the peril of arms, still keeps his soul armed; so that the better man is even he who has fallen upon the stricken field and poured out his life-blood for a Cause."[405] One last example will serve to show Cicero's penchant for the moralizing reflection. He writes in defense of a friend who has been brought up on the charges of corruption: "But there is nothing which is so volatile as slander, nothing which slips abroad so readily, is caught up so greedily, or disseminated so widely."[406] These maxims are arguments to bolster one's proof of a point. They also serve to give a high moral tone to the character of the speaker and the content of the speech.

In addition to enthymemes and maxims, the other half of rhetorical reasoning is rhetorical induction or the example, whether historical or invented.

---

[403]Cic. *Amic.* 23.90.

[404]Cic. *Amic.* 19.67. He is quoting from Arist. *Eth. Eud.* 7.2; also *Eth. Nic.* 8.3.8.

[405]Cic. *Marcell.* 31.

[406]Cic. *Planc.* 57.

Audiences like examples, since they are more tangible, as it were, more within

the compass of one's experience, more easily grasped than the sometimes

convoluted reasoning of the syllogism, even though the latter is more cogent.

The audience more immediately "sees" the connection as the speaker proves a

point by moving from particular case to particular case from which an inference

is drawn.[407] Isocrates sets the tone for the use of example by saying: "In your

deliberations, let the past be an exemplar for the future; for the unknown may

be soonest discerned by reference to the known."[408] In other words, if past

events of a similar nature are shown to have happened, then there is a relatively

sure chance that the same thing will happen in the future.

Demosthenes draws up an excellent argument from the citation of a number

of past cases to prove to Aeschines that those traitors who take bribes from

those grasping for power are ultimately loathed and discarded by them once they

have attained power:

> Look at the instances . . . Lasthenes was hailed as a friend—until
> he betrayed Olynthus; Timolaus, until he brought Thebes to ruin;
> Eudicus and Simus of Larissa, until they put Thessaly under
> Philip's heel. Since then the whole world has become crowded
> with men exiled, insulted, punished in every conceivable way.
> What of Aristratus at Sicyon? or Perilaus at Megara? Are they

---

[407]See Arist. *Top.* 1.12 for Aristotle's words on this point: "Induction is more convincing and clear and more easily grasped by sense-perception and is shared by the majority of people, but reasoning is more cogent and more efficacious against argumentative opponents." See also 8.2, where he says induction should be used against the multitude.

[408]Isoc. Discourse 1 (*Demonicus*) 35.

not outcasts?[409]

In an another example, Demosthenes warns the Athenians of flirting with Philip's friendship. He gives them numerous examples of a "strange and distressing epidemic" invading Greece which is causing various cities to give up their independence:

> Yet this infatuation, this hankering after Philip, men of Athens, until very recently had only destroyed the predominance of the Thessalians and their national prestige, but now it is already sapping their independence, for some of their citadels are actually garrisoned by Macedonians. It has invaded Peloponnesus and caused the massacres at Elis. . . . It has entered Arcadia, and turned Arcadian politics upside down. . . . The Argives have followed their example. Holy Mother Earth! if I am to speak as a sane man, we stand in need of the utmost vigilance, when this infection, moving in its circuit, has invaded our own city.[410]

Aeschines gets in his licks at Demosthenes by the same argument from example, in order to show that the words of Ctesiphon's motion, "because he [Demosthenes] continually speaks and does what is best for the people," is a "monstrous assertion." Aeschines does this by a brief review of Demosthenes' private life in which the latter had betrayed relatives and friends to advance his

---

[409]Dem. *De Cor.* 48.

[410]Dem. *De Falsa Leg.* 259-61. See also 263-67 where Demosthenes reviews the experience of the Olynthians who could not be conquered by superior naval forces but were ultimately conquered by their own citizens accepting bribes, exactly Demosthenes' point regarding Aeschines. See also 294-97 for another excellent illustration of example. See also Dem. 23 (*Against Aristocrates*) 102, 104, 107, 118, 130, 141 where Demosthenes shows that his point can be learned from many examples or by relating a piece of history. See also Dem. 24 (*Against Timocrates*) 139: "I should like, gentlemen of the jury, to give you a description of the method of legislation among the Locrines. It will do you no harm to hear an example, especially one set by a well-governed community."

career.[411]

Isocrates affords many illustrations of example. There is a lengthy one in his address to Philip in whose personal genius he had hopes of a united Greece: "That it is not, therefore, impossible for you to bring these cities together, I think has become evident to you from what I have said. But more than that, I believe I can convince you by many examples that it will also be easy for you to do this." He proceeds to give him the examples of Alcibiades, Conon, Dionysius, and Cyrus, and then concludes the argument with:

> Now if Alcibiades in exile, and Conon after a disastrous defeat, and Dionysius, a man of no repute, and Cyrus, with his pitiable start in life, advanced so far and achieved such mighty deeds, how can we fail to expect that you, who are sprung from such ancestors, who are king of Macedonia and master of so many peoples, will effect with ease this union which we have discussed?[412]

Sometimes, examples may be used, as Aristotle says, as "part to part, of like to like, when both come under the same genus, but one of them is better known than the other" to argue deductively to a conclusion. Aristotle himself gives a very good illustration of this:

> For example, to prove that Dionysius is aiming at a tyranny, because he asks for a bodyguard, one might say that Pisistratus before him and Theagenes of Megara did the same, and when

---

[411]Aeschin. *In Ctes.* 51-53.

[412]Isoc. Discourse 5 (*To Philip*) 57-67. See also his other works: 4 (*Panegyricus*) 140-43; 6 (*Archidamus*), 41-46; 8 (*On the Peace*) 106-113; 14 (*Plataicus*) 40-50; 15 (*Antidosis*) 155, 231-39. See also Lys. 19 (*On the Property of Aristophanes: Against the Treasury*) 4, where he says: "I think you all know that there have been many cases in the past" of false accusations; also 34-52 in which he gives a long series of examples in which the jury had been mistaken about peoples' wealth based on rumors.

they obtained what they asked for made themselves tyrants. All the other tyrants known may serve as an example of Dionysius, whose reason, however, for asking for a bodyguard we do not yet know. All these examples are contained under the same universal proposition, that one who is aiming at a tyranny asks for a bodyguard.[413]

Aristotle argues deductively based on a major premise that is a universal proposition established inductively. The entire argument would go something like the following: All those who aim at a tyranny ask for a bodyguard. This is based on past experience, as for example Pisistratus and Theagenes and all other tyrants that one knows. The minor premise is: Dionysius asks for a bodyguard. The conclusion: Dionysius is aiming at a tyranny. Demosthenes gives a similar illustration of this type of argument from example when he attempts to prove that Timocratus wants to overthrow democracy by the way all conspirators begin, by subtly introducing laws that are inimical to the established constitution.[414]

Cicero cites numerous historical parallels to demonstrate and refute a point.[415] In defending Milo he tries to prove that homicide is justifiable and

---

[413]Arist. *Rh.* 1.2.19.

[414]Dem. 24 (*Timocrates*) 205-6. Aeschin. *In Ctes.* 235 is another example of this where the orator argues, as Palmer (*Aristotle's* τόποι, 39, n. 2) paraphrases it: "Any one who gains more strength than the courts is on his way to overthrow the state." Aeschines had cited the short reign of terror of the Thirty who had murdered more than 1500 citizens without trial.

[415]Cicero (*Top.* 44) cites the *causa Curiana* (92 B.C.E.) in which Lucius Licinius Crassus, the famous orator, "in his defense of Curius cited many cases of men who, having been named as heirs in the event that a son was born within ten months and died before attaining his majority, would have taken the inheritance. Such a citation of parallel cases carried the day, and you jurists make frequent use of it in your

even inevitable to defend oneself against violence:

> Once a soldier in the army of Gaius Marius suffered an indecent assault at the hands of a military tribune, a relative of the commander; and the assailant was slain by his intended victim, who, being an upright youth, preferred to act at his peril rather than to endure his dishonour. What is more, the great general absolved the offence and acquitted the offender.[416]

Again he uses a case from history to defend Flaccus against the charge of extortion based on Flaccus' devoted service to the nation: "Our ancestors discharged Manius Aquilius who had been proved guilt by a succession of witnesses on numerous charges of extortion because he had prosecuted with such energy the war against runaway slaves." He then goes on to cite Piso, whom he had defended and who had been given an innocent verdict "because he had been a stout and steadfast consul." In these and other cases, the jury is being asked through these historical precedents to consider their vote of not-guilty for Flaccus as one cast for the safety and best interests of the country. As one last example, Cicero attacks Publius Lentulus, a prominent praetor and supporter of Cataline's conspiracy, who was allowed to resign from office so the Senate could try him as a private citizen "without the restraint of any religious scruple, even though such scruples did not prevent the illustrious Gaius Marius from killing the praetor Gaius Glaucia without his being named in any resolution."[417]

---

responses."

[416]Cic. *Mil.* 4.9.

[417]Cic. *Cat.* 3.15.

These illustrations of example give one the flavor of the quality of reasoning inherent in rhetorical induction. The invented ones are as numerous as the historical ones cited above. Together with comparisons, similes, and analogous cases from fables and tales, they present a likeness to the subject under argumentation or persuasion which the speaker hopes the audience will accept as true. A universal statement is inferred based on similitude in at least one particular instance, although more individual cases add weight to the inference. With this background on the theory and practice of the enthymeme and example, the two components of rhetorical reasoning, we proceed now to see how Paul conducts his proof to the Corinthians through the method of λόγος.

C. The Use of Λόγος in 2 Corinthians 10-13

The λόγος of Paul's offense and defense in 2 Corinthians 10-13 is filled with proofs that answer his opponents and dissolve suspicion among the Corinthians that he is an opportunistic imposter. Paul uses a mixture of demonstrative and refutative enthymemes, maxims, and examples to argue for the authenticity of his apostleship and to persuade the Corinthians that his gospel is more expedient and advantageous for them than the claims of his adversaries. Already in his response he has projected himself as a person of outstanding character who is authoritatively stamped with the divine seal by reason of his extraordinary gifts and hardships. At the same time he has aroused in them a sense of outrage and indignation, fear and shame at their trifling acceptance of another gospel. Now by the very same speech he must cognitively convince the Corinthians through rational appeals that the false apostles are extremely dangerous for their spiritual existence and that his apostolic authority holds the promise of their approval before God.

Paul uses, first of all, the argument from authority throughout his response to the Corinthians. It had already been noted earlier in the section on $\mathring{\eta}\theta o\varsigma$ that Paul associated himself with God's power, knowledge, and trustworthiness to lend credibility and competence to his character as a genuine apostolic leader. He now strives to demonstrate this to the Corinthians through rational proofs that will convince them that he has been directly certified by God to work on their behalf. Paul uses this argument to promote his own standing before the Corinthians, to show his superiority to the pseudo-apostles, and to support his theology and his behavior as an apostle. His witness to all of this is none other than God, whom he calls upon any number of times to validate his statements (10:4, 8, 13; 11:11; 12: 2-3, 19). Paul asserts to the Corinthians that God has spoken to him directly, a fact that should to be motive enough for the Corinthians to give their consent to his leadership and theology (12:3-9). Paul's argument would syllogistically go something like this: You Corinthians recognize that extraordinary visions and revelations directly from God validate the origin, genuineness, and leadership of an apostle. Furthermore, you believe that one who undergoes and overcomes an almost overwhelming amount of hardships is a person stamped with God's approval and esteem. I have been the recipient of such blessings and sufferings to an unparalleled degree (11:23-29; 12:1-4, 12). Therefore, God is the source of my authority as an apostle and the original witness to the content of my gospel. The major premise is based on the universal proposition that these signs and wonders presume a special relationship with God, a presupposition already accepted by the Corinthians in their reception of the false apostles and their fascination with their letters of recommendation.

Paul accommodates himself to this universal proposition for the sake of the argument (10:8), although he does not believe it to be valid from his perspective (11:17). He bases his argument from authority for the validity of his gospel and the legitimacy of his apostleship on some other inductive fact, namely the one particular but comprehensive experience of the crucified Christ which then becomes a universal law in the domain of faith. The argument syllogistically would go something like this: The weakness of the crucified Jesus is the source of Jesus' power from God (13:4). I, Paul, have experienced weaknesses in this same spirit and "willingly boast of my weaknesses" instead of boasting in my accomplishments. Therefore, "the power of Christ rests upon me" (12:9). That is the validating stamp of approval of my gospel and ministry. Paul subtly offers this latest syllogism to the Corinthians as one which paradoxically supersedes the original argument intended to convince the Corinthians. He comes at this indirectly since he needs first to entertain the original universal proposition already accepted by the Corinthians, namely that signs and wonders are the legitimating marks of a true apostle, and use it on the level of their immature faith in order ultimately to contradict its inductive content and replace it with new experiential data. It is a subtle transposition of major premises which in either form establishes the fact of his delegated power from God and the motive for the allegiance of the Corinthians. They are to obey Paul, accept his gospel, reject the values of the false apostles because God has spoken in behalf of Paul.

Throughout his response Paul consistently braces up his statements with references to God as a knowledgeable and intimate partner on whom he can call for verification of his life and ministry. He frequently uses phrases like: "God knows I do" love you (11:11); "the God and Father of the Lord Jesus knows that I do not lie" (11:31); "only God can say" (12:2); "God knows" (12:3); "before God I tell you, in Christ, I have done everything to build you up" (12:19); "I begged the Lord. . . . He said to me" (12:8). These act as arguments from authority. And as Aristotle says, "it would be unseemly to contradict the gods."[418] Paul augments these authoritative expressions with others: "the power the Lord has given us" (10:8); my weapons "possess God's power" (10:4); "we will stay within the bounds the God of moderation has set for us" (11:13); "that the power of Christ may rest upon me" (12:9); "the proof

---

[418]Arist. *Rh*. 2.23.12.

of the Christ who speaks in me" (13:3); "we live in [Christ] by God's power in us" (13:4). It is the overwhelming ambience of the witness of God in Paul's defense that imparts to his argumentation a certitude that cannot be compromised or contradicted. His slanderers are necessarily silenced as he takes issue with their theology and methodology. They have no approval outside their own self-recommendation. The Corinthians should recognize the limited quality of such a witness. They now know that Paul has gone up to heaven to hear ineffable secrets and returned with this knowledge. What have his opponents to offer in comparison with this intimate, unmediated contact with the divine? The Corinthians must have to conclude that Paul knows the true meaning of God's wisdom expressed in Christ. The inferences from Paul's argument from authority lie under the surface, unexpressed formally by Paul but undoubtedly understood by the Corinthians. Paul's argumentation is almost one sustained enthymeme throughout using the τόπος ἐκ κρίσεως to prove his credentials.

There is a complex of thought surrounding the use of the word δόκιμος and the language of approval in 2 Cor 13:5-10 which is related to the argument from authority. The argument Paul uses concomitantly establishes once again his divine credentials while denigrating those of the false apostles who come self-recommended. At the same time the argument confronts the Corinthians as to their own practice of the faith. The argument refers to the *scrutinium* or δοκιμασία in the Greek political system whereby public officials were required to submit to an examination before taking office to determine their worthiness.

They had to be approved by an examining body before assuming their duties.

Likewise they had to undergo an examination (εὔθυνα) at the end of their term

to determine their conduct while in office.[419] Through his play on the word

δοκιμάζω which refers to the scrutiny of candidates for official state functions,

Paul argues that he has been examined and tested by God, mainly through his

sufferings, and has been approved an authentic apostle. His visions and

revelations are the proof (δοκιμή, 13:3) of his divine approbation. Paul says

of himself: "We are not ἀδόκιμοι." Paul argues that he is God-commended,

while the false apostles are counterfeits (10:18: self-boasting does not make one

δόκιμος; see also 11:13-15). Paul warns the Corinthians to test themselves

(ἐαυτοὺς πειράζετε, 13:5) in the faith lest they become ἀδόκιμοι (13:5). The

implication of Paul's argument is that the Corinthians, so long as they follow

the authority of the false apostles, will be unapproved by God.

Concomitant with this topic Paul uses another argument, one derived from

the more and the less or the a fortiori argument. This argument works quite

effectively since Paul claims such a startling contrast between himself and his

opponents in character, behavior, and theology. One of the more dramatic

inclusionary statements is the identification of the false apostles with Satan; it

is meant as a strong warning to the Corinthians to avoid such people. Paul's

---

[419]Aristotle (Constitution of Athens 55) describes what the examination might be like. Isoc. 7 (Areopagiticus) 38 refers to the "examination of magistrates" and Aechin. In Tim. 28 cites Solon's thoughts contained in his "Scrutiny of public men."

argument would go something like this: If the great deceiver Satan disguises himself as an angel of light, "it comes as no surprise that his ministers disguise themselves as ministers of the justice of God" (11:13-15). This is an example of the greater to the lesser. Another way to word this is through the following syllogism based on the presumed truth of the accepted premise that Satan is a master disguiser who can trick people into thinking he is a minister of Christ: those who disguise themselves as apostles of Christ are Satan; the false apostles disguise themselves as apostles of Christ (i.e., angels of light); therefore the false apostles are Satan. There is no overt statement that the false apostles are Satan but the conclusion is all the more chilling because the Corinthians are forced to the conclusion; they foresee it as soon as the syllogism is set up. There is a further corollary to this argument: the false apostles, as a result of their behavior and deception, will end up in the same way and place as Satan. This is another enthymeme expressed through one premise (11:15). In a few words Paul has demonstrated the utter baseness of his opponents. It is a devastating argument because it inculcates at the same time a profound fear in the Corinthians at their own destiny, if they follow such a crowd.

At the same time, if the false apostles are capable of assuming such morally depraved disguises and furthermore of exploiting the Corinthians (11:20), what is hindering them from further encroachments on the freedom of the Corinthians? If they do not hesitate to do these things, what is to say they will not hesitate to do other things more dreadful to the Corinthians? A corollary of this is Paul's rebuke, expressed in elliptical form: it is shameful that you honor such people who take advantage of you but you will not honor me, the one who loves you and has proved it in a selfless way (11:11; 12:15).

Continuing this contrast between his behavior and that of his opponents, Paul challenges the so-called wisdom of the Corinthians by the anomaly of their endurance of the exploitation of the false apostles (11:19-20) and their rejection of his alleged unimpressive person (10:1, 10). He ironically plays upon the verb ἀνέχομαι. He finds their choice most illogical, arguing with a good dose of irony: if their wisdom leads them to endure this kind of abusive treatment (11:19-20), then they are in no position to pass judgment on him (11:16). Paul asks them to endure a little of his folly, since they endure a lot more from others (11:19). Ironically, the Corinthians ought to be grateful to Paul that he lives up to their perception of him, powerful in his letters but weak in appearance; for if he did not, then he would treat them as abusively as the false apostles. Paul thus discredits their notions of appearance and reality and calls for a redefinition of wisdom and power.

Paul further uses this argument to refute the charge that he was "crafty," catching the Corinthians by guile and taking advantage of them (12:16-17). He argues that it would be madness in him if, after preaching the gospel free of charge and making sure he was no burden to them, he should turn around now and take advantage of the Corinthians. Why should he do something illegal and underhanded now when he could earlier have accomplished the same end with social approbation? The slander of the false opponents is not logical. With this argument, Paul implies his opponents have twisted his motives in declining support from the Corinthians.

Furthermore, Paul argues, the false apostles claim authenticity based on letters of recommendation and self-appraising *synkrisis* with one another in a closed circle (10:12). His legitimacy, on the other hand, is based on an authenticating principle outside of himself, namely on God (10:18). If the Corinthians can give their allegiance to these false apostles with human pretensions (11:18), they should even more so give their devotion to Paul who comes recommended by God. Conversely, Paul is arguing that in this world of God-recommended apostles, there is no room for human boasting; there is only the weakness of Christ crucified who now lives by the power of God. If this gospel is the only reality, then the much-vaunted ministry of the false apostles is an illusion, sheer ignorance (10:12). The obvious conclusion based on this argument from the more and the less is that if the Corinthians have the right gospel and the divinely deputized leader to begin with, why do they settle for something else? Why settle for less when they have it all? The appeal is to their notions of advantage and expediency on the basis of a logical argument.

The next argument Paul uses is based on the topic of definition. He deliberately plays into the hands of the Corinthians by tentatively accepting their definition of the legitimate apostle as one endowed with signs and wonders, applies it to himself, and then abruptly redefines apostolic criteria on the experience of Christ. The first part he does very directly by saying: "If anyone is convinced that he belongs to Christ, let him reflect on this: he may belong to Christ but just as much do we" (10:7) and "Even though I am nothing, I am in no way inferior to the super-apostles" (12:11). He says frankly: "I am more of a minister of Christ than they" (11:23). Paul's argument runs something like this: if, as you say, signs and wonders make an apostle, I fit the definition perfectly by reason of my many more hardships for the gospel and my many revelations from God. "I have performed among you with great patience the signs that show the apostle" (12:12). He uses this argument to exonerate himself and to clear himself of the slanders that have attached to his name. He catches the Corinthians off-guard by meeting them on their own terms. He matches their expectations completely, even exceeding those they held for Paul's opponents.

Paul, in spite of his reluctance to talk about his personal experiences, lays the facts out frankly, since he is being tried, as it were, on precisely what the Corinthians call the signs of an apostle. He meets his audience at their own level, the definition of a legitimate apostle. However, in the course of his self-revelations he shifts the grounds of the criteria and begins formulating a new definition which meets his own criteria based on his experience of the crucified Christ who died out of weakness but now lives by the power of God (13:4). The argument from this new definition sounds something like the following: the community is able to recognize the true apostle based on the "Jesus . . . we preached" and on "the gospel you accepted" (11:4). The true apostle is defined as one who boasts of and is "content with weakness, with mistreatment, with distress, with persecution, and difficulties for the sake of Christ" (12:10). The true apostle is recognized as one who looks powerless on the outside but is strong in the way the crucified and risen Christ is strong: "We too are weak in him, but we live with him by God's power in us" (13:4). It is a choice of reality over appearances and one must choose wisely, lest one fail the challenge (13:5). Such a definition outrightly condemns the tactics of the false apostles and their different gospel and supplants them with another model. Paul does not say directly that he fits this new model perfectly but this is the obvious conclusion, unexpressed but understood. From this judgment the Corinthians are to give their allegiance to Paul.

Flowing from this is the damning accusation hurled at the false apostles. How does one recognize they are false? They are in disguise as minions of Satan, although they claim they work on the same terms as Paul (11:12) and even claim his work as their own, as implied by 10:15. There will be many signs: they will recommend themselves and they will compare themselves to others (10:12), they will boast immodestly (10:12), they will abuse their disciples (11:20), they will raise their definition "against the knowledge of God" as preached and experienced by Paul (10:5), they will slander Paul who has been to heaven and back with unutterable revelations (12:11). Just as these formerly were parts of the earlier definition used against Paul, they are no longer part of the new definition which Paul gives the Corinthians. He challenges them not to be superficial (10:7) but to test themselves to see whether they are living in faith (13:5). Paul's argument from definition becomes an exercise in revising their notions of the gospel of Jesus.

Paul's use of the μέτρον τῆς κανόνος in 2 Cor 13:12-15 becomes part of the persuasive argument from definition. Paul details the parameters of boasting; it cannot exceed the bounds established by God (10:13). *Self*-commendation is contrary to this μέτρον. The false apostles measure themselves by their own standards (10:12). Therefore the false apostles exceed the legitimate rule; they boast εἰς τὰ ἄμετρα (10:15) They are not approved (see use of δόκιμος in 10:18). Paul, on the other hand, is approved because he stays within the measure of the rule established by God. He attempts no *synkrisis* or *self*-commendation. In this argument Paul re-defines an apostle for the Corinthians as one who is approved by God (10:18). He makes the necessary conclusions concerning the status of the false apostles based on their invalid standard. They don't measure up. They cannot be authentic.

Another topical argument Paul uses is one that consists in examining inconsistencies in the words and actions of his adversaries in order to demonstrate their hypocritical stance and in showing the contradictions between their slander and his actual behavior. This refutative argument has the twofold purpose, therefore, of discounting the character of his opponents in the eyes of the Corinthians and of discrediting their aspersions against him. Paul goes on to show that the false apostles are not what they claim to be nor is he what they claim him to be. Both of these points have already been touched upon from other aspects. Here Paul uses enthymemes to prove his point rationally.

Paul has already set the tone of the self-contradictions of his opponents in his potent image of their masquerade as ministers of Christ. Like Satan, "they practice deceit" (11:13). This declaration consequently calls into question everything they say about themselves or about Paul. Nothing of what they preach, Paul is saying to the Corinthians, can be believed. As for the inconsistencies in his opponents' words and actions, Paul gives evidence. He uses a climactic series of verbs in 11:20 to point out their exploitation, their imposition on the hospitality of the Corinthians, their proud demeanor, and even their physical abuse. These are not the actions of an authentic apostle. Cast in syllogistic form, the argument runs as follows: an authentic apostle does everything to build the Corinthians up (12:19), not take advantage of them. His opponents take advantage of the Corinthians by proclaiming superiority and by behavior that is demeaning. They boast they are authentic apostles but their actual conduct shows them to be otherwise. Paul refutes their inflated claims by pointing out to the Corinthians what his opponents are actually doing. Their actions reveal their intentions.

Paul mainly uses this argument, however, to answer the charges against him and to amplify his own character as an authentic apostle. He not only makes his claim but he shows by his conduct that he is truly what he says he is.

The disclosures of his hardships and extraordinary revelations minutely answer the accusations against him. He points out to the Corinthians that the slanders of his opponents that he is not an authentic apostle stand in stark contradiction to his almost superhuman endurance and experience of supernatural gifts. Paul argues that if his opponents say he does not show the signs and wonders of an apostle, how does one explain then his actual experience? Their statements, therefore, are false and cannot be substantiated.

Besides pointing out the falsity of statements which do not measure up with reality, Paul uses this argument for yet a third reason, namely to point up the contrast between his selfless behavior toward the Corinthians and their exploitation by his opponents. Paul argues that his opponents have never shown the Corinthians their disinterested love; but he constantly stresses that he has shown them extraordinary love and a desire to build them up (11:11; 12:19). This thought is implied in his statement: "I will gladly spend myself and be spent for your sakes. If I love you too much, will I be loved the less for that?" (12:15). The argument throughout is that words must be supported by action and that his actions have been far more evidentially based than those of his opponents who speak well but who do not live up to their claims. The overriding irony of the entirety of chapters 10-13 is that the false apostles are actually guilty of the opposite of what they accuse Paul of. They accused Paul of being strong in his letters but weak in his presence (10:10). They, by way of contrast, are strong in their rhetoric in the presence of the Corinthians but weak in the actual fact of their deeds.

The last topic Paul uses is one employed in cases of slander where the speaker denies and then refutes the charges by explaining why they arose in the first place. Paul is sensitive to the criticisms that he displays "weak human behavior" (10:2), that he does not belong to Christ (10:7), that he does not show the signs of an apostle (12:12), that his refusal to accept support was wrong (11:7). He denies all these charges based on the definitions given to these accusations. The slanders are predicated on a different gospel and spirit and on another Jesus than the one he first preached to the Corinthians. It is no wonder the Corinthians have given credence to them. Paul spends the majority of his argument slowly re-educating the Corinthians. He vehemently denies all the charges, while showing that the charges were seemingly true because the Corinthians did not understand or accept Paul's theology of a Christ crucified in weakness but now living by the power of God. This seems to be the meaning of his remark to the Corinthians: "You view things superficially" (κατὰ πρόσωπον, 10:7).

Paul, by his own admission, is not inclined toward the self-appraising boasting of his opponents (10:12). He has a different spirit. He wants approval from God for his work in the ministry (10:17). This is the reason for his modesty in not vaunting himself. However, he is a realist enough to know that he must answer the charges and do it on the terms demanded by his accusers before he can inculcate a different attitude. Paul's reluctance to meet his accusers on their own terms, which to him is foolishness, gives credibility to the slanders. At the end of his catalogue of hardships and disclosure of his rapture into paradise, he says somewhat enigmatically: "Do you think throughout this recital that I am defending myself to you?" (12:19). He has been defending himself above all by showing the reasons for the attacks. His explanation, namely that he is more interested in boasting of his weaknesses so that the power of Christ may be on him (12:9), refutes the charges.

In using this topic, Paul exposes a fallacy in the argumentation of his opponents, one that Aristotle mentions in his discussion of apparent enthymemes. This is the fallacy of consequence. The example Aristotle gives illustrates the fallacy: "Since a man pays attention to dress and roams about at night, he is a libertine, because libertines are of this character."[420] Paul points out to the Corinthians this fallacy in the contention of his opponents that he is not an apostle just because he does not speak well or have the outward appearances and behavior of one.

In addition to his use of the topics as sources for enthymemes, Paul also includes maxims in his arsenal of proofs. One, 10:17-18, has the ring of a solemn pronouncement, which actually is a citation of Jer 9:22-23: the one who boasts in the Lord is approved. The Corinthians are able and obliged to fill in the missing premises. In doing so, they make a judgment against the false apostles as well as against themselves. Another maxim is one that Paul uses to

---

[420]Arist. *Rh.* 2.24.7.

show his love for the Corinthians by choosing not to be a burden to them. He says in 12:14: "Children should not save up for their parents but parents for children." This maxim makes a general observation about the natural order of things.[421] Paul transfers this truth to another plane to signify to the Corinthians that he is their parent in Christ, telling them not only of his unselfish love in contrast to the exploitation of the false apostles but calling them to obedience.

Another maxim, paradoxical in its meaning, carries much of Paul's argument in 2 Corinthians 10-13 and presupposes some previous catechizing of the Corinthians along this theological thought, although he has had to remind them of it in light of the different gospel they received from the false apostles. In 12:9, Paul, after praying that the thorn in his side would be removed, received this message from the Lord: "My grace is enough for you, for in weakness power reaches perfection." Such a statement exposes the uselessness of boasting about one's achievements or extraordinary gifts, since they in no way demonstrate the authenticity of the apostle. In 13:3-5 Paul applies the truth borne by this maxim as a litmus test of the faith of the Corinthians and as a proof that Paul has not failed the Corinthians or in his own self-understanding (13:6). One of the advantages of maxims, as Aristotle observed, is that "it makes speeches ethical." They show moral purpose and consequently the moral

---

[421]This may be a traditional proverb which Paul took from a collection of γνῶμαι. The thought echoes a passage from Philo, *Moses* 2.245, which Furnish (*II Corinthians*, 558, n. 14) quotes: "But since, in the natural order of things children are the heirs of their fathers and not fathers of their children . . ."

character of the speaker, while at the same time they convince by reason of their immediate appeal to the audience's moral sense.

Paul uses examples to advance the argumentation of his letter. They are useful even though they don't strictly demonstrate the point at hand but mainly corroborate it. A comparison or simile can act cogently to underscore an argument. Paul uses a persuasive example in 11:3 to emphasize for the Corinthians the seriousness of giving in to the seductive blandishments of the false apostles. He takes a past example of historic consequences for the human race in its relationship to God and applies it as a future possibility for the Corinthians. The Corinthians are poised at this moment like Eve of old. The false apostles are the cunning serpent. Should the Corinthians listen to the serpent's voice, they will fall away from Christ, a condition of inconceivable dislocation such as Adam and Eve experienced in being put out of the garden of Paradise. Paul's use of this historical precedent is sufficient warrant for the Corinthians to end their relationship with the false apostles. As a contrast to the activity of the false apostles, Paul uses another example to prove his own genuineness to them. He says he has the jealous love of God for them. As such, he is the one, acting *in loco parentis*, to give them in marriage to Christ (11:2). No one else has this right. The example implies that the false apostles are satanic seducers and the Corinthians potential adulterers should they flirt with them.

The above discussion is representative of how Paul arranges the λόγος of his response to persuade the Corinthians to accept his own judgment of the dangerous situation in the community. Paul approaches the Corinthians with logical proofs, arguments based on enthymeme and example, to appeal to their reason. Paul designs his logical proofs to show the Corinthians that his gospel and his person are rooted in the kind of evidence that induces belief and to demonstrate that he is approved by God. As such, he is the only one with credentials and authority to speak as an authentic apostle. His critics, on the other hand, are not approved by God. Therefore their recommendation and their self-approving comparisons and gifts, however real, are useless to show any divine apostolic commission. Paul logically turns on its head his critics' argument in 13:3 that there is no proof of the Christ speaking in him.

At this point in his response Paul has demonstrated his slanderers to be false apostles and deceitful workers (11:3) and himself to be more a minister of Christ than they (11:23) because he acts in the same spirit as Christ did—crucified through weakness but now living by the power of God (13:4). This is Paul's recommendation and consequently the reason for his approved status as an apostle. Paul, through the use of enthymemes and the example of Christ, produces evidence of his authority and his gospel. Paul's λόγος, the logical part of his response, when interwoven with his reciprocal use of ἦθος and πάθος, makes a persuasive argument for his case.

CONCLUSION

This study has analyzed the three methods of proof, ἦθος, πάθος, and λόγος, mentioned by Aristotle and other ancient theorists of rhetoric as foundational in any rhetorical act of persuasion, and Paul's rhetorical use of them in 2 Corinthians 10-13. My argument was that Paul was probably aware of the theory and practice of these methods and used them to advantage in addressing the rhetorical situation in Corinth. Although he used the letter form, which prevented him from the oratorical benefit of direct delivery in front of a live audience, he nevertheless incorporated in 2 Corinthians 10-13 all the salient rhetorical techniques and literary conventions for effective persuasion to create the virtual experience of personal address.

The study concentrated on Paul's use of these three constituent and interactive methods of proof without concern for the parts and basic division of a rhetorical speech. My object was primarily to see how Paul exercised the power of persuasion through the interplay of the strength of his personal character (as well as his knowledge of the character of the audience), the use of emotions, and the quality of his rhetorical reasoning; and through this analysis to come to a deeper understanding of the text. My aim was a strictly historical one. This is to say that I examined only those literary sources containing the theory and practice of rhetoric antecedent to and contemporaneous with Paul as possible influences on his use of the three methods of proof characteristically utilized in any act of persuasion, always with the understanding that Paul adapted these methods to the exigencies of the situation at hand. First, I extracted the definition, nature, and understanding of ἦθος, πάθος, and λόγος from the ancient theorists notable for their critical analysis of the rhetorical act. Second, I examined representative speeches of select famous orators for the actual practice of these methods of proof. And last, I investigated 2 Corinthians 10-13 for Paul's use of these techniques traditional to any persuasion for the purpose of coming to a deeper understanding of the function and meaning of the text. Some tentative conclusions can be drawn from this investigation:

1. Far from rejecting rhetoric, Paul took advantage of the leverage rhetorical skills gave him on occasion and used them in the service of the Gospel. His statement that he was an ἰδιώτης τῷ λόγῳ (11:6), however one interprets what he was an "amateur" in, cannot be minimally taken as a realistic or serious appraisal of his inability to argue persuasively in writing but should be considered as a form of *praeteritio*, a rhetorical technique used by many speakers of his times. Paul himself acknowledges that his critics think his letters are βαρεῖαι καὶ ἰσχυραί (10:10) and that he is bold (θάρρος) *in absentia* (ἀπὼν) but makes a poor showing (ταπεινός) in person (κατὰ πρόσωπον, 10:1). These statements indicate that he has at least rhetorical writing skills if not necessarily rhetorical presence.

Paul's use of λόγος (11:6) can mean eloquence in the sense of assured and inspired delivery[422] and it can also connote persuasive writing. My assertions of Paul's skilled use of rhetorical techniques in 2 Corinthians 10-13 does not draw any conclusions about his ability at public speaking, which may have been the criticism leveled against him (10:10). My point was to prove, from the rhetorical investigation of the text, that Paul most probably had serious training in rhetorical skills through exposure to the *progymnasmata* and advanced lessons available in Tarsus. There he learned the cogency of logical proofs, the knowledge and effectiveness of the use of the emotions, and the psychological advantage of good character as crucial components in any persuasive argument.

The key point in my rhetorical analysis has been that he used such rhetorical techniques as proofs to re-establish his competence and credibility, to refute the accusations of his critics, and re-claim the allegiance of the Corinthians. His self-defense, which stands out prominently in the text, has been precisely for the larger cause of the upbuilding (οἰκοδομή) of the Corinthians (10:8; 12:19; 13:10). What was at stake was a serious challenge, in Paul's mind, to the Corinthians' authentic faith in Christ. This challenge attenuated the power of the weak and crucified Christ (13:4) and supplanted it with enthusiasm for the self-made credentials of human beings. This was the

---

[422]Munck (*Paul and the Salvation of Mankind*, 158, n.2) gives an extensive enlightening footnote on the quality of θάρσος (Att. θάρρος) demanded in the bearing of an orator. He further suggests that the Corinthians may have been guilty of deifying their Christian leaders based on their ability to persuade, which was a mark of a great sophist. Paul apparently did not have the style of a professional orator and it is perhaps this lack he is referring to in 11:6 and not to the eloquence (λόγος) expressed in literary form.

pragmatic exigence which called forth Paul's rhetorical response with the intention of altering the dysfunctional reality. My point has been that Paul, to use Lloyd Bitzer's phrase, introduced a set of constraints, necessarily operative in a rhetorical situation, to re-create reality through discourse.[423] These constraints were the so-called artistic or speaker-created proofs of Aristotle and other rhetorical theorists, namely proof through character ($\mathring{\eta}\theta o\varsigma$), emotions ($\pi\acute{\alpha}\theta o\varsigma$), and rhetorical reasoning ($\lambda\acute{o}\gamma o\varsigma$).

2. In this regard, New Testament critics need to take these categories of proof into consideration when interpreting 2 Corinthians 10-13, since it has been the underlying assumption of my investigation that the rhetorical situation faced by Paul invited and dictated the kind of response his discourse ultimately took. The situation of slander against Paul, the kind of gospel advocated by the false apostles, the threat to his personal authority, and the crisis of faith for the Corinthians clearly prescribed the matter, form, and style of his answer. Looking at 2 Corinthians 10-13 through the lens of these three classical methods of proof brings focus to the understanding of the text and shows that Paul's response was a serious and straightforward one. He was not attempting to parody the self-laudation techniques of his opponents in order to show the emptiness of such an approach. Neither was he merely using rhetoric for the sake of display before the Corinthians. The rhetorical situation demanded

---

[423]See Bitzer, *The Rhetorical Situation*, 8. Some of the following conclusions utilize the insights of Bitzer regarding the rhetorical situation.

precisely the kind of conventional use of the classical tripartite method of proof in order to mediate change in the Corinthians.

As a way of illustrating the above statements, we can say that Isocrates filled his *Antidosis* with arguments from character, emotions, and reasoning because this was the proper and relevant response to attacks against his method of teaching. His response was apropos to the situation in which his enemies were assailing his good name through invective, emotional pleading, incorrect facts about his wealth, and specious logic concerning the value of good speaking for a citizen. From the only example we have in antiquity of litigation between a plaintiff (Aeschines) and a defendant (Demosthenes), we can see spelled out clearly the kind of response on Demosthenes' part invited by the situation generated by Aeschines. We can extrapolate from Paul's words the rhetorical situation which ultimately determined the form of his response, a reply, I contend, drawn from the classical methods of proof.

3. In doing rhetorical analysis of 2 Corinthians 10-13 or even of other selected Pauline texts to probe for deeper understanding, critics will have to introduce some outside controls on their exegesis by investigating historical parallels using these rhetorical methods of proof or other Greco-Roman rhetorical conventions. Without such controls, the rhetorical analysis will become an overlay of a modern paradigm or an imaginative re-creation. I have been at pains to show both from actual theory and from numerous literary precedents that Paul utilized traditional techniques of argumentation familiar to

his audience. He used standard methods of proof which mediated his message and through which he influenced his rhetorical audience to change its perceptions. The apposition of both ancient rhetorical theory and practice to 2 Corinthians 10-13 makes this mode of argumentation immediately apparent. One additional benefit of such a comparative analysis has been the exposition of the socio-rhetorical contexts, cultural conventions, intellectual categories, institutional roles, and political alignments existing in the Greco-Roman world of the Corinthian community which honored, expected, delighted in, and were convinced by the use of such rhetorical proofs.

4. Paul's manner of addressing the rhetorical situation through the use of the three methods of proof should make the critic more cautious in defining the enemies in 2 Corinthians 10-13. Who were they and were they as bad as Paul portrays them? Paul's emotional language and his negative imagery of them, flowing from his perceived sense of their self-absorption and threats to his authority and gospel, convey a censorious attitude which makes it hard to sift for the truth. We cannot conclude from Paul that this is the way his antagonists were in actuality. If we had only the speech of Aeschines or only that of Demosthenes, we would have to conclude from their respective portraits that both were traitors and reprobates. Even with both speeches before us, it is hard to filter out the truth. We can get a sense of how rhetorical proofs can color the listeners' judgments by the manner in which Aeschines pictures Timarchus. Whatever the content of the resulting portrait, we can see the form of the three

proofs at work. There is a tendency, perhaps exemplified at times by my own analysis, to side with Paul and to believe he is righteous and true in his attitude toward those whom he dubs as false apostles (11:13). However, one needs to exercise caution in being swayed by Paul's rhetoric. It was an accepted convention of classical rhetorical argumentation to paint the other side in derisive and deprecatory tones. This was part of the delight an ancient audience felt at accomplished orators crossing swords.

Paul twice calls his antagonists super-apostles (11:5; 12:11: τῶν ὑπερλίαν ἀποστόλων) and he becomes somewhat apologetic to the Corinthians in his claim that he is in no way inferior to them. Both references seem to indicate that Paul recognized, with some tinge of irony, their gifts, however inappropriately they used them to manipulate the Corinthians. Paul's ultimate condemnation of them, however, rests on the notion of approval. They are not approved by God (10:18). Though they might have been tested in hardships like himself and have received spiritual gifts, yet these credentials were not enough to make them apostles of Christ (11:13) or ministers of the justice of God (11:15). Paul claims that even Satan comes with the same references (11:14). Something else is needed. That something else only Paul has and this is what makes him their authentic apostle, namely approbation by God (13:3-9). Paul's conviction of this status of approval makes him intransigent in his condemnation of his antagonists and thus colors the kind of language and style he uses to characterize them. Be that as it may, given the theory and examples in the paper on how orators try to win allegiance to their point of view, the reader has to weigh Paul's rhetorical approach and beware of adopting wholesale Paul's denunciation of his critics.

5. The chief rhetorical genre or species of rhetoric exemplified in 2 Corinthians 10-13, although this was not a main thrust of the paper, is that of *deliberative* rhetoric. Paul mainly exhorts the Corinthians to what he feels is expedient and advantageous in terms of present and particularly future belief and behavior as a community in alliance with its founder and conversely dissuades them from a mentality that is based upon false wisdom and false allegiance. Paul persuades them not to be ἀδόκιμοι (13:5), that is, outside the pale of approbation by God and therefore outside the community. If they are not in affiliation with him who has been approved by God, they are in danger (11:3). There is no middle ground. Consequently, the Corinthians must make the right judgment (13:5).

In conclusion, then, my primary focus has been on Paul's rhetorical strategy in 2 Corinthians 10-13 and the techniques of persuasion he employed to respond to a situation of challenge from opponents and dissidents concerning theology and authority. The challenge was so commanding that it obligated Paul to respond. Moreover, the situation was so controlling that it dictated that way Paul needed most effectively to argue, namely, through the use of the three classical methods of proof in any persuasive discourse. In order properly to understand Paul's meaning in 2 Corinthians 10-13, one must grasp the nature and needs of his audience as well as the standard and familiar sources of proof needed to modify the situation. Like his audience, Paul was aware that his opponents had predetermined the conditions in which he was obliged to defend himself ($\mathring{\eta}\theta o\varsigma$), to dispose the Corinthians emotionally to see the situation as he saw it ($\pi\acute{\alpha}\theta o\varsigma$), and to offer them solid reasons for his legitimacy as their only authentic apostle ($\lambda\acute{o}\gamma o\varsigma$). His opponents had the boldness ($\tau\acute{o}\lambda\mu\alpha$, 2 Cor 10:12; 11:21) to set up this situation; he would have similar boldness to answer, however foolish the charade (11:21). Paul would do anything for the upbuilding of the Corinthians (10:8; 12:19; 13:10), even to an exercise in rhetorical argumentation. My purpose was to show how Paul made his appeal through the three proofs well-known to rhetorical transactions, in which persuasion, acceptance of Paul's view of reality, was the ultimate goal.

BIBLIOGRAPHY

Ancient Texts

Aeschines. *The Speeches of Aeschines*. Translated by Charles D. Adams. LCL. Cambridge: Harvard University Press, 1988.

Aristotle. *The Poetics*. Translated by W. H. Fyfe. LCL. Cambridge: Harvard University Press, 1982.

--------. *The Art of Rhetoric*. Translated by John H. Freese. LCL. Cambridge: Harvard University Press, 1926.

--------. *Rhetorica Ad Alexandrum*. Translated by H. Rackham. Rev. ed. LCL. Cambridge: Harvard University Press, 1983.

--------. *Topica*. Translated by E. S. Forster. LCL. Cambridge: Harvard University Press, 1989.

Cicero. *De Amicitia*. Translated by William A. Falconer. LCL. Cambridge: Harvard University Press, 1992.

--------. *Brutus*. Translated by G. L. Hendrickson. Rev. ed. LCL. Cambridge: Harvard University Press, 1988.

--------. *In Catalinam I-IV*. Translated by C. Macdonald. New ed. LCL. Cambridge: Harvard University Press, 1989.

--------. *De Domo sua*. Translated by N. H. Watts. LCL. London: William Heinemann, 1923.

--------. *Pro Flacco*. Translated by C. Macdonald. New ed. LCL. Cambridge: Harvard University Press, 1989.

--------. *De Haruspicum Responsis*. Translated by N. H. Watts. LCL. London: William Heinemann, 1923.

--------. *De Inventione*. Translated by H. M. Hubbell. LCL. Cambridge: Harvard University Press, 1976.

--------. *Pro Ligario*. Translated by N. H. Watts. Rev. ed. LCL. Cambridge: Harvard University Press, 1992.

--------. *The Letters to His Friends Including the Letters to Quintus*. Vol. III. Translated by W. Glynn Williams. LCL. London: William Heinemann, 1929.

--------. *Pro Milone*. Translated by N. H. Watts. Rev. ed. LCL. Cambridge: Harvard University Press, 1992.

--------. *Pro Murena*. Translated by C. Macdonald. New ed. LCL. Cambridge: Harvard University Press, 1989.

--------. *Orator*. Translated by H. M. Hubbell. Rev. ed. LCL. Cambridge: Harvard University Press, 1988.

--------. *De Oratore Books I, II*. Translated by E. W. Sutton and completed by H. Rackham. LCL. Cambridge: Harvard University Press, 1988.

--------. *De Oratore Book III*. Translated by H. Rackham. LCL. Cambridge: Harvard University Press, 1982.

--------. *De Partitione Oratoria*. Translated by H. Rackham. LCL. Cambridge: Harvard University Press, 1982.

--------. *Pro Plancio*. Translated by N. A. Watts. LCL. London: William Heinemann, 1923.

--------. *Post Reditum ad Quirites*. Translated by N. H. Watts. LCL. London: William Heinemann, 1923.

--------. *Pro Sulla*. Translated by C. Macdonald. New ed. LCL. Cambridge: Harvard University Press, 1989.

--------. *Topica*. Translated by H. M. Hubbell. LCL. Cambridge: Harvard University Press, 1976.

--------. *The Verrine Orations*. Vol. I. LCL. London: William Heinemann, 1928.

Demetrius. *On Style*. Translated by W. Rhys Roberts. Rev.ed. LCL. Cambridge: Harvard University Press, 1982.

Demosthenes. *De Corona and De Falsa Legatione*. Translated by C. A.

Vince and J. H. Vince. LCL. Cambridge: Harvard University Press, 1971.

--------. *Against Meidias, Androtion, Aristocrates, Timocrates, Aristogeiton I and II.* Translated by J. H. Vince. LCL. Cambridge: Harvard University Press, 1986.

--------. *Private Orations 50-58.* Translated by A. T. Murray. LCL. Cambridge: Harvard University Press, 1964.

Isaeus. *Speeches.* Translated by Edward S. Forster. LCL. Cambridge: Harvard University Press, 1983.

Isocrates. *On the Peace, Areopagiticus, Against the Sophists, Antidosis, Panathenaicus.* Vol. II. LCL. Cambridge: Harvard University Press, 1982.

--------. *Orations and Letters.* Vol. III. Translated by Larue Van Hook. LCL. Cambridge: Harvard University Press, 1986.

Longinus. *On the Sublime.* Translated by W. H. Fyfe. LCL. Cambridge: Harvard University Press, 1982.

Lysias. *Orations.* Translated by W. R. M. Lamb. LCL. Cambridge: Harvard University Press, 1988.

Plato. *The Dialogues of Plato.* Translated by B. Jowett. 2 vols. New York: Random House, 1920.

Plutarch. *Moralia I.* Translated by Frank Cole Babbitt. Cambridge: Harvard University Press, 1986.

Quintilian. *The Institutio Oratoria of Quintilian.* Translated by H. E. Butler. Four volumes. LCL. Cambridge: Harvard University Press, 1989.

[------]. *Rhetorica Ad Herennium.* Translated by Harry Caplan. LCL. Cambridge: Harvard University Press, 1989.

Elder Seneca. *Controversiae and Suasoriae.* Translated by M. Winterbottom. 2 vols. LCL. Cambridge: Harvard University Press, 1974.

Seneca. *Moral Essays.* Translated by John W. Basore. 3 vols. LCL. Cambridge: Harvard University Press, 1985.

Spengel, Leonard. *Rhetores Graeci.* 3 vols. BT. Leipzig: Teubner, 1853-56.

Walz, Christian. *Rhetores Graeci.* 9 vols. Stuttgart und Tübingen: J. G. Cottae, 1832-36.

Secondary Literature

Alewell, K. *Über das rhetorische PARADEIGMA. Theorie Beispielsammlung. Verwendung in der römischen Literature der Kaiserzeit.* Leipzig: Hoffmann, 1913.

Amante, David J. "The Theory of Ironic Speech Acts." *Poetics Today* 2 (1981) 77-96.

Atkins, J. W. H. *Literary Criticism in Antiquity.* Gloucester, MA: Peter Smith, 1961.

Aune, David E. *The New Testament in Its Literary Environment.* Library of Early Christianity 8. Philadelphia: Westminster, 1987.

Bailey, James L. and Lyle D. Vander Broek. *Literary Forms in the New Testament: A Handbook.* Westminster, MD: John Knox, 1992.

Baird, William. *1 Corinthians, 2 Corinthians.* Knox Preaching Guides. Atlanta: Knox, 1980.

Baldwin, C. S. *Ancient Rhetoric and Poetic.* New York: Macmillan, 1924; reprinted, Westport, CT: Greenwood, 1971.

--------. *Medieval Rhetoric and Poetic.* New York, 1924; reprinted, Westport, CT: Greenwood, 1971. Hermogenes' *Progymnasmata* in English, 23-38.

Baird, William. "Visions, Revelation, and Ministry: Reflection on 2 Cor 12:1-5 and Gal 1:11-17." *JBL* 104 (1985) 651-662.

Barré, M. L. "Paul as 'Eschatologic Person': A New Look at 2 Cor 11:29." *CBQ* 37 (1975) 500-26.

Barrett, C. K. "Christianity at Corinth." *Essays on Paul.* Philadelphia: Westminster, 1982. 1-27.

--------. *The Second Epistle to the Corinthians.* HNTC. New York: Harper & Row, 1973.

--------. "Paul's Opponents in II Corinthians." *NTS* 17 (1971) 233-254.

--------. "PSEUDAPOSTOLI (2 Cor 11:13)." *Essays on Paul.* Philadelphia: Westminster, 1982. 87-107.

--------. "Boasting (καυχᾶσθαι, κτλ.) in the Pauline Epistles." *L'Apôtre Paul; personnalité, style et conception du ministère.* Ed. A. Vanhoye. BETL 73. Leuven: Leuven University Press, 1986. 363-368.

Bates, W. H. "The Integrity of II Corinthians." *NTS* 12 (1965) 56-59.

Batey, Richard. "Paul's Interaction with the Corinthians." *JBL* 84 (1965) 139-146.

Baur, Karl Ludwig. *Rhetorica Paullina.* 2 vols. Halae: Orphanotrophei, 1782.

Beck, I. "Untersuchungen zur Theorie des Genos Symbuleutikon." Ph.D. diss., Hamburg, 1970.

Benoit, William. *Uneigentliches Sprechen. Zur Pragmatik und Semantik von Metaphor, Metonymie, Ironie, Litotes und rhetorischer Frage.* Tübingen Beitrage zur Linguistik, 102. Tübingen: G. Narr, 1978.

Betz, Hans Dieter. *Der Apostle Paulus und die sokratische Tradition: Eine exegetische Untersuchung zu seiner 'Apologie' 2 Kor 10-13.* BHT 45. Tübingen: Mohr/Siebeck, 1972.

--------. "Eine Christus-Aretalogie bei Paulus (2 Kor 12,7-10)." *ZTK* 66 (1969) 288-305.

--------. *Paul's Apology, II Corinthians 10-13 and the Socratic Tradition.* The Center for Hermeneutical Studies in Hellenistic and Modern Culture. Berkeley: Graduate Theological Union and University of California, 1970.

--------. "The Problem of Rhetoric and Theology according to the apostle Paul." *L'Apôtre Paul: personnalité, style et conception du ministère.*

Ed. S. Vanhoye. BETL 73. Leuven: Leuven University Press, 1979.

--------. *Galatians: A Commentary on Paul's Letter to the Churches of Galatia*. Hermeneia. Philadelphia: Fortress, 1979.

--------. ed. *Plutarch's Ethical Writings and Early Christian Literature*. SCHNT 34. Leiden: Brill, 1978.

--------. *2 Corinthians 8 and 9: A Commentary on Two Administrative Letters of the Apostle Paul*. Hermeneia. Philadelphia: Fortress, 1985.

Bitzer, Llyod. "The Rhetorical Situation." *PhRhet* 1 (1968) 1-12.

Bjerkelund, C. *Parakalô: Form, Funktion und Sinn der parakalô-Sätze in den paulinischen Briefen*. Bibliotheca theologica Norvegica 1. Oslo: Universitetsforlaget, 1967.

Black, C. Clifton II. "The Rhetorical Form of the Hellenistic Jewish and Early Christian Sermon: A Response to Lawrence Wills." *HTR* 81/1 (1988) 1-18.

Blass, Friedrich. *Die Rhythmen der asianischen und römischen Kuntsprosa*. Leipzig: Deichert, 1905.

Blaiklock, E. M. "The Irony of Paul." *New Testament Studies in Honor of Ray Summers*. Eds. H. L. Drumwright and C. Vaughan. Waco, TX: Markham Press Fund, 1975.

Blumenthal, A. von. "*TYPOS* und *PARADEIGMA*." *Hermes* 63 (1928) 391-414.

Boor, Werner de. *Der zweite Brief an die Korinther*. 4th ed. Wupperthaler Studienbibel. Wuppertal: Brockhaus, 1978.

Booth, Wayne C. *The Rhetoric of Fiction*. 2nd ed. Chicago: University of Chicago, 1982.

--------. *The Rhetoric of Irony*. Chicago: University of Chicago, 1974.

Bornkamm, Günther. "The History of the Origin of the So-Called Second Letter to the Corinthians." *NTS* 8 (1962) 258-63.

Bosch Sánchez, Jorge. *"Gloriarse" segun san Pablo: Sentido y teología de καυχάομαι*. AnBib 40. Rome: Biblical Institute Press, 1970.

Bradley, D. G. "The *Topos* as a Form in the Pauline Parenesis." *JBL* 72 (1953) 238-46.

Brandt, William. *The Rhetoric of Argumentation.* New York: Bobbs-Merrill, 1970.

Bruce, F. F. *1 and 2 Corinthians.* NCBC. Grand Rapids: MI: Eerdmans, 1971.

Bryant, Donald C., ed. *Ancient Greek and Roman Rhetoricians: A Biographical Dictionary.* Columbus: MO, 1968.

Bünker, Michael. *Briefformular und rhetorische Disposition in 1. Korintherbrief.* GTA 28. Göttingen: Vandenhoeck & Ruprecht, 1984.

Bultmann, Rudolf. *Der Stil der paulinischen Predigt und die kynisch-stoische Diatribe.* Göttingen: Vandenhoeck & Ruprecht, 1984.

--------. *The Second Letter to the Corinthians.* Minneapolis: Augsburg Publishing Co., 1985.

--------. "καυχάομαι." *TDNT* 3.645-54.

--------. *Exegetische Probleme des zweiten Korintherbriefes. Zu 2. Kor 5,1-5; 5,11-6,10; 10-13; 12,21.* SymBU 9. Uppsala: Wretman, 1947.

Burgess, T. C. *Epideictic Literature.* Ph.D. diss., University of Chicago. Chicago: University of Chicago Press, 1902.

Burke, Kenneth. *A Rhetoric of Motives.* Berkeley: University of California, 1969

Butts, James R. *The Progymnasmata of Theon: A New Text with Translation and Commentary.* Ph.D. diss., Claremont Graduate School, 1986.

Caird, G. B. *The Language and Imagery of the Bible.* London: Gerald Duckworth, 1980.

Campbell, Karlyn Kohrs. *The Rhetorical Act.* Belmont, CA: Wadsworth, 1982.

--------. and K. H. Jamieson, eds. *Form and Genre: Shaping Rhetorical Action.* Annadale, VA: Speech Communication Association, 1978.

Carson, D. A. *From Triumphalism to Maturity: An Exposition of 2 Corinthians 10-13*. Grand Rapids, MI: Baker Book House, 1984.

Castelli, Elizabeth. *Mimesis as a Discourse of Power in Paul's Letters*. Ph.D. diss., Claremont Graduate School, 1987.

Chance, Bradley. "Paul's Apology to the Corinthians." *PerspRelS* 9/2 (1982) 145-55.

Church, F. Forrester. "Rhetorical Structure and Design in Paul's Letter to Philemon." *HTR* 7/1-2 (1978) 17-33.

Clark, Donald Lemen. *Rhetoric in Greco-Roman Education*. New York: Columbia University Press, 1957.

Clarke, M. L. *Rhetoric at Rome: A Historical Survey*. London: Cohen & West, 1953.

Collins, John N. "Georgi's 'Envoys' in 2 Cor 11.23." *JBL* 93 (1974) 88-96.

Cope, E. M. *An Introduction to Aristotle's Rhetoric*. London: Macmillan & Co., 1867.

Corbett, Edward P. J. *Classical Rhetoric for the Modern Student*. 2nd ed. New York: Oxford, 1971.

Corrington, Gail Peterson. *The "Divine Man": His Origin and Function in Hellenistic Popular Religion*. AUS. Frankfurt: Peter Lang, 1986.

Cosby, Michael R. "Paul's Persuasive Language in Romans 5." *Persuasive Artistry: Studies in New Testament Rhetoric in Honor of George Kennedy*. Ed. Duane F. Watson. JSOT 50. Sheffield: JSOT, 1991. 209-226.

Crafton, Jeffrey. *The Agency of the Apostle: A Dramatistic Analysis of Paul's Response to Conflict in 2 Corinthians*. JSNTSup 51. Sheffield: JSOT, 1991.

D'Alton, J. F. *Roman Literary Theory and Criticism*. London/New York: Longmans, Green, 1931.

Danker, Frederick W. *Benefactor: Epigraphic Study of a Graeco-Roman and New Testament Semantic Field*. St. Louis: Clayton Publishing House, 1982.

--------. *II Corinthians*. Augsburg Commentary on the New Testament. Minneapolis: Augsburg, 1989.

--------. "Paul's Debt to the *De Corona* of Demosthenes: A Study of Rhetorical Techniques in Second Corinthians." *Persuasive Artistry: Studies in New Testament Rhetoric in Honor of George Kennedy.* Ed. Duane F. Watson. JSOT 50. Sheffield: JSOT, 1991. 262-80.

Daube, David. "Rabbinic Methods of Interpretation and Hellenistic Rhetoric." *HUCA* 22 (1949) 239-64.

Dixon, P. *Rhetoric*. London: Methuen, 1971.

Dockhorn, Klaus. *Macht und Wirkung der Rhetorik.* Respublica Literaria, 2. Bad Hamburg: Gehlen, 1968.

Donnelly, Francis P. *The Oration of Demosthenes "On the Crown": A Rhetorical Commentary.* New York: Fordham, 1941.

Doty, William G. *Letters in Primitive Christianity.* Philadelphia: Fortress, 1973.

--------. "The Classification of Epistolary Literature." *CBQ* 31 (1969) 183-99.

Douglas, Alan E. *The Intellectual Background of Cicero's Rhetoric: A Study in Method.* ANRW, 1.3. Berlin/New York: De Gruyter, 1973. 95-137.

Duncan T. St. "Rhetorical Elements in the Letters of St. Paul." *TAPhLA*, 1925.

Du Toit, A. B. *Hyperbolical Contrasts: A Neglected Aspect of Paul's Style.* Colloquim Biblicum Lovaniense, 73. Leuven: Leuven University Press, 1985.

Eagleton, Terry. *Literary Theory.* Minneapolis: University of Minnesota, 1983.

Eco, Umberto. *The Role of the Reader. Explorations in the Semiotics of Texts.* Bloomington, IN: Indiana University Press, 1979.

Erickson, Keith, ed. *Aristotle: The Classical Heritage of Rhetoric.* Meteuchen, NJ: Scarecrow, 1974.

Exler, F. *The Form of the Ancient Greek Letter: A Study in Greek Epistolography*. Washington, DC: Catholic University Press, 1923.

Fahy, Thomas. "St. Paul's 'Boasting' and 'Weakness'." *ITQ* 31 (1964) 214-17.

Fallon, Francis T. *2 Corinthians*. New Testament Message, 11. Wilmington, DE: Michael Glazier, 1980.

Farenga, Vincent. "Periphrasis on the Origin of Rhetoric." *MLN* 94/5 (1979) 1033-55.

Farrar, F. W. "The Rhetoric of St. Paul." *Exp* 10 (1879) 1027.

Fiore, Benjamin. *The Function of Personal Example in the Socratic and Pastoral Epistles*. AnBib 105. Rome: Biblical Institute Press, 1986.

Fiorenza, Elizabeth Schüssler. "Rhetorical Situation and Historical Reconstruction in 1 Corinthians." *NTS* 33 (1987) 386-403.

Fischel, Henry. "Story and History: Observations on Greco-Roman Rhetoric and Pharisaism." *Essays in Greco-Roman and Related Talmudic Literature*. Ed. Henry Fischel. New York: KTAV, 1977.

Fisher, Fred L. *Commentary on 1 & 2 Corinthians*. Waco: TX: Word, 1965.

Fitzgerald, James T. *Cracks in an Earthen Vessel: An Examination of the Catalogues of Hardship in the Corinthian Correspondence*. SBLDS 99. Atlanta: Scholars Press, 1988.

Forbes, Christopher. "Comparison, Self-Praise, and Irony: Paul's Boasting and the Conventions of Hellenistic Rhetoric." *NTS* 32 (1986) 1-30.

Fridrichsen, Anton. "Zum Stil des paulinischen Peristasenkatalogs zu 2 Cor 11.23ff." *SO* 7 (1929) 25-29.

--------. "Peristasenkatalog und Res Gestae: Nachtrag zu Cor 11,23ff." *SO* 8 (1929) 77-82.

Friedrich, Gerhard. "Die Gegner des Paulus in 2 Korintherbrief." *Abraham under Vater: Juden und Christen im Gespräch über die Bibel (Michel Festschrift)*. Eds O. Betz, M. Hengel and P. Schmidt. AGJU 5. Leiden; Brill, 1963. 181-215.

Furnish, V. P. *II Corinthians*. AB32A. Garden City, NY: Doubleday, 1984.

Gale, Herbert M. *The Use of Analogy in the Letters of Paul*. Philadelphia: Westminster, 1964.

Georgi, Dieter. *The Opponents of Paul in Second Corinthians*. Philadelphia: Fortress, 1986.

Gill, Christopher. "The Ēthos/Pathos Distinction in Rhetorical and Literary Criticism." *CQ* 34/1 (1984) 149-66.

Godet, Georges. *La Seconde Épître aux Corinthiens*. Neuchâtel: Attinger, 1914.

Goldstein J. A. *The Letters of Demosthenes*. New York: Columbia University Press, 1968.

Grant, R. M. "Hellenistic Elements in 1 Corinthians." *Early Christian Origins: Studies in Honor of Harold R. Willoughby*. Ed. A. Wikgren. Chicago: Quadrangle Books, 1961. 60-66.

Grimaldi, William M. A. *Aristotle, Rhetoric II: A Commentary*. New York: Fordham University Press, 1988.

Gunther, John J. *St. Paul's Opponents and Their Background: A Study of Apocalyptic and Jewish Sectarian Teachings*. NovTSup 35. Leiden: Brill, 1973.

Hafemann, Scoot J. *Suffering and the Spirit: An Exegetical Study of II Cor 2.14-33 within the Context of the Corinthian Correspondence*. WUNT, 19. Tübingen: Mohr, 1986.

Halmel, Anton. *Der zweite Korintherbrief des Apostles Paulus: Geschichtliche und literarkritsche Untersuchungen*. Halle: Niemeyer, 1904.

Halperin, David L. "Heavenly Ascension in Ancient Judaism: The Nature of the Experience." *SBLSP* 26 (1987) 218-232.

Hanson, A. T. *Studies in Paul's Technique and Theory*. Grand Rapids: Eerdmans, 1974.

Hanson, Richard P. C. *The Second Epistle to the Corinthians: Christ and Controversy*. Torch Bible Commentaries. London: SCM, 1967. '

Harada, Makota. *Paul's Weakness: A Study in Pauline Polemics (2 Cor 10-13)*. Ph.D. diss., Boston University, 1968.

Harding, Mark. "The Classical Rhetoric of Praise and the New Testament." *The Reformed Theological Review* 3 (1986) 73-82.

Hauser, Gerald A. *An Introduction to Rhetorical Theory*. New York: Harper & Row, 1986.

Hay, David. "What is Proof?--Rhetorical Verification in Philo, Josephus, and Quintilian." *SBLSP* 17 (1979) II, 87-100.

Heinrici, C. F. G. *Der zweite Brief an die Korinther*. 8th ed. KEK 6. Göttingen: Vandenhoeck & Ruprecht, 1900.

Hellwig, Antje. *Untersuchungen zur Theorie der Rhetorik bei Platon und Aristoteles*. Hypomnemata 38. Göttingen: Vandenhoeck & Ruprecht, 1973.

Héring, Jean. *The Second Epistle of St. Paul to the Corinthians*. London: Epworth, 1967.

Hester, James D. "The Use and Influence of Rhetoric in Galatians 2:1-14." *TZ* 42 (1986) 386-408.

--------. "The Rhetorical Structure of Galatians 1:11-2:14." *JBL* 103/2 (1984) 223-33.

--------. "Placing the Blame: The Presence of Epideictic in Galatians 1 and 2." *Persuasive Artistry: Studies in New Testament Rhetoric in Honor of George Kennedy*. Ed. Duane F. Watson. JSOT 50. Sheffield: JSOT, 1991. 281-306.

Himmelfarb, Martha. "Apocalyptic Ascent and the Heavenly Temple." *SBLSP* 26 (1987) 210-217.

Hisey, Alan. "Paul's 'Thorn in the Flesh': A Paragnosis." *JBL* 29 (1961) 125-29.

Hock, Ronald F. and Edward N. O'Neil. *The Chreia in Ancient Rhetoric: The Progymnasmata*. Atlanta: Scholars Press, 1986.

Hodgson, Robert. "Paul the Apostle and First Century Tribulation Lists." *ZNW* 74 (1983) 59-80.

Hollenbach, William. *Paul's Self-Understanding as Ascertained through an Analysis of Certain Dramatic Figures of Speech.* Ph.D diss., Drew University, 1965.

Holmberg, Bengst. *Paul and Power: The Structure of Authority in the Primitive Church as Reflected in the Pauline Epistles.* Lund: Gleerys, 1978.

Horsley, R. A. "Wisdom of Words and Words of Wisdom in Corinth." *CBQ* 39 (1977) 224-239.

Hudson-Williams, H. L. "Political Speeches in Athens." *CQ* n.s. 1 (1951) 68-73.

--------. "Thucydides, Isocrates, and the Rhetorical Method of Composition." *CBQ* 42 (1948) 76-81.

Hübner, Hans. "Der Galaterbrief und des Verhältnis von antiker Rhetorik und Epistolographie." *TLZ* 109/4 (1984) 241-50.

Hughes, Frank Witt. *Early Christian Rhetoric and Second Thessalonians.* Sheffield: Academic Press, 1989.

--------. "The Rhetoric of Reconciliation: 2 Corinthians 1.1-2.13 and 7.5-8.24." *Persuasive Artistry: Studies in New Testament Rhetoric in Honor of George Kennedy.* Ed. Duane F. Watson. JSOT 50. Sheffield: JSOT Press, 1991. 246-61.

Hughes, Philip E. *Paul's Second Epistle to the Corinthians.* NICNT. Grand Rapids: Eerdmans, 1962.

Humphries, Raymond. *Paul's Rhetoric in 1 Corinthians 1-4.* Ph.D. diss., Graduate Theological Union, Berkeley, CA, 1979.

Jaeger, Werner. *Early Christianity and Greek Paideia.* Cambridge, MA: Harvard University Press, 1961.

--------. *Paideia: The Ideals of Greek Culture.* 3 vols. New York: Oxford University Press, 1939.

Jewett, Robert. *The Thessalonian Correspondence: Pauline Rhetoric and Millenarian Piety.* Philadelphia: Fortress, 1987.

--------. *Paul's Anthropological Terms. A Study of Their Use in Conflict*

282

Settings. AGJU 10. Leiden: Brill, 1971.

Judge, E. A. "Paul's Boasting in Relation to Contemporary Professional Practice." *AusBR* 16 (1968) 37-50.

--------. "St. Paul and Classical Society." *JAC* 15 (1972) 19-36.

Käsemann, Ernst. *Die Legitimatät des Apostles: Eine Untersuchungen zu II Korinther 10-13.* Darmstadt: Wissenschaftliche Buchgesellschaft, 1956.

Kaufer, David. "Irony and Rhetorical Strategy." *PhRhet* 10 (1978) 1-13.

Kee. Doyle. "Who Were the 'Super-Apostles' of 2 Corinthians 10-13? *RestQ* 23 (1980) 65-76.

Kennedy, George. "The Earliest Rhetorical Handbooks." *AJP* 80 (1959) 169-78

--------. "Focusing of Arguments in Greek Deliberative Oratory." *TAPA* 90 (1959) 131-38.

--------. *The Art of Persuasion in Greece.* Princeton: Princeton University Press, 1963.

--------. *The Art of Rhetoric in the Roman World.* Princeton: Princeton University Press, 1972.

--------. *New Testament Interpretation through Rhetorical Criticism.* Chapel Hill, NC: University of North Carolina Press, 1984.

--------. *Classical Rhetoric and its Christian and Secular Tradition from Ancient to Modern Times.* Chapel Hill, NC: University of North Carolina Press, 1980.

Kim, Chan-Hie. *Form and Structure of the Familiar Greek Letter of Recommendation.* Missoula, MT: Scholars Press, 1972.

Kinneavy, James L. *Greek Rhetorical Origins of Christian Faith: An Inquiry.* Oxford: Oxford University Press, 1976.

Klek, J. "Symbuleutici qui dicitur sermonis historica critica." *Rhetorische Studien* 8. Paderborn: Schöningh, 1919.

Köster, Helmut. *Introduction to the New Testament.* 2 vols. Philadelphia: Fortress, 1982.

Kraftchick, Steven. *Ethos and Pathos Appeals in Galatians Five and Six: A Rhetorical Analysis.* Ph.D. diss., Emory University, 1985.

Kroll, W. "Rhetorik." *PWSup* 8 (1940) 1039-1138.

Kümmel, Werner G. *Introduction to the New Testament.* Rev. ed. Nashville: Abingdon, 1975.

Kustas, George L. *Diatribe in Ancient Rhetorical Theory.* Berkeley: Center for Hermeneutical Studies, 1976.

Lang, F. *Die Brief an die Korinther.* NTD 7. Göttingen: Vandenhoeck & Ruprecht, 1986.

Lanham, Richard A. *A Handlist of Rhetorical Terms: A Guide for Students of English Literature.* Berkeley: University of California, 1968.

Lausberg, Heinrich. *Handbuch der literarischen Rhetorik: Eine Grundlegung der Literaturwissenschaft.* Munich: Max Hüber, 1973.

--------. *Elemente der literarischen Rhetorik.* Munich: Hüber, 1967.

Libermann, Saul. *Hellenism in Jewish Palestine: Studies in the Literary Transmission, Beliefs and Manners of Palestine in the I Century B. C. E. - IV Century C. E.* New York: The Jewish Theological Seminary of America, 1950.

--------. *Greek in Jewish Palestine: Studies in the Life and Manners of Jewish Palestine in the II-IV Centuries C. E.* New York: Philipp Feldheim, 1965.

--------. "How Much Greek in Jewish Palestine?" *Essays in Greco-Roman and Related Talmudic Literature.* Ed. Henry Fischel. New York: KTAV, 1977.

Liddell, Henry G. and Robert Scott. *A Greek-English Lexicon.* New (9th) ed. Henry S. Jones. Oxford: Clarendon Press, 1940.

Lincoln, Andrew T. "Paul the Visionary: The Setting and Significance of the Rapture into Paradise in II Corinthians 12:1-10." *NTS* 25 (1979) 204-220.

Loheit, Fritz. *Untersuchungen zur antiken Selbstapologie.* Rostock: Adlers Erben, 1928.

Lumpe, A. "Exemplum." *RAC* 6 (1966) 1229-57.

Lunsford, Andrea A. and Lisa S. Ede. "On Distinctions between Classical and Modern Rhetoric." *Essays on Classical Rhetoric and Modern Discourse.* Eds. Robert J. Connors, Lisa S. Ede and Andrea Lunsford. Carbondale: Southern Illinois University, 1985.

Machalet, Christian. "Paulus und seine Gegner. Eine Untersuchungen zu den Korintherbriefen." *Theokratia: Jahrbuch des Inst. Judaicum Delitzschianum II, 1970-72 (Rengstorf Festgabe).* Eds. W. Dietrich and others. Leiden: Brill, 1973. 183-203.

Mack, Burton L. *Anecdotes and Arguments: The Chreia in Antiquity and Early Christianity.* Occasional Papers 10. Claremont, CA: Institute for Antiquity and Christianity, 1987.

--------. *Rhetoric and the New Testament.* Minneapolis: Fortress, 1990.

--------. "Decoding the Scripture: Philo and the Rules of Rhetoric." *Nourished with Peace: Studies in Hellenistic Judaism in Memory of Samuel Sandmel.* Eds. F. E. Greenspahn, E. Hilgert, and B. L. Mack. Chico, CA: Scholars Press, 1984. 81-115.

--------. and Vernon K. Robbins. *Patterns of Persuasion in the Gospels.* Literary Facets. Sonoma, CA: Polebridge, 1989.

Malherbe, A. J. *Ancient Epistolary Theorists.* SBLSBS 19. Atlanta: Scholars Press, 1988.

--------. *Moral Exhortation, A Greco-Roman Sourcebook.* Library of Early Christianity. Philadelphia: Westminster Press, 1986.

--------. "'Gentle as a Nurse': The Cynic Background to 1 Thess 2." *NovT* 12 (1971) 203-17.

--------. "Antisthenes and Odysseus, and Paul at War." *HTR* 76 (1983) 143-73.

Malina, T. W. "The Corinthian Correspondence." *Studies in the Gospels and Epistles.* Ed. M. Black. Philadelphia: Westminster, 1962. 190-224.

Marshall, Peter. *Enmity in Corinth: Social Conventions in Paul's Relations with the Corinthians.* WUNT 2/23. Tübingen: J. C. B. Mohr (Paul Siebeck), 1987.

Martin, Clarice J. "The Rhetorical Function of Commercial Language in Paul's Letter to Philemon (Verse 18)." *Persuasive Artistry: Studies in New Testament Rhetoric in Honor of George Kennedy.* Ed. Duane F. Watson. JSOT 50. Sheffield: JSOT Press, 1991. 320-37.

Martin, Josef. *Antike Rhetorik, Technik und Methodie.* HKAW II/3. Munich: Beck, 1974.

McCall, Marsh. *Ancient Rhetorical Theories of Simile and Comparison.* Cambridge, MA: Harvard, 1969.

Marrou, H. I. *A History of Education in Antiquity.* New York: The New American Library, 1964.

McCant, Jerry W. "Paul's Thorn of Rejected Apostleship." *NTS* 34 (1988) 550-572.

McGuire, Martin R. P. "Letters and Letter Carriers in Christian Antiquity." *CW* 53 (1960) 148-53; 184-86; 199-200.

Menzies, Allan. *The Second Epistle of the Apostle Paul to the Corinthians.* London: Macmillan, 1912.

Miller, Arthur B. "Aristotle on Habit (ethos) and Character (ethos): Implications for the *Rhetoric.*" *Speech Monographs* 41 (1974) 309-16.

Miller, Carolyn. "Aristotle's 'Special Topics' in Rhetorical Theory and Pedagogy." *RSQ* 17/1 (Winter, 1987) 61-70.

Mitchell, Margaret. *Paul and the Rhetoric of Reconciliation: An Exegetical Investigation of the Language and Composition of 1 Cor.* Tübingen: J. C. B. Mohr (Paul Siebeck), 1991.

Mott, Stephen. "The Power of Giving and Receiving: Reciprocity in Hellenistic Benevolence." *Current Issues in Biblical and Patristic Interpretation (Tenney Festschrift).* Ed. G. F. Hawthorne. Grand Rapids: Eerdmans, 1975. 60-72.

Muilenberg, James. "Form Criticism and Beyond." *JBL* 88/1 (1969) 1-18.

Mullins, Terrence Y. "Disclosure: A Literary Form in the New Testament." *NovT* 7 (1964) 44-50.

--------. "Paul's Thorn in the Flesh." *JBL* 76 (1957) 299-303.

--------. "*Topos* as a New Testament Form." *JBL* 99 (1973) 350-58.

Munck, Johannes. *Paul and the Salvation of Mankind*. Richmond, VA: John Knox Press, 1959.

Murphy, James J., ed. *A Synoptic History of Classical Rhetoric*. Davis, CA: Hermagoras Press, 1983.

Murphy-O'Connor, Jerome. *St. Paul's Corinth. Texts and Archaeology*. Good News Studies, 6. Wilmington, DE: Michael Glazier, 1983.

Nadeau, R. "On *Stases*: A Translation with an Introduction and Notes." *SM* 13 (1964) 361-424.

Natali, Carlo. "Paradeigma: The Problems of Human Acting and the Use of Example in Some Greek Authors of the 4th Century B.C." *RSQ* 19/2 (Spring, 1989) 141-52.

Nida, E. A. and others. *Style and Discourse, with special reference to the text of the Greek New Testament*. Cape Town: Bible Society, 1983.

Nisbet, Patricia. "The Thorn in the Flesh." *ExpTim* 80 (1969) 126.

Nock, Arthur D. *Early Christianity and its Hellenistic Background*. New York: Harper & Row, 1964.

Norden, Eduard. *Die antike Kunstprosa vom VI. Jahrhundert v. Chr. bis in die Zeit der Renaissance*. 3rd reprint. Stuttgart: Teubner, 1915.

O'Collins, Gerald G. "Power Made Perfect in Weakness: 2 Cor 12,9-10." *CBQ* 33 (1971) 528-37.

Olson, Stanley N. *Confidence Expressions in Paul: Epistolary Conventions and the Purpose of 2 Corinthians*. Ph.d. diss., Yale Unversity, 1976.

--------. "Epistolary Uses of Expressions of Self-Confidence." *JBL* 103 (1984) 585-97.

Palmer, Georgiana. *The τόποι of Aristotle's Rhetoric as Exemplified in the*

Orators. Ph.D. diss., University of Chicago, 1932. Chicago: University of Chicago Libraries, 1934.

Peabody, David. "Boasting in the Lord. A Study of KAYXAOMAI in Paul's Letters." Unpublished seminar papers, Southern Methodist University, 1974.

Perelman, Chaim and L. Olbrechts-Tyteca. *The New Rhetoric: A Treatise on Argumentation.* Notre Dame: Notre Dame University Press, 1969.

--------. *The Realm of Rhetoric.* Notre Dame: Notre Dame University Press, 1982.

--------. "Rhetoric and Philosophy." *PhRhet* 1 (1986) 15-24.

--------. *The New Rhetoric and the Humanities. Essays on Rhetoric and Its Applications.* Dordrecht: Reidel, 1979.

Peristiany, J. G. *Honour and Shame: The Values of Mediterranean Society.* Chicago: University of Chicago Press, 1966.

Perlman, S. "The Historical Example, Its Use and Importance as Political Propaganda in the Attic Orators." *ScrHier VII: Studies in History.* Eds A. Fuks and I. Halpern. Jerusalem: Magnes, 1961. 150-66.

Petersen, Norman. *Rediscovering Paul: Philemon and the Sociology of Paul's Narrative World.* Philadelphia: Fortress, 1985.

Pfitzer, V. C. *Paul and the Agon Motif. Traditional Athletic Imagery in Pauline Literature.* NovTSup 16. Leiden: Brill, 1967.

Plank, Karl A. *Paul and the Irony of Affliction.* Atlanta: Scholars Press, 1987.

Plett, Heinrich F. *Einführung in die rhetorische Textanalyse.* 3rd ed. Hamburg: Buske, 1975.

Plummer, Alfred. *A Critical and Exegetical Commentary on the Second Epistle of Paul to the Corinthians.* ICC. Edinburgh: T & T Clark, 1915.

Power, Mark Allan. *What is Narrative Criticism?* Minneapolis: Fortress, 1990.

Preminger, Alex, O. B. Hardison, Jr., and Kevin Karrane, eds. *Classical and Medieval Literary Criticism.* New York: Frederick Ungar Publishing Co., 1974.

Price, Bennett J. *Paradeigma and Exemplum in Ancient Rhetorical Theory.* Ph. D. diss., University of California at Berkeley, 1975.

Price, Robert M. "Punished in Paradise (An Exegetical Theory on II Corinthians 12:1-10)." *JSNT* 7 (1980) 140-60.

Pross. Edward L. "Practical Implications of the Aristotelian Concept of Ethos." *Southern Speech Journal* 17 (1952) 257-64.

Rabe, Hugo. *Rhetores Graeci.* Leipzig: Teubner, 1913-.

Roberts, W. Rhys. *Greek Rhetoric and Literary Criticism.* New York: Longsman, Green & Co., 1928.

Robertson, Edwin H. *Corinthians 1 and 2.* J. B. Phillip's New Testament Commentaries. New York: Macmillan, 1973.

Rowland, Robert and Deanna Womack. "Aristotle's View of Ethical Rhetoric." *RSQ* 15/1-2 (1985) 13-31.

Russell, D. A. *Greek Declamation.* Cambridge: Cambridge University Press, 1983.

Ryken, Leland, ed. *The New Testament in Literary Criticism.* New York: Frederick Ungar, 1984.

Saake, Helmut. "Paulus als Ekstatiker. Pneumatologische Beobachtungen zu 2 Kor 12:1-10." *NovT* 15 (1973) 153-60.

Sampley, J. Paul. "Paul and His Opponents in 2 Corinthians 10-13, and the Rhetorical Handbooks." *The Social World of Formative Christianity and Judaism.* Eds. Jacob Neusner, Peder Borgen, Ernest S. Frerichs and Richard Horseley. Philadelphia: Fortress Press, 1988. 162-77.

Sattler, William M. *Conceptions of Ethos in Rhetoric.* Ph.D. diss., Northwestern University, 1941.

Schelke, Karl H. *The Second Epistle to the Corinthians.* New York: Crossroad, 1981.

Schmeller, Thomas. *Paulus und die "Diatribe": eine vergleichende Stilinterpretation.* NTAbh n.s. 19. Münster: Aschendorff, 1987.

Schneider, Bernardin. "HE KOINONIA TOU HAGIOU PNEUMATOS (II Cor 13:13)." *Studies Honoring Ignatius Charles Brady, Friar Minor.* Franciscan Institute Publications, Theology Series, 6. Eds. R. S. Almagno and C. L. Harkins. St. Bonaventure, NY: Franciscan Institute Press, 1976. 421-447.

Schneider, Norbert. *Die rhetorische Eigenart der paulinischen Antithese.* HUT 11. Tübingen: J. C. B, Mohr (Paul Siebeck), 1970.

Scroggs, Robin. "Paul as Rhetorician: Two Homilies in Rom 1-11." *Jews, Greeks and Christians: Religious Cultures in Late Antiquity: Festschrift for W. D. Davies.* Ed. R. G. Hammerton-Kelly. SJLA 21. London: Brill, 1976. 271-298.

Segal, Alan F. "Heavenly Ascent in Hellenistic Judaism, Early Christianity and Their Environment." *ANRW* II.23/2 (1980) 1333-94.

--------. "Paul and Ecstasy." *SBLSP* 25 (1986) 555-80.

Semler, J. S. *Paraphrasis II. epistolae ad Corinthios.* Halae Magdeburgicae: Hemmerde, 1776.

Sevenster, J. N. *Do You Know Greek? How Much Greek Could the First Jewish Christians Have Known?* Leiden: E. J. Brill, 1968.

Siegert, Folker. *Argumentation bei Paulus, gezeigt an Römer 9-11.* Tübingen: J. C. B. Mohr (Paul Siebeck), 1985.

Smith, Morton. "Palestinian Judaism in the First Century." *Essays in Greco-Roman and Related Talmudic Literature.* Ed. Henry Fischel. New York: KTAV, 1977.

Smith, Neil Gregor. "The Thorn that Stayed: An Exposition of 2 Cor 12:7-9." *Int* 13 (1959) 409-16.

Soller, Richard P. *Personal Patronage in the Early Empire.* Cambridge: Cambridge University Press, 1982.

Solmsen, Frederick. "The Aristotelian Tradition in Ancient Rhetoric." *Rhetorika: Schriften zur aristotelischen und hellenistischen Rhetorik.* Hildesheim: Georg Olms Verlagsbuchhandlung, 1968.

--------. "Aristotle and Cicero on the Orators Playing Upon the Feelings." *CP* 33 (1938) 390-404.

Spencer, Aida Besançon. *Paul's Literary Style: A Stylistic and Historical Comparison of II Corinthians 11:16-12:13, Romans 8:9-39 and Philippians 3:2-4:13.* Evangelical Theological Society Monograph. Jackson, MS: Evangelical Theological Society, 1984.

--------. "The wise fool (and the foolish wise): A Study of Irony in Paul (2 Cor 11:16-12:13)." *NovT* 23 (1981) 349-60.

Spittler, Russell P. "The Limits of Ecstasy: An Exegesis of 2 Corinthians 12:1-10." *Current Issues in Biblical and Patristic Interpretation (Tenney Festschrift).* Ed. Gerald F. Hawthorne. Grand Rapids: Eerdmans, 1965. 259-66.

Standaert, Benoît. "Analyse rhetorique des Chapitres 12 a 14 de 1 Cor." *Charisma und Agape* (2 Kor 12-14). Ed. L. de Lorenzi. Rome: Abbey of St. Paul-Outside-the-Walls, 1983. 23-50.

--------. "La rhetorique ancienne dans saint Paul." *L'Apôtre Paul: personnalité, style et conception du ministère.* Ed. S. Vanhoye. BETL 73. Leuven: Leuven University Press, 1986, 78-92.

Stephenson, Alan M. G. "Partition Theories on II Corinthians." *Studia Evangelica. II/1: The New Testament Scriptures.* Ed. F. L. Cross. TU 87. Berlin: Akademie-Verlag, 1964. 639-46.

--------. "A Defense of the Integrity of 2 Corinthians." *The Authorship and Integrity of the New Testament.* S. P. C. K. Theological Collections, 4. London: S. P. C. K., 1965. 82-97.

Stirewalt, Martin Luther. "The Form and Function of the Greek Letter-Essay. *The Romans Debate.* Rev. and exp. Karl P. Donfried. Edinburgh: T & T Clark, 1991.

Stowers, Stanley K. "Social Typification and the Classification of Ancient Letters." *The Social World of Formative Christianity and Judaism.* Eds. Jacob Neusner, Peder Borgen, Ernest S. Frerichs, and Richard Horsley. Philadelphia: Fortress, 1988.

--------. *The Diatribe in Paul's Letter to the Romans.* Chico, CA: Scholars Press, 1981.

--------. *Letter Writing in Greco-Roman Antiquity*. Philadelphia: Westminster Press, 1986.

Strachan, R. H. *The Second Epistle of Paul to the Corinthians*. MNTC. New York/London: Harper, 1935.

Süss, Wilhelm. *Ethos: Studien zur älteren griechischen Rhetorik*. Leipzig: Teubner, 1910.

Tabor, J. D. *Things Unutterable: Paul's Ascent to Paradise in Its Greco-Roman, Judaic, and Early Christian Contexts*. Studies in Judaism. Lanham, MD: University Press of America, 1986.

Talbert, Charles. *Reading Corinthians: A Literary and Theological Commentary on 1 and 2 Corinthians*. New York: Crossroad, 1989.

Theissen, Gerd. *The Social Setting of Pauline Christianity: Essays on Corinth*. Ed. J. H. Schütz. Philadelphia: Fortress, 1982.

Thierry, Jean J. "Der Dorn im Fleische (2 Kor. 12:7-9)." *NovT* 5 (1962) 301-310.

Thrall, Margaret E. "Super-Apostles, Servants of Christ, and Servants of Satan." *JSNT* 6 (1980) 42-57.

Travis, Stephen H. "Paul's Boasting in 2 Corinthians 10-12." *SE VI* (1973) 527-32.

Veyne, Paul. *Bread and Circuses*. New York: Viking Penguin, 1990.

Volkmann, R. *Die Rhetorik der Griechen und Römer in systematischer Übersicht*. 2nd ed. Reprint of 1885 edition. Hildesheim: Olms, 1963.

Ward, Richard F. *Paul and the Politics of Performance: A Study of 2 Corinthians 10-13*. Ph.D. diss., Northwestern University, 1987.

Warner, Martin, ed. *The Bible as Rhetoric: Studies in Biblical Persuasion and Credibility*. Warwick Studies in Philosophy and Literature. London/New York:Routledge, 1990.

Watson, Duane F. "1 Corinthian 10:23-11:1 in the Light of Graeco-Roman Rhetoric: The Role of Rhetorical Questions." *JBL* 108 (1989) 301-318.

--------. *Invention, Arrangement and Style: Rhetorical Criticism of Jude and 2 Peter*. SBLDS 104. Atlanta: Scholars Press, 1988.

--------. "A Rhetorical Analysis of Philippians and Its Implications for the Unity Question." *NovT* 30 (1988) 57-88.

--------. "A Rhetorical Analysis of 3 John: A Study in Epistolary Rhetoric." *CBQ* 51 (1989) 479-501.

Watson, Francis. "2 Cor 10-13 and Paul's Painful Letter to the Corinthians." *JTS* 35 (1984) 324-346.

Weiss, Johannes. *Beiträge zur paulinischen Rhetorik*. Göttingen: Vandenhoeck & Ruprecht, 1897.

Welborn, L. L. "On the Discord in Corinth. 1 Corinthians 104 and Ancient Politics." *JBL* 106 (1987) 83-113.

Wendland, Hans. *Der zweite Korintherbrief*. MeyerK 6. Göttingen: Vandenhoeck & Ruprecht, 1924.

--------. *Die hellenistisch-römische Kultur in ihren Beziehungen zum Judentum und Christentum*. HNT 2. Tübingen: Mohr/Siebeck, 1972.

White, J. L. *The Form and Function of the Body of the Greek Letter. A Study of the Letter-Body in Non-Literary Papyri and in Paul the Apostle*. SBLDS 1. Missoula, MT: Society of Biblical Literature, 1972.

--------. *Light from Ancient Letters*. Philadelphia: Fortress, 1986.

--------. "Ancient Greek Letters." *Greco-Roman Literature and the New Testament*. Ed. David Aune. SBLSBS 21. Atlanta: Scholars Press, 1988.

Wilder, Amos. *Early Christian Rhetoric: The Language of the Gospel*. 2nd ed. Cambridge, MA: Harvard University Press, 1971.

--------. *The Bible and the Literary Critic*. Minneapolis: Fortress, 1991.

Wills, Lawrence. "The Form of the Sermon in Hellenistic Judaism and Early Christianity." *HTR* 77 (1984) 277-299.

Windisch, Hans. *Der zweite Korintherbrief*. KEK 6. Abteilung. Göttingen:

Vandenhoeck & Ruprecht, 1924; rep. 1970.

Wire, Antoinette. *The Corinthian Women Prophets: A Reconstruction through Paul's Rhetoric*. Minneapolis: Fortress, 1990.

Wischmeyer, Oda. *Der höchste Weg*. SNT 13. Gütersloh: Mohn, 1981.

Wuellner, Wilhelm. "The Rhetorical Structure of Luke 12 in Its Wider Context." *Neot* 22 (1989) 283-310.

--------. "Paul's Rhetoric of Argumentation in Romans." *CBQ* 38 (1976) 330-51.

--------. "Greek Rhetoric and Pauline Argumentation." *Early Christian Literature and the Classical Tradition*. Eds. William R. Schoedel and Robert L. Wilken. Paris: Edition Beauchesne, 1979. 177-88.

--------. "Paul as Pastor: The Function of Rhetorical Questions in First Corinthians. *L'Apôtre Paul: personnalité, style et conception du ministère*. Ed. S. Vanhoye. BETL 73. Leuven: Leuven University Press, 1986. 49-77.

--------. "Hermeneutics and rhetorics: from 'truth and method' to 'truth and power'." *Scriptura* 53 (1989) 1054.

--------. "Where is Rhetorical Criticism Taking Us?" *CBQ* 49 (1987) 448-63.

Yoos, George E. "A Revision of the Concept of Ethical Appeal." *PhRhet* 12/1 (1979) 41-58.

Zmijewski, Josef. *Der Stil der paulinischen "Narrenrede": Analyse der Sprachgestaltung II Kor. 1-12 als Beitrag zur Methode von Stiluntersuchungen neutestamentlicher Texte*. Köln/Bonn: Peter Hanstein, 1978.

--------. "Kontextbezug und Deutung von 2 Kor 12:7a." *BZ* 21 (1977) 265-272.

INDEXES

Greek and Latin Authors Cited

Modern Authors

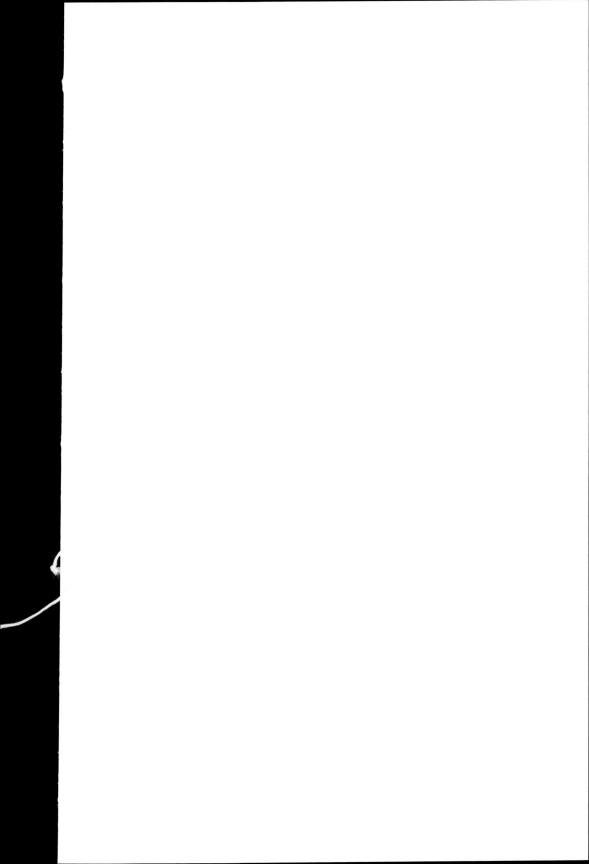